Makeover Television

2009

Reading Contemporary Television

Series Editors: Kim Akass and Janet McCabe

janetandkim@hotmail.com

The Reading Contemporary Television series aims to offer a varied, intellectually groundbreaking and often polemical response to what is happening in television today. This series is distinct in that it sets out to immediately comment upon the TV zeitgeist while providing an intellectual and creative platform for thinking differently and ingeniously writing about contemporary television culture. The books in the series seek to establish a critical space where new voices are heard and fresh perspectives offered. Innovation is encouraged and intellectual curiosity demanded.

Published and Forthcoming:

Reading *CSI*: Crime TV Under the Microscope *edited by Michael Allen*

Reading *Deadwood*: A Western to Swear by *edited by David Lavery*

Reading *Desperate Housewives*: Beyond the White Picket Fence
        edited by Janet McCabe and Kim Akass

Makeover TV: Realities Remodelled *edited by Dana Heller*

Reading 'Quality' TV *edited by Janet McCabe and Kim Akass*

Reading *Sex and the City* *edited by Kim Akass and Janet McCabe*

Reading *Six Feet Under*: TV to Die For
        edited by Kim Akass and Janet McCabe

Reading *The L Word*: Outing Contemporary Television *edited by*
        Kim Akass and Janet McCabe, with an introduction by Sarah Warn

Reading *The Sopranos*: Hit TV from HBO *edited by David Lavery*

Reading *24*: TV against the Clock *edited by Steven Peacock*

Third Wave Feminism and Television: Jane Puts It in a Box
        edited by Merri Lisa Johnson

MAKEOVER TELEVISION

Realities Remodelled

edited by

Dana Heller

I.B. TAURIS

LONDON · NEW YORK

Published in 2007 by I.B.Tauris & Co Ltd
6 Salem Road, London W2 4BU
175 Fifth Avenue, New York NY 10010
www.ibtauris.com

In the United States of America and in Canada distributed by
Palgrave Macmillan, a division of St Martin's Press
175 Fifth Avenue, New York NY 10010

ISBN 978 1 84511 330 8

A full CIP record for this book is available from the British Library
A full CIP record for this book is available from the Library of Congress

Library of Congress catalog card: available

Typeset in Goudy Old Style by Steve Tribe, Andover
Printed and bound in India by Rakesh Press

Contents

Acknowledgements

Above all, I want to express my gratitude to the authors of these essays for their excellent work: Kim Akass, Jack Z. Bratich, Joanna L. Di Mattia, Caroline Dover, Kathryn Fraser, Elizabeth Gailey, Jennifer Gillan, Annette Hill, Anne Jerslev, Janet McCabe, Joanne Morreale, Nigel Morris, Gareth Palmer, Helen Powell, Sylvie Prasad, Guy Redden, and Vanessa Russell.

In addition, I am indebted to our series editors at I.B.Tauris, Kim Akass and Janet McCabe. Without their wisdom this volume might never have been. Without their wit it most certainly would never have been such fun. I am also grateful to Ashley Graham Kennedy, Research Assistant extraordinaire, for her invaluable help in preparing the manuscript.

Finally, thanks to Galya for all the little daily rituals of transformation and revelation that ultimately amount to the best and most challenging makeover of all.

Contributors

KIM AKASS has co-edited and contributed to *Reading* Sex and the City (I.B.Tauris, 2004), *Reading* Six Feet Under: *TV to Die For* (I.B.Tauris, 2005), *Reading* The L Word: *Outing Contemporary Television* (I.B.Tauris, 2006) and *Reading* Desperate Housewives: *Beyond the White Picket Fence* (I.B.Tauris, 2006). She is currently researching the representation of motherhood on American TV and is co-editor of the new television journal *Critical Studies in Television* (MUP) as well as (with McCabe) series editor of 'Reading Contemporary Television' for I.B.Tauris.

JACK Z. BRATICH is Assistant Professor of Journalism and Media Studies at Rutgers University. He is co-editor of *Foucault, Cultural Studies, and Governmentality* (SUNY, 2003). His writings analyse conspiracy theories, audience studies, reality television, and the culture of secrecy. His book, *Conspiracy Politics: Political Rationality and Popular Culture* is forthcoming from SUNY Press. He is now working on a cultural study of public secrecy.

JOANNA L. DI MATTIA has a PhD in Women's Studies from Monash University, Australia. She has recently published essays in *Reading* Sex and the City (I.B.Tauris, 2004) and *Reading* Six Feet Under: *TV to Die For* (I.B.Tauris, 2005). Essays on HBO's *Angels in America* and *Queer as Folk* are forthcoming. Her current research is on the place of sexual practice and pleasure in debates about queer visibility.

CAROLINE DOVER is a Research Fellow in the Communications and Media Research Institute, University of Westminster, UK. She is also a Research Consultant on the Economic and Social Research

Council 'Identities and Social Action' project: *Urban Classroom Culture & Interaction* based at King's College London.

KATHRYN FRASER is an independent scholar. She has published in the areas of visual and popular culture and film studies and has written extensively on the makeover phenomenon. She received her PhD from McGill University in 2003.

ELIZABETH ATWOOD GAILEY is an Associate Professor at the University of Tennessee in Chattanooga (UTC). Her research interests include representation of women in popular culture, the links between gender, consumption, and popular culture and the role of the media in social change. She is the author of *Write to Death: News Framing of the Right to Die Conflict from Quinlan's Coma to Kevorkian's Conviction* (Praeger, 2003).

JENNIFER GILLAN is an Associate Professor of English and Media Studies at Bentley College. She has published essays on Television, Film and Native American Studies in *Cinema Journal, American Literature, Arizona Quarterly*, and in a number of other journals and anthologies. She is working on a book on Reality Television and is the co-editor of several award-winning multicultural anthologies, *Unsettling America, Identity Lessons, and Growing Up Ethnic in America* (Penguin, 1994, 1999, 1999) and *Italian American Writers on New Jersey* (Rutgers, 2003).

ANNETTE HILL is Professor of Media, and Research Director of the School of Media, Arts and Design, University of Westminster, UK. Her books include *Restyling Factual TV* (forthcoming, 2007), *Reality TV: Audiences and Popular Factual Television* (2005), *TV Living* (with David Gauntlett, 1999) and *Shocking Entertainment* (1997), as well as a variety of articles on audiences and popular culture. She is the co-editor (with Robert C Allen) of *The Television Studies Reader* (Routledge 2003). Her current research interests include interactive media audiences.

ANNE JERSLEV is Associate Professor and Head of the Section of Film and Media Studies at University of Copenhagen, Denmark. Her latest book publication in English (edited together with Danish art historian, Rune Gade) is *Performative Realism: Interdisciplinary Studies in Art and Media* (Museum Tusculanum Press, 2005). In addition, Jerslev is the author of books on David Lynch, cult films, and music video youth communities. Her latest book in Danish is about media and intimacy. She is currently the director of a research programme funded by a grant from the Danish Research Council for the Humanities about contemporary popular media culture.

JANET McCABE is Research Associate (TV Drama) at Manchester Metropolitan University. Author of *Feminist Film Studies: Writing the Woman into Cinema* (Wallflower, 2004), she is co-editor of and contributor to *Reading* Sex and the City (I.B.Tauris, 2004), *Reading* Six Feet Under: *TV to Die For* (I.B.Tauris, 2005), *Reading* The L Word: *Outing Contemporary Television* (I.B.Tauris, 2006) and *Reading* Desperate Housewives: *Beyond the White Picket Fence* (I.B.Tauris, 2006). She is managing editor of the new television journal *Critical Studies in Television* (MUP) as well as (with Akass) series editor of 'Reading Contemporary Television' for I.B.Tauris.

JOANNE MORREALE is an Associate Professor of Communications Studies at Northeastern University. She is editor of *Critiquing the Sitcom* (2002), a compilation of essays addressing race, class, and gender issues in the television situation comedy, and has published several articles on ideological analysis of televisual texts. She is also the author of two other books, *A New Beginning: A Rhetorical Frame Analysis of the Presidential Campaign Film* (1987), and *A History and Criticism of the Presidential Campaign Film* (1992), and she is a contributing author to *The Persuasion Society* (2001).

NIGEL MORRIS is Principal Lecturer in Media Theory and Teacher Fellow in the Department of Media Production, University of Lincoln. He is the author of *The Cinema of Steven Spielberg* (Wallflower Press, 2007). His other publications include articles and chapters on aspects of American, British, German and Welsh cinema, literary adaptation, and cinematic and literary modernism.

GARETH PALMER is Postgraduate Tutor for Research in Media and the Creative Arts at the University of Salford. His recent publications have centred on questions of consumption and lifestyle. In 2003 he published *Discipline and Liberty* with Manchester University Press. His next book will consider how media employ modes of enchantment to circulate and sustain pre-rational discourses around magic (astrology,

makeover as alchemy/transformation, showbiz as magical kingdom etc).
At present he serves as an associate editor with SurveillanceandSociety.
org. Palmer is also occupied with practical work as a writer/producer
with three projects in progress. His next book will consider the ways in
which lifestyle television works through class and models of the self.

HELEN POWELL is a Senior Lecturer at the University of East London
and is Programme Leader for Media & Advertising. Prior to lecturing,
she gained a PhD from the British Film Institute and has worked within
the advertising industry. Her research interests include commodification
and celebrity culture, creativity and advertising, and the role of the
celebrity expert in the development and promotion of a post-War DIY
culture in the United Kingdom. At present she is working on two
publications, one looking at processes of identification in relation to the
celebrity (Palgrave, forthcoming) and a co-authored book, *The Advertising
Handbook* (Routledge, 2007).

SYLVIE PRASAD teaches Media and Cultural Studies at the University
of East London and is Programme Leader for Media Production. She
writes on photography and cultural politics and research interests include
the role of celebrity experts in knowledge transfer and the photograph
and commodity culture. Her work as a photographer has been exhibited
widely including *Shadow Cities* (2004) a solo show for the London
Biennale, UK, and *Night Flight* (2005) at Museum Man and the Institute
of International Visual Arts, Liverpool, UK. She is currently working on
a book and photographic project, *Making it Real: Exterior Design, Lifestyle
and the Self*, which examines transformations on a housing estate in the
north-west of England.

GUY REDDEN teaches Media and Cultural Studies at the University of
Lincoln. His research revolves around the moral dimensions of consumer
culture. He has done work on the commodification of personal guidance
(self-help and alternative spirituality) and on expressive gift economies
on the Internet (activism, blogging etc). Recent publications include:
'The New Agents: Personal Transfiguration and Radical Privatisation in
New Age Self-Help' in *Journal of Consumer Culture*, and 'Read the Whole
Thing: Journalism, Weblogs and the Re-mediation of the War in Iraq' in
Media International Australia.

VANESSA RUSSELL is a Melbourne writer and is completing postgraduate studies at the University of Melbourne with a thesis on 'Losing My Religion: Studies in Deconversion'. Her research interests range from celebrity exercise videos to graphic novels to literary deconversion narratives. Her recent work has been published in *Meanjin*, *Island*, and *Anthology of Australasian Short Stories* and an article about the illusion of the attainable body in celebrity exercise videos was published in *Interactions*.

Introduction

READING
THE MAKEOVER

Dana Heller

Everyone loves a good transformation.' Or so claims Anita Gates
(2005) in her critical assessment of the recent explosion of popular
home makeover shows that have overtaken American cable television
since the Learning Channel's (TLC) 2000 premiere of *Trading Spaces* (the
US adaptation of the popular British show *Changing Rooms*). Suddenly,
or so it seemed, everything and everyone was in need of a makeover, or
at least the experience of watching one performed on television. And
the practice seemed to cut across all genres and time slots, insinuating
itself into local news programmes, serial dramas, talk shows, soap operas,
sitcoms, game shows, and thus into the daily viewing rituals of multiple
niche markets and demographics. With the 2003 success of ABC's
Extreme Makeover: Home Edition, the genre became an established network
hit. Not long afterwards, I recall a segment of the popular ABC morning
show *Live With Regis and Kelly* (2004) that featured 'nursery makeovers',
thus proffering the ideal solution for style-deficient infants – and their
parents – in need of a self-enhancing lift. More recently, *The New York
Times* reports that suburban homeowners have made 'garage makeovers'
(Kocieniewski 2006) one of the newest, fastest-growing segments of the
home-improvement market. And the very next day, as if determined to
keep thematically on point, a well-known op ed columnist and critic of

the George W. Bush administration proclaims that it is high time for an 'extreme makeover at the White House' (Kristof 2006).

The television makeover rage, and the popular idiom of reinvention that it has spawned, shows no signs of abating. 'It's not hard to understand the genre's popularity,' Gates explains. 'Combine the traditional importance of home with a hunger for security in the post-September 11 era and a growing middle class sense of entitlement, and you get a huge potential audience eager for home improvement' (2006). But on second glance it isn't only American television that has been overtaken by makeover shows, and it isn't only homes and gardens that audiences in the United Kingdom, Europe, and around the world have set their sights on remaking. In fact, beyond the private space of the home (e.g. *Extreme Makeover: Home Edition, Design on a Dime, Trading Spaces, While You Were Out*), makeover television is transforming the body by means of cosmetic surgery or rigorous self-discipline (e.g. *Extreme Makeover, The Biggest Loser, The Swan, I Want a Famous Face*). It is reconfiguring the dynamics of intimacy, heterosexual courtship, and family life (*The Bachelor, The Bachelorette, Supernanny, Wife Swap, Nanny 911*). It is remaking ordinary people into celebrities and well-known celebrities into ordinary people (e.g. *American Idol, I Want to Be a Hilton, The Osbournes, Britney & Kevin: Chaotic, Newlyweds, The Simple Life, Ashlee Simpson*). It is performing a virtual overhaul of consumer principles, strategies and lifestyle (*Pimp My Ride, Made, Camp Jim, ToddTV*). And it is recasting critical elements of social identity, in particular gender, race, and class (*Faking It, The Apprentice, Queer Eye for the Straight Guy/Girl*, and the soon-to-premiere *Black.White*, in which 'two families – one black and one white – come together under one roof in Los Angeles' [2006] as they prepare to trade races and experience the world through the eyes of the other).

Of course, narrative investment in extreme transformation of the subject – occurring virtually overnight – is nothing new, as readers of Charles Dickens well know. However, while literary makeover cases such as Ebenezer Scrooge awaken one morning to find their cynical, miserly impulses replaced by purity of heart and giddy generosity of spirit, today's televisual makeovers emphasize physical change and material/ service acquisition as the paths to genuine expression of one's inner self and better nature. Perhaps, as several contributors to this volume suggest, it is true that makeover television programming provides the new consumerist fairy tales for our times. However, if this is so, what sorts of lessons are we really to learn from them and what kinds of social, historical, technological, and epistemological conditions inform their production and reception? Or as one of my students recently asked, in an effort to comprehend the astounding success of ABC's *Dancing with the Stars* (a show that stages a competition of celebrities determined to make themselves over into master ballroom dancers), 'what is the problem to which mastering the Cha Cha is suddenly the solution?'

Makeover Television: Realities Remodelled is a collection that explores these questions within the over-arching context of global television's own ongoing, evolutionary makeover of its constituent, hybrid parts, otherwise known as genres. Indeed, as Anna Everett rightly observes in her discussion of HGTV and TLC home improvement shows, makeover programming is only one of the latest 'contributions to reality TV's new global programming gold rush' (2004: 158). *Makeover Television* thus examines the international explosion of reality television programming by focusing on the largely British and American phenomenon of 'makeover' formats. Our argument, broadly phrased, is that contemporary makeover programming provides the paradigmatic example of reality television's prominence and far-reaching mass appeal. Specifically, that appeal lies in what Jack Z. Bratich in this volume calls 'powers of transformation,' or a televisual performance that does not merely attempt to capture reality but transform it, with the ultimate aim of remodelling reality.

Of course, the perennial popularity of makeover formats is apparent not only among television producers but with audiences as well. Here, in the United States, ratings for shows such as *Extreme Makeover: Home Edition* have posted higher than popular scripted dramas, gaining audiences in a surge that has stunned both critics and industry executives. With this in mind, one of the aims of *Makeover Television* is to investigate the pleasures of the makeover text, particularly as many of the contributors to the volume approach their objects not only as scholars and critics but as regular viewers and fans. Of interest are not only the ways in which makeover television remakes its subjects, but the ways in which it reconfigures the role of audiences as both passive and active. This reconfiguration of audience participation is centrally related, as several authors note, to the historical processes by which makeover television has itself been made by borrowing and mixing elements of other media genres, such as exercise videos (following Vanessa Russell's essay in this volume), high fashion photography (a visual link that Anne Jerslev herein investigates), and advice columns from traditional women's lifestyle magazines (as Kathryn Fraser observes in her essay on the makeover as modern Pygmalion myth). In fact, as Nigel Morris argues, it is this reshuffling of elements that results in makeover television's seemingly unique televisual structures and narratives, many of them advancing the politics of identity in their seemingly unscripted representations of gender, class, sexuality, race, and nation.

With so much at stake, and with such a dazzling proliferation of sub-genres that are all at once clearly part of what Rachel Moseley famously termed the 'makeover takeover', *Makeover Television* is organized into four sections. The first section looks at the problem of defining makeover television for the purposes of understanding broadcaster, audience, and wider societal investments in its discursive forms and practices. Here, as Annette Hill and Caroline Dover's empirical research shows, makeover television – while remaining an imprecise category – demonstrates an unequivocal character in its tendency to eliminate 'real life' from lifestyle television.

The volume's second section considers the dominant principle of celebrity in reality makeover narratives. Helen Powell and Sylvie Prasad's study of the 'expert' host of makeover programming along with Jennifer Gillan's reading of Britney Spears' contribution to Rock Star Reality Television, *Chaotic*, reveals celebrity aura as an imagined link between ordinary and extraordinary social identities and as a practical guide in the transformative process of media self exposure. The third section focuses squarely on questions of social identity, or the gendered, sexualized, nationalized, and class-based elements of makeover narrative that deliver the ethos of transformation in both 'fictionalized' (as in Kim Akass and Janet McCabe's feminist analysis of *Nip/Tuck*) and 'non-fictionalized' (as in Joanne DiMattia's study of the masculinities produced by *Queer Eye for the Straight Guy*) formats. And the last section considers the commercial traffic in makeover myths, across fields of media production and neo-liberal propaganda, in an effort to identify the larger ideological contexts in which the industrial and national appeal of the makeover formula circulates. Here, for example, Gareth Palmer considers the hugely popular series *Extreme Makeover: Home Edition* as a modern day American fairy tale that champions right-wing political interests in its celebration of nuclear families and the commercial market as a magical cure-all for their hardships and sorrows, while Guy Redden argues that makeover shows, particularly in the British context, form their own 'makeover morality' around the logic of liberal consumer capitalism and its marketing of personalized choice and values.

As editor, then, my hope is that readers will discover in this volume an arrangement of essays that sustain and advance the current critical discussion of reality television while offering something fresh and innovative in their emphasis on the makeover ambitions that drive the reality television movement to perennially remodel its realities anew. Happy reading!

Chapter One

PROGRAMMING REALITY

Control Societies, New Subjects and the Powers of Transformation

Jack Z. Bratich

In spring 2005 the television show *Intervention* premiered on A&E. The programme followed the lives of addicted protagonists, who thought they were just being filmed for a documentary. However, the programme was part of an effort by the families to perform a 'real' intervention (getting the individual to rehabilitation). The show thus was not simply a document of an intervention – it was a co-conspirator and collaborator in the process. The show's goal was not to represent changes in the world, but to directly *produce* those changes via a televisual format.

Intervention could be placed into the 'makeover show' category, but this means expanding our notion of makeover. For instance, 'real' interventions themselves would have to be seen as psychological and biological makeovers. *Intervention* is not an exceptional programme: it condenses into one programme the processes that, I will argue, run throughout reality TV. Essentially, its subject matter and its techniques of representing that subject matter fuse together. My argument here is that 'makeover' goes beyond the shows typically associated with it: 'making over' and transformation define the very essence of reality TV itself.

The oft-heard initial responses to reality TV – that it is 'really' constructed, that it still depends on codes of representation, that it is highly stylized and artificial – miss the crucial innovations that the genre brings. Reality television (RTV) may be less about representing reality than intervening in it; less mediating and more *involving*. Less an aesthetic genre than a set of techniques and social experiments, RTV is more accurately a televisual version of 'reality programming'. This article examines the interventionist tendency for its social and political ramifications. I analyse the ways RTV transforms subjects, highlighting how programmes test the physical and mental limits of individuals. The goal of these transformations is the creation of malleable subjects adequate to new economic and social conditions. Finally, I argue that the closest cultural form to RTV is actually the fairy tale. With its emphasis on metamorphosis and transformation, RTV takes on the cultural function of the archaic fairy or wonder tale. But rather than dismiss RTV in this way (as ideological mystification, as fantastical escapism), I highlight the new potentials emerging from RTV's *inscapism*, or the *immersion* into everyday life.

The Reality Transformation Programme

Since its emergence, television has had an intimate relation with the reality of everyday life. From its early integration into the everyday rhythms of the domestic sphere to its long-standing interest in capturing events in real time, from its proliferation into mundane mobile spaces to its mobilization of viewers to consume, vote, wage war, television has sought to represent, capture, and alter its perceived other – reality. Reality TV is a culmination of this long history, seeking to finally embed itself in everyday life.

Numerous scholars have noted that RTV is much more than a representational vehicle (Couldry 2004; Andrejevic 2003; Scannell 2002; Lewis 2004; Murray and Ouellette 2004; Palmer 2002; Fetveit 1999). What these studies show is that RTV alters the medium's organization and logic: its relation to everyday life, to audiences, and to the contexts from which it emerges. I am not arguing that TV and reality are one and the same, but that we can displace the debates over realism, reality, and representation altogether. In other words, RTV does not *represent* the current conjuncture – it interjects itself into the conjuncture and enhances particular components required by it.

One televisual precedent that can shed some light on this pragmatic feature is the early 1990s trend of makeover-themed daytime talk shows. On *Jenny Jones*, *Sally Jessie Raphael* and *Ricki Lake*, among others, deviant teens found themselves transformed in style thanks to parental collaboration with the show. The 'boot camp' episodes of talk shows were also important predecessors. Unruly children would be brought onto the show with their frustrated parents, and then collectively transferred to privatized military camps for behaviour modification. The programme, having assisted in sending them off (to cheers from the audience) would also follow-up on how successful the camps were. These boot camp episodes did not just represent these practices; they enacted them. The programmes were *performative* acts: distribution mechanisms for the boot camps. Boot camps, and now RTV, function as a *promise*: 'this can happen to you, too', 'we will offer you the chance to participate', and 'you, too, can solve familial problems'. Perhaps to pay homage to this ancestor, ABC aired a show called *Brat Camp* in summer 2005, which followed troubled teens as they were led into the wild to transform themselves. *Brat Camp* crystallizes that feature of RTV found in *Intervention* and elsewhere: making over subjects. RTV can thus be conceived of as a performative phenomenon that captures, modifies, reorganizes, and distributes what I am calling 'powers of transformation'. These powers obviously don't 'belong' to RTV. As other contributors to this volume note, the capacity for reinvention is part of the American mythos. From the Jeffersonian self-made citizen to melting-pot ideologies, the American character has been defined around the ability to alter oneself in accordance with changing contexts. In addition, I will trace these practices of metamorphosis to the archaic function of the fairy tale.

Plenty of RTV shows are arranged around this power of transformation: the home improvement and redesigning shows make a game out of domestic rearrangement (*Extreme Makeover: Home Edition*, *Design on a Dime*, *Trading Spaces*, *While You Were Out*, *Garden Police*, and much of the line-up on the Home & Garden, Style, and Discovery Home channels). The design shows render the spatial arrangement of things and people in the home malleable, redefining 'home-work' as a fusion of labour, spatial rearrangement, and know-how. Other programmes encourage personal transformation via property improvements (*Pimp My Ride*, *American Chopper*, *Movin' Up*). This persistent reconfiguration of private spaces and objects becomes a means of self-improvement that reshapes subjects in their relationships to masculinity (Hay 2004), kinship (Tincknell and Raghuram 2002), and citizenship (Ouellette 2004).

Transformations occur by turning ordinary people into celebrities (*American Idol*, *I Want a Famous Face*, *America's Next Top Model*, *I Want to Be a Hilton*) and celebrities into ordinary people (*The Osbournes*, *Newlyweds*, *The Anna Nicole Show*, *The Simple Life*, *The Surreal Life*, *Ashlee*

Simpson, *Being Bobby Brown, Hogan Knows Best, My Fair Brady, Breaking Bonaduce*). Personal transformations occur through style overhauls (*Queer Eye for the Straight Guy/Girl, Ambush Makeover, What Not to Wear, How do I look?, Starting Over*), seduction training (*From Wack to Mack, Wanna Come In?, Beauty and the Geek*), corporeal alterations (*Extreme Makeover, The Swan, I Want a Famous Face, The Biggest Loser, Celebrity Fit Club*) and entire life overhauls (*Made, Camp Jim, Changing Lives, ToddTV*). For women, transformations go from unattractive to beautiful (*The Swan*) and then 'from beautiful to sexy' (*America's Next Top Model*). For men, from loser to winner (*Average Joe*) and from loser to player (*Wanna Come In?*).

And this just covers *individual* transformations. Programmes like *Renovate My Family, Wife Swap, Trading Spouses, Nanny 911, Supernanny*, and *Meet Mr. Mom* make the nuclear family the unit of transformation. CNN's *Turnaround* targets small businesses for a makeover, and the unit keeps getting larger – as *Town Haul* makes over a small (economically depressed) town.

Even shows whose purported content is not about transformation end up iterating just that value through their participants' statements. We often hear about the 'learning process' and maturation of youth in their encounter with various social identities in MTV's *The Real World* and *Road Rules*. Contestants consistently speak of personal growth through self-knowledge on *Big Brother* and *Survivor*. Losers on these programmes often have more compelling parting words than the winners. Nick Couldry (2004) has directed our attention to these moments in RTV, namely the rituals by which contestants morph from players back into 'real world' subjects. In *The Amazing Race*, emotional outpourings during this ritual produce grand statements about self-transformation via the intense time with their partner (romantic, familial, platonic). On *The Biggest Loser*, achieving official numerical victory also takes a backseat to the processes undergone by contestants. Players and their families regularly stress that it is not the physical change that matters but the rejuvenated self-value and revived spirit. And this change is not contained within the programme's televisual run. As many put it, it is all a 'work in progress'. Losing is not defeat, but an opportunity for learning, a process and not an outcome.

Contestants often define the resistance to transformation as a character defect. On *Beauty and the Geek*, for instance, Richard was consistently singled out as someone who was annoyingly asserting his quirky personality rather than undergoing a change as required by the unstated codes of the game. *American Idol* locates progress not only in the contestant's improved vocal skills, but also in their ability to open up their expressive selves and find their unique voice. 'Not opening up' is a flaw that will get contestants on *America's Next Top Model* eliminated, as well as a more informal concern among participants on *The Real World*. In sum, regardless of the explicit goals of a programme (money, victory, romance, an entertainment industry contract), the informal processes include a demand for learning about oneself, for 'getting out of the comfort zone', for assessing character flaws in oneself, and ultimately committing to a metamorphosis based on these processes.

Beyond finding the theme of transformation within the content of programmes, we should also consider RTV's relation to its audience. RTV, as many scholars have noted, is marked by an increase in audience interactivity (Andrejevic 2003; Tincknell and Raghuram 2002; Holmes 2004; Griffen-Folley 2004). RTV's integration of audiences into its programming design turns seemingly passive viewers into labouring subjects, whose participation alters programming outcomes (e.g. winners). More importantly, it transforms their own place in the televisual medium – audiences are now considered 'co-programmers' and 'co-producers'. RTV has altered 'audience power', the mediated capacities to affect and be affected, by harnessing those powers as the shows' life-blood (Bratich 2005).

In addition to audience feedback, interactivity comes via the fact that most RTV programmes are comprised of ordinary people. The audience doesn't just interact as voters: it functions as a pool of potential contestants and participants. No longer positioned as receivers of communication, no longer assigned to the role of spectators or consumers (no matter how active), no longer relegated to producing fan sites and subcultural communities, audiences now constitute the 'texts' themselves. Obviously this does not mean ordinary people typically get to design the scenarios, cast the programme, edit the text, or reap the profits that producers do. But it does mean that the audience is incorporated as a variable into the design itself, that ordinary people are transformed into players/participants whose actions can alter future arrangements.

Finally, reality TV's human subjects have become increasingly replaceable and interchangeable. Shows now turn subjects into variables, allowing expelled contestants to return (*The Contender, The Apprentice, Survivor: Pearl Island,* and *Big Brother*) and replacing others (*Road Rules X-Treme, Forever Eden*). *Trading Spouses* and *Wife Swap* make parenthood an interchangeable variable, while *Who Wants to Marry My Dad?* reverses the traditional roles of the subjects of arranged marriages. Ordinary people can transform into fictional characters (*The Real Gilligan's Island*) and fictional characters come to stand in for living ones (*My Fair Brady*, with TV mom Florence Henderson acting as Christopher 'Peter Brady' Knight's mother when meeting future fiancé, Adrian Curry). The most direct example of interchangeability was on *ToddTV* when the producers, facing a diffident and unruly protagonist, introduced him to his potential replacement – some random guy also named Todd. Transformation in these examples refers not to a single, isolated individual with flexible capacities, but versatility in the position itself: *the capacity to be replaced*. These powers of transformation are thus embedded in the very design of RTV and seek to become embedded in the programming of reality itself.

'Reality ain't what it used to be': Pimp my Society

These showy makeovers are the visible symptoms of a larger condition of making over relations between television and reality itself. The fact that individuals, families, businesses, and towns can all be made over demonstrates that reality itself may be, at bottom, identified by this malleability. But how is it that reality can be equated with the modifiable? Doesn't it by definition refer to the grounded, the sturdy terrain, and the stable strata of being itself?

Dislodging reality from these connotations need only go to the genealogy of the term. The phrase, 'reality ain't what it used to be', takes on new significance if we recall that the etymology of 'reality' belongs to a tradition of sovereign power. Reality has its roots not only in the *res* but also in the *rex*: 'of the king' or belonging to the king. In its link to 'realty', reality came to mean 'fixed or immutable property'. 'Reality', 'realty', and 'royalty' conceptually emerge in this matrix of land and power. Reality was the province of the Godhead: the kingdom as both land and legitimate existence. The power to define rested with the sovereign's power over territory. This etymological lineage means that 'reality' has been less a matter of truth and veracity than about the authority and power to *make things happen*. In other words, thinking of reality as a neutral source of representation is only a recent historical development.

And what are the characteristics of current configurations of reality and power? Gilles Deleuze argues that in the post-Second World War era there has been a general transformation in the ways power operates

(1990a; 1990b). Power no longer emanates primarily from a sovereign subject at centre (or top), nor is it housed in a series of institutions with internal rules and procedures (as in Michel Foucault's notion of disciplinary power). The disciplinary power once fixed inside discrete sites and institutions now flows throughout the networks of society (Rose 1999: 234). Phenomena like the rise of outpatient therapy, work-at-home labour, continuous education, and house arrest are examples of this social spread. Deleuze calls this current configuration a 'control society', defined by its ceaseless modifications, instantaneous communications across space, and decentralized diffusion into everyday life. Reality, in this formula, is not a stable field of objects, each with representable essences. It is instead a mobile network of forces defined by their exteriors, by the *relations* among forces. Control works by modulating and experimenting on these relations. Objects become variables, targets of modification, and are increasingly integrated into the social design: as Deleuze puts it, 'in a control-based system nothing's left alone for too long' (1990a: 175).

A number of autonomists elaborate on this analysis by highlighting the economic conditions for these control mechanisms (Dyer-Witheford 1999; Hardt and Negri 2000 & 2004). Flexible labour, the fusion of labour/leisure, the mobile precarious workforce, and digital information infrastructures are all part of this post-Fordist landscape. Labourers are trained to work together in temporary groups, to respond to tasks quickly, to assess their progress through continuous reports, and to enhance their interpersonal communicative skills. These processes create subjects who are increasingly interconnected, nomadic, self-reflexive, and flexible.

Control societies need to shape and encourage this flex-subject, and I argue that RTV is a key cultural form where this occurs. Other scholars have noted this relationship. Alison Hearn (2004) argues that contemporary 'gamedocs' like *The Apprentice*, *Survivor*, *Big Brother*, *Fear Factor*, *Real World: Road Rules Challenge*, and others are built on the management strategies of post-Fordism. As John Ellis notes, participants are 'thrown together by circumstances, they are mutually dependent but in order to survive have to stab each other in the back. The experience is akin to a modern workplace with its project-based impermanence, appraisal processes, and often ruthless corporate management' (2001: 12).

To make this discussion of reality and power clearer, we can note another prominent characteristic of contemporary societies – information and communication technologies. For Deleuze (1990a; 1990b), each age has a particular machine associated with it, and in control societies that machine is the computer. Operations performed on reality are thus akin to those in cybernetics. Michael Hardt continues this analogy by referring to this regime of control societies as 'social software', where ultimately what is sought is an 'infinitely programmable machine' (1998: 36). Reality, rather than being tied to land and agriculture, is more like a *reality software*.

And if this notion of 'reality programming' seems far-fetched, we can note the research being done on programmable atoms and solid matter engineering to understand how far the 'software' metaphor meshes with the physical world. See, for instance, the best-selling *Hacking Matter* (McCarthy 2003), which could have been subtitled 'Molecular Makeovers'. RTV, I argue, is a type of reality software, where subjects are both variables of the programme as well as users granted partial access to that code.

Game Shows and Everyday Life

A brief look at changes in game shows over the years might give us a sense of how reality TV seeks to become reality. Past game shows worked with a high level of abstraction, even transcendence, from reality. This earlier generation of game shows (*Jeopardy*, *Wheel of Fortune*, *The Price is Right*, *The Newlywed Game*, *Card Sharks*, *The Joker's Wild*) was characterized by digitized number displays, hyper artificial spaces (the stage and segmented seats), and disembodied skills (trivia retrieval, price estimation, relationship knowledge, and word association). These programmes established a clear distinction between contestants (with individual seats, boxes, or desks). And while celebrities joined the programmes to assist players, they were conspicuously cordoned off from the ordinary people (often spatially separated a la *Password*, *Match Game*, *Hollywood Squares*, *The $25,000 Pyramid*). These older game shows created a sphere severed from everyday life by taking contestants and viewers into a hyper virtual space.

Today's gamedocs have the opposite trajectory: rather than taking the game into a separate constructed sphere, they seek to immerse game dynamics into everyday life. Programmes like *Survivor* and *Big Brother*, while obviously highly contrived scenarios, depend on melding game dynamics with mundane interpersonal relations (Haralovich and Trosset 2004). And the spaces, while fabricated, also act as experiments in forms of living (domestic and survival zones).

Take, for instance, the imprisonment in the synthetic house of *Big Brother*. Some would say this artifice undermines the programme's claim to reality because it creates a highly controlled zone detached from recognizable relationships (kinship, workplace, institutions) (Tincknell and Raghuram 2002). What could be less real than the contrived stunts and spaces of *Big Brother*? Yet this is precisely what makes RTV the genre for control societies. Yes, it creates extremely constructed scenarios, but these are simply distillations of scenarios occurring across other social sites. With the recent inclusion of sleep deprivation and week-long 'slop' diets, the experience is becoming closer to a televisual version of a 'camp' (Agamben 2005). Yes, it is a laboratory, but that lab is now in the mundane space of the household (the one on the TV screen and the one that surrounds the TV screen). In fact, it is all the more real because this virtual scenario could potentially infuse *any* of those other scenarios and organizations, while belonging to none. In condensing and intensifying human interactions, *Big Brother* transforms these relations in reality. The constructedness of a design might not accurately reflect reality, but that is not its purpose, which is to make it over.

Even shows that have highly artificial competitive events (like *Real World: Road Rules Challenge*) make the parallel dynamics of interpersonal attachment and conflict significant, if not central, to the programme. While early seasons of *Real World: Road Rules Challenge* focused on the athletic competitions, recently these activities have not only become secondary, they are incorporated as variables within the players' subjective dynamics. For instance, a team often tries to 'throw' a challenge when they wish to eliminate one of their own team mates because of interpersonal conflicts. The formal game, rather than being background for or determining personal interactions, is subsumed into the informal games of the subjects.

The historical transformation from highly abstract game shows to the embedded sphere of gamedocs is now seeing a backlash of hyperreal game sets (*Deal or No Deal*, *1 vs. 100*). Overall though, we have witnessed a transformation of the relationship between the genre and everyday life. The 'game', rather than being an escape or separation from reality, now intertwines with reality's details, becoming *immanent* to it.

Testing Limits: The Prank'd Subject

Making over reality involves not only making subjects interchangeable, but also breaking down their boundaries. Just as the factory and other institutions' walls crumble in control societies, so do the borders of individual subjects. They are repeatedly prodded, tinkered with, and eventually made porous to their outside. RTV has been linked to a boom in programmes that 'test character' (Hill and Palmer 2002). These procedures are often corporeal: they probe the body's limits, either for endurance capacities (like standing or hanging upside-down for hours on end, being covered in live worms, bees, and insects) or for gastro-intestinal tolerance (eating exotic animal parts, extremely hot peppers, or live insects). These challenges comprise the micro-practices of a show's contests (*Amazing Race*, *Road Rules*, *Survivor*, *Real World: Road Rules Challenge*) and at times entire programmes are built around them (*Fear Factor*, *Eco-Challenge*, *Brat Camp*).

When it comes to breaking down the limits of subjectivity, there is perhaps no better example than the prank show. Like their predecessors (*Candid Camera*, *Candid Microphone*), these programmes (*Spy TV*, *Scare Tactics*, *The Jamie Kennedy Experiment*, *Boiling Points*) create disruptions in the fabric of everyday life as a way of testing the capacities of the pranked subject. How far will someone go to accommodate these disruptions? These subjects, in good RTV fashion, include celebrities (a.k.a. the 'former ordinary') as well as ordinary people (a.k.a. 'virtual celebs'). A variety of abilities and limits are challenged, such as fear reactions (*Scare Tactics* and *Mad Mad House*), sexual desire and romantic loyalty (*Women Behaving Badly*, *One Bad Trip*), hospitality (*Damage Control*) and patience (*Crank Yankers*, *Boiling Points*). Other programmes take the prank out of the vignette form and arrange entire seasons around it (*Joe Millionaire*, *Joe Schmo*, *My Big Fat Obnoxious Fiancée*, *Big Shot*, *Invasion Iowa*).

One particular prank/hidden camera programme, *Boiling Points*, is especially relevant here. On the show, money is awarded to unaware youths that can tolerate timed patience-testing scenarios. Situations often involve rude and incompetent service workers (bartenders who cut off customers after one drink, exceptionally slow cashiers, bowling attendants who give marks' shoes away), nauseating bodily behaviour (flatulent strangers in waiting rooms) and transgressive interpersonal interactions (pushy beachcombers, ill-mannered blind dates, public exhibitionists). Rewards are given to those who can most placidly negotiate conflict scenarios. Whether they are in spaces of work or leisure, the victims quickly learn that 'it pays to be patient' (the programme's tagline) with violators of social protocol.

Boiling Points is MTV's attempt to produce a tolerant youth through a series of tests designed to push subjects to their patience limits. Individuals who demonstrate civil and polite behaviour are rewarded. Those who don't exhibit this are forced to reflect on their habitually impatient responses, rendering their conduct modifiable. Even more, the interruption of their routine should be welcomed. As Paolo Virno puts it, in our society we have become *accustomed* to 'no longer having fixed customs', to sudden change, and to regularly being 'exposed to the unusual and to the unexpected' (Virno 2004: 33). *Boiling Points*, like other prank shows, performs this acclimation culturally.

More specifically, *Boiling Points* works in tandem with MTV's *The Real World*, a show that also, as Jon Kraszewski (2004) points out, promotes liberal tolerance as a social solution. In this way, MTV (a self-nominated educator of youths) is a training ground for co-operative encounters, for plugging behaviours into 'circuits of civility' (Rose 1999: 246). The title of the show itself tells us much about the general functioning of RTV's boundary-testing practices. A boiling point, we'll recall, is not just a limit or endpoint, but a threshold of transformation (from liquid to gas). Making subjects over means turning youth into a *phase transition* (in physics, the changes between the solid, liquid, and gaseous states), which seeks to transform an entire generation into a set of modifiable and controllable powers.

Breaking down the body/mind through severe challenges is nothing new. Tests of endurance, exhaustion, sleep deprivation, and starvation have historically been part of initiation rites in military organizations, religious orders, and fraternal groups. But this is precisely where we can once again see the shift from disciplinary society to control society. These earlier makeovers were housed in enclosed spaces and bounded institutions. The limit testing was functionally designed to establish loyalty to and identification with that very organization.

This phase transition subject is very different from the one targeted in the first wave of *Candid Camera* and Stanley Milgram's filmed simulations (as analysed by Anna McCarthy 2004). Whereas the earlier subjects were tested for their loyalty and adherence to an anonymous 'them' (especially of the disciplinary society's bureaucracies) the new subjects are tinkered with to see how they perform with others *without* bureaucratic norms for guidance. Challenging social relations to promote tolerance is central. Gendered behaviour, courtship practices, sexual identification, and diversity encounters are all stakes in these experiments.

Rather than breaking down an individual's barriers in order to have that subject identify with the disciplinary institution's own fixed positions, the new limit testing seeks 'openness' as its goal. However, this openness is not a freedom-enhancer; it refers instead to 'ceaseless control in open sites' (Deleuze 1990a: 175). We see a move here from obeying orders to implementing self-organized solutions based on programmatic commands. Individuals, through their bodies and minds, are fragmented and then recomposed as flexible and open-ended, ready to absorb command mechanisms as if they were their own. Deleuze calls this new subject of control a 'dividual'. Rather than being a Self with solid interiority, subjects are broken down into a variety of capacities, and then recombined with others in permanent fluctuation. Whether the rewards are money, social acceptance, self-knowledge, or celebrity, RTV prank shows make the makeover itself a source of pleasure and learning. The pranked subject – learning by being at the ready, able to respond quickly to emergent commands and unfamiliar scenarios – is the subject par excellence of control societies.

Faireality Tales

Interestingly enough, this genre of the powers of transformation has an antecedent that precedes not just television, but mass media and even writing itself. In a significant way, RTV takes up the mantle left by the ancient function of the *fairy tale*. How could this be, given the argument so far about RTV's interventionism? Aren't fairy tales the most extreme version of pure representation we have? Only if we are talking about the commonsensical notion of the escapist narrative. When we typically call something a fairy tale, we are highlighting its most illusory qualities. We dismiss it as a flight of fancy or as a deluded fantasy; something that is most detached from reality. But if we look at the fairy tale's specific definition and history, we can find in its original qualities the keys to understanding RTV today.

The fairy tale was, in its essence, about the powers of transformation. First, much of its narrative content involves magical realms, supernatural powers of inhabitants, and a world imbued with enchanted properties. The world of the fairy tale is made up of spells, charms, invocations, wish-grantings, and other direct transformative actions. In other words, the fairy tale conveys a realm of profound modification and makeovers (as long as the protagonist had the right knowledge and allies).

The characters in fairy tales include chimera, monsters, and hybrids, as well as those who appear in masks and disguises. Fairy tales highlight shape shifters (wolves into grandmas, frogs into princes, Greek gods into animals, transmigration of souls), transpositions of characters (servants into princesses, living to dead and back again), and wishes granted that change the past/present/future. The wish-granters (in recent versions, the fairy godmother) also protect, assist, and guide. Jack Zipes (2002) describes the narrative subject of these tales: 'The success of the protagonist usually leads to marriage; the acquisition of money; survival and wisdom... Whatever the case may be, the protagonist is transformed in the end. The functions form a transformation' (online interview, see also Zipes 1979; 1991). Fairy tales at their thematic core are allegories of metamorphosis (especially subjective ones), which have implications for western conceptions of identity. As Marina Warner puts it, the emphasis on transmutation 'runs counter to notions of unique, individual integrity of identity in the Judeo-Christian tradition' (2).

Second, and more importantly, the fairy tale's social function was not primarily representational. The narratives had an ethical function – namely to transform the *recipients* of the stories. The fairy tale is more accurately called the 'wonder folk tale' or magic tale or marvellous tale. Jack Zipes defines it in this way, 'The characters, settings, and motifs are combined and varied according to specific functions to induce wonder and hope for change in the audience of listeners/readers, who are to marvel or admire the magical changes that occur in the course of events. It is this earthy, sensual, and secular sense of wonder and hope that distinguished the wonder tales from other oral tales as the legend, the fable, the anecdote, and the myth' (2002). Changes to the protagonist of the tale corresponded to changes in the listener upon hearing the tale.

Later, the fairy tale gathered a more specific instructional and moral function (of the Victorian type). Be it training in gender relations, in warning against demonized activities, or in learning lessons about the limit and expansion of the possible, fairy tales were a technique to modify conduct. And these are the more above-board versions of these tales. On the darker side, wonder tales were part of a 'faery' tradition whose main function (for its human participants) was an underworld initiation (see Stewart 1998; 1999).

In other words, the metamorphosis that the wonder tale narrativizes is also its wish for transformation potentials in the world. As Warner puts it, 'stories of this kind promise us change, too' (19). The fairy tale's gesture is thus to become immanent, to turn the word into world, and to make its transformative themes constitutive of everyday life. The very act of transmitting the fairy tale involved a 'blurring between art and nature in order to convey migrating forms of life' (Warner: 2). In essence, the fairy tale performed as well as represented metamorphosis.

As Warner and others see it, these powers of transformation were eventually formalized in literature, especially in the genre of magical realism. But perhaps now with a shift from the printed word to television we have a 're-oralization' (as medium theorists put it). Perhaps now we can even speak of real magicalism? RTV, in its reshaping of subjects, operates as fairy tale or wonder tale. Many shows, as I have detailed above, make the transformation of their protagonists (contestants, participants) central. Even the 'narrative' goals are often similar to fairy tales (success, marriage, survival). The attainment of wisdom today comes in the form of learning about oneself.

Some programmes explicitly draw from the fairy tale genre, including *The Swan* and *Bachelor/ette*. *Joe Millionaire* was set in a castle and included a segment that highlighted how the female contestants kept calling their experience a fairy tale. *Extreme Makeover: Home Edition* typically defines its project as 'making dreams come true' (repeated across a variety of programmes). References to 'prince charmings' and princesses (*Love is in the Heir*) abound. Perhaps as an inaugural ceremonial nod to its tradition, the series premiere of *The Apprentice: Martha Stewart* had its contestants compete by rewriting and updating fairy tales.

Much like the element of surprise central to the wonder tale, RTV also distributes 'twists' widely in its programmes, continually 'breaking rules of the wonder world' (Warner: 18). RTV has its own fairy godmothers; experts in fashion and design who assist individuals in making their wishes come true. In some RTV zones, the fairy tale element has been christianized into the 'miraculous' (where divine intervention takes the form of the Dream Team). On *Extreme Makeover: Home Edition*, for instance, the recipients of aid are often defined as 'deserving'. Their previous personal sacrifice gets rewarded (now on earth rather than in heaven). This particular immanentization of the divine is akin to bringing heaven to earth. And as Gareth Palmer's contribution to this volume argues, this religiously inflected programme also contains the ideological function usually attributed to fairy tales; namely that it mystifies the social conditions of the programme's existence, providing a private, for-profit solution (by corporations like ABC and Sears) under the guise of charitable works.

But the similarities between fairy tales and RTV just enumerated remain representational. More significant is the second aspect of fairy tales – their transformative function within society. As watchers, we are to learn from the protagonists' own transformations, to learn *about* the powers of transformation. Whereas the instructional and transformative component of traditional fairy tales came through authoritative vehicles (tribal storytellers, parental figures) today these techniques are dispersed via the medium of everyday life. RTV makes over its audience as much as its protagonists. Fairy tales are the code for reality software. The powers of transformation once embodied in the wonder tale now find expression in reality television's immersion in everyday life. And in case we lose sight of this connection between the ancient and the postmodern, RTV has given us its own reminder: in late 2005, NBC premiered the reality series titled simply *Three Wishes*.

Conclusion: Making Over Reality

From makeovers to making stars, from making people wealthy to matchmaking, RTV ultimately makes *making* happen. We can think of RTV less as a genre than as a televisual mechanism for conducting powers of transformation. Programming has left television, and the whole of reality itself has become *programmable*. Challenging bodies' limits, interchanging roles and people, collectivizing activities, and testing tolerance thresholds are just a few of the technical procedures deployed in RTV's makeovers. Their effects include breaking down the interiorities of subjects, dissolving them into 'dividuals', and reconnecting capacities with others; in sum, turning subjects into variables, a set of modifiable powers. In Virno's terms, 'what we have then, at every moment and no matter what, is a reality which is repeatedly innovated' (33). Reality programming is an experiment demonstrating that reality is programmable.

From one angle, RTV is a nightmarish cybernetic dystopia. But the control society is not simply the latest in a line of pessimistic scenarios. Television's immanence is not a tale of total information domination. Control itself has changed, making it 'not a question of worrying or hoping for the best, but of finding new weapons' (Deleuze 1990b: 178). Reality programming, in its obsession with metamorphosis (especially of subjects), finds its niche as the fairy tale that provides another dimension of possibility.

According to Jack Zipes, these wonder tales had a populist and political bent to them. They embodied a utopian impulse: 'it is the celebration of miraculous or fabulous transformation in the name of hope that accounts for its major appeal. People have always wanted to improve and or change their personal status or have sought magical intervention on their behalf' (2002). Because of these aspirations for a better life, the wonder tales 'were always considered somewhat suspect by the ruling and educated classes. The threatening aspect of wondrous change, turning the world upside down, was something that ruling classes always tried to channel through codified celebrations like Carnival and religious holidays'. This transformative potential within fairy tales is retained in reality programming.

RTV, as a set of experiments in transformation, ultimately cannot contain the meanings and directions of those experiments. Containment itself belongs to a disciplinary society model of power. While RTV seeks to transform the world into its experiment, it is simultaneously impossible to harness all impulses into the game dynamic. If control societies 'interweave' reality and television, then this interweaving can be undone, and the threads reworked to make new meshworks (Dyer-Witheford 1999: 71).

There is thus an 'ambivalence' at the heart of the absorption of reality (Virno: 84). According to Toni Negri (2004), with the current developments in technology and labour practices:

> we have finally attained an incredible power that used to belong
> to the domain of literary anthropology and that is now ours:
> metamorphosis. The monster can be recognized as the possibility of
> metamorphosis. Once again, as with every open possibility, one finds
> oneself faced with a terrible ambiguity. [115]

In other words, the powers of transformation, once unleashed and nourished, are not easily controlled. As Marina Warner, speaking about the work of Philip Pullman's *His Dark Materials*, puts it: contemporary fairy tales convert the negative shadows of the uncanny 'into a paean to the pure virtuality of transformation as energy itself' (207). With this virtual unformed energy, which knowledges and alliances can emerge? What forms of collaboration are possible? What transformations can be enhanced that don't follow prescribed trails?

Reality ain't what it used to be, but neither is control. Ultimately, RTV depends on popular powers of transformation. These capacities have no necessary goals; no one can own powers of transformation. Fairy tales, a popular storytelling form, cannot simply be used as weapons against people. They invoke and provoke makeovers not reducible to their intended pathways. Those pathways and instruments themselves can be made over, taking unexpected and democratic routes. This is itself a fairy tale. Its end, if there is one, depends on the capacities of new subjects to create their own forms of reinvention.

Note

Parts of this chapter have previously appeared as '"Nothing is left alone for too long": reality programming and making malleable subjects in control societies' in the *Journal of Communication Inquiry* (30:1, Jan. 2006, 65–83).

Chapter Two

MAPPING GENRES

Broadcaster and Audience Perceptions of Makeover Television

Caroline Dover and Annette Hill

Introduction

Like all television genres, 'makeover television' is an imprecise category. By examining broadcaster definitions and audience perceptions of this popular programming phenomenon, we will map the genre within the context of recent changes in British factual programming. This will enable us to examine makeover programmes, not simply through their content, but also through their production and reception in order to get a sense of the makeover format as a whole and, ultimately, its impact on viewers. Whilst text-based studies are able to explore constructions of class, sexuality, nationality and so forth within specific programmes or series, our focus here is on exploring what producers and viewers see as significant characteristics of the genre. And these characteristics are, to a large extent, determined by comparisons with other types of programming. The way audiences have learned to live with all television genres is as much to do with the broadcasting environment – in particular the commissioning and scheduling of a variety of hybrid formats – as the actual content of the programmes themselves.

In our analysis we draw upon surveys of British broadcaster categories within non-factual television, the range of lifestyle and makeover programmes, and quantitative and qualitative research into British audience perceptions of lifestyle. We use a nationally representative sample of all British television viewers and their attitudes towards all types of factual and reality programming. This large sample allows us to map general attitudes to lifestyle, and compare those across significant social groups, and television genres. Our production and reception analysis requires that we select a specific geographical and temporal framework for our study. We will be considering programmes commissioned and broadcast on British television between 2003 and 2006. This timescale encompasses a period in which both new and traditional types of lifestyle programmes co-existed, in which makeover programmes were prominent in the schedules, and in which the characteristics of the makeover format developed. Whilst such an approach is necessarily context-related, we hope that the broadcaster and viewer perceptions of makeover programmes presented here will offer an insight into contemporary and non-British studies of the makeover genre. Many of the series referred to, for example *Changing Rooms*, are successful within a number of different national contexts and have been imported and exported between countries. Similarly, the changes taking place within factual or non-fictional programming are culturally specific to Britain, but also represent general trends in the dominance of popular factual television in many countries around the world (Hill 2007).

Our production and audience analysis suggests that makeover shows take the real life out of lifestyle programming. The popularity of makeover formats has weakened their association with other traditional factual genres and the depiction of 'real life'. Contemporary makeover shows now have a greater association with light entertainment genres. This shift has, to some extent, been reflected in the changing commissioning structures of broadcasters and it has certainly been recognized by viewers. Those who enjoy makeover shows do so because of the programmes' emotional and entertaining content; they do not tend to have high expectations of watching informative or true-to-life content. Our research shows that lifestyle programme viewers are not isolated viewers of this particular genre, but savvy viewers who are aware of general trends within non-fictional television. Thus, a production and reception analysis is valuable in understanding general trends in television genres, and challenging assumptions of lifestyle viewers based on textual analysis alone.

British Makeover Television

Programmes addressing lifestyle issues have existed on British television since the 1950s (and the cookery programmes of Fanny Craddock) but in recent years high audience ratings have been achieved with makeover formats. Expert presenters guide participants to 'improved' homes (*Changing Rooms*), 'improved' personal appearances (*What Not to Wear*), 'better' social skills (*Would Like to Meet*) or all of these things together (*Queer Eye For The Straight Guy*). The many variations of makeover have also been extended to participants' partners, children and pets. Indeed, 'the ability to makeover itself means lifestyle programming continues to perform well in the ratings' (Hill 2005: 31). But, in spite of the prevalence of makeover shows, the category 'makeover television' is curiously absent from the organizing strategies employed by commissioners. Lifestyle and makeover programmes are largely undifferentiated (hence our concern with both here), and are variously referred to as Feature Formats, Feature Series, Factual Features, Leisure Documentaries and Factual Entertainment. They can fall under the jurisdiction of different organizational departments – Factuals, Features or Entertainment – and the lines between genres are now blurred across all non-fiction television. Not only are formats shared across previously distinct categories such as 'documentaries' and 'game shows' but popular topics also appear in a variety of formats. For example, property programmes range from makeover shows (*House Doctor*) to surveillance features (*Homes From Hell*) and reality game shows (*The Block*).

So, although genre boundaries are always imprecise, it would seem that the makeover and lifestyle formats are particularly problematic. British television is, in spite of the growth of a multichannel industry, still very much rooted in the ideas of public service broadcasting. The balance between information and entertainment perceived in factual sub-genres such as the makeover format has political resonance, both within the industry and amongst viewers. Indeed, these two qualities (often perceived as an oppositional binary) are, as we shall see, central to perceptions of all factual genres. Whilst British terrestrial broadcasters compete with each other for audiences using attractive, entertaining formats they are also legally obliged to produce their quota of informative programming (however imprecisely this is actually defined and measured).

By way of an illustration, an interesting area of investigation is the comparison of lifestyle makeover shows and what we might call 'life experiment shows'. In series such as *Wife Swap* and *Faking It*, participants are subjected to life-altering circumstances for a few weeks' filming. Although there are no expert presenters conducting the makeover, the participants do undergo physical and/or emotional transformations as a result of the experiments. Our research shows that such series tend to be categorized by broadcasters as documentaries. As such, they are presented as public service programmes documenting social issues, and are not directly associated with lifestyle features. However, audiences recognize the similarities in format between the two types of programming and tend to associate them as entertainment genres in which the informative content is generally low. Subsequently, the concomitant social value of these shows, as framed by audiences' concepts of public service broadcasting and factual programmes, is also low.

It is through the examination of both broadcast ecologies and audience perceptions that such consistencies and contradictions are highlighted and explored. And it is through such an engagement with the 'contingent and transitory' construction of genre, by both producers and consumers, that further understanding of changes in television can be developed (Mittel 2001: 11). We will begin by considering the commissioning context and by presenting two broadcaster case studies.

Commissioning Departments

In spite of the take-up of digital, cable and satellite services amongst UK householders, the terrestrial channels (BBC1, BBC2, ITV1, Channel 4 and Five) have, so far, retained a significant share of the audience. All of the terrestrial channels are governed, to varying degrees, by public service requirements. It is on the BBC and Channel 4 (the broadcasters with the greatest public service associations) that the makeover and lifestyle shows with the highest ratings are shown. An episode of *Changing Rooms*, the long-running British home makeover show (that has generated formats in the USA and Australia), was able to gain a 21 per cent share of multichannel viewers when it was aired on BBC1 during the period of our initial research in 2003. On non-terrestrial channels such as UKTV Style, Discovery Real Time and Living TV, there is a wealth of makeover programmes but all of them are either repeats of episodes first shown on British terrestrial channels or they are American imports (all of which receive a very small percentage of the audience share). For the purposes of our research here, the BBC and Channel 4 are therefore the most suitable broadcaster case studies.

At the end of the 1990s, most primetime lifestyle programmes followed the traditional magazine show format of presenters/experts featuring in a series of instructional segments about home decoration, cooking or fashion. It was predominantly on daytime talk shows that members of the public were seen in quick 'before and after' makeover items which resembled articles in women's print magazines. In Britain, the focus on ordinary people and their everyday lives (and latterly, celebrities revealing their 'everyday selves') first developed within popular documentary series (Dover 2004; Dovey 2000; Kilborn 2000). It is now seen across the range of factual entertainment genres and over recent years the formula has been successful in conjunction with a variety of repeatable formats.

Consumer reports (such as *Watchdog*, BBC1) present the best value products and investigate company malpractice. Some of the traditional lifestyle magazine programmes shared with such programmes a focus on domestic topics and both addressed the audience primarily as consumers. But as lifestyle programmes increasingly adopted narrative drives, they came to look less and less like consumer reports and more like other reality formats (following public participants in a created-for-television experience). As an indication of the range seen on British television, we can organize factual entertainment programmes into the following (non-official) categories: CCTV/accident reconstruction shows (for example, *999*, *The Planet's Funniest Animals*); list/clip compilation shows (for example, *100 Best TV Ads*); celebrity profiles and 'showbiz' documentaries; formatted social experiments (for example, *Wife Swap*, *Faking It*); reality games/talent shows (for example, *Big Brother*, *The Apprentice*, *I'm a Celebrity Get Me Out Of Here!*). These categories are not, however, entirely discreet, with many series using a mix of formats. Within factual television, the flexibility of traditional sub-genres such as documentary has been seen for some time (Dover 2004). And now, when looking across British factual television, hybrid formats are common (not least in the primetime schedules). *Wife Swap*, for example, combines social experiment and observational documentary with melodrama, whilst *I'm a Celebrity Get Me Out Of Here!* combines formatted social experiment and observational documentary with the game show and celebrity profile. This flexibility may help explain why so many series are successful within a number of different national contexts and have been imported and exported between countries (primarily the USA and UK).

The environment within which British factual programmes are commissioned, made and scheduled to audiences is both confusing and contradictory. In the increasingly competitive multichannel market, the range of programmes produced is now primarily determined by broadcast commissioners (rather than producers). Whilst commissioners are still concerned with genre as a means of identifying and managing desired programming, they are now also closely concerned with scheduling and channel identity (Ellis 2000). The latter requires an emphasis on target audiences and the tone of a channel's collective programming (its brand image). This new environment has urged commissioners to develop strategies for their respective departments and channels but has not necessarily led to greater clarity in their producer guidelines (see below). Indeed, it is possible that the blurring of lines between genres and the replication of formats has been encouraged by the fact that genre and content are no longer such clearly determining factors in the commissioning process.

In order to investigate broadcasters' own categories of factual sub-genres such as the makeover format, we referred to schedules and the Producer Notes published by the BBC and Channel 4 at the time of our initial research in 2003 and also tracked any changes in organization evident at the end of 2005. Producer Notes are intended to help independent producers develop programme proposals in line with the commissioners' aims and also to submit them to the appropriate department. In some cases they also outlined the re-structure of departments. A common feature of all, however, was the absence of any specific definitions of genres/sub-genres.

BBC

Initially, primetime makeover and lifestyle programmes emanated from three different commissioning departments within the BBC, all of which came under the umbrella of Documentaries and Contemporary Factual. Whilst the dating makeover series *Would Like to Meet* and the fashion makeover series *What Not to Wear* were commissioned by Leisure/Popular Documentaries, the home and garden makeover series *Changing Rooms* and *Ground Force* were categorized as Factual Entertainment. Meanwhile, more traditional lifestyle magazine programmes such as *Holiday* as well as consumer affairs series were controlled by the Features department, also within Documentaries and Contemporary Factual.

The Leisure/Popular Documentaries department claimed to be the home of programmes addressing the following topics: motoring, relationships, lifestyle, travel, DIY, home improvement, health and beauty, history, technology, food and gardening. With the exception of 'history' (which is more usually a Specialist Documentary area of concern), these are all obvious lifestyle topics (which in the last couple of years have extended to parenting, pet training, household cleanliness and personal finance). So why were the lifestyle makeover series *Changing Rooms*, *Ground Force*, and *DIY SOS* categorized not as Leisure Documentaries but as Factual Entertainment? The answer is not at all clear from the programme requirements described within the Producer Notes but may be found in the scheduling. Whilst the majority of lifestyle programmes on the BBC have traditionally been shown on the niche channel BBC2, those that counted as Factual Entertainment, listed above, were broadcast on the mainstream, family-viewing channel BBC1. This is reflective of the rise of entertainment-led factual programmes from the end of the 1990s in primetime slots that had been left available by the failure of game shows and sitcoms at that time (Dover 2004). Furthermore, the BBC1 programmes are 30 minutes in length, whilst the BBC2 programmes are sometimes 60 minutes, adopting what the Producer Notes refer to as sectional narrative. This implies that there is an overall narrative that drives the programme for an hour but viewers can join the programme at any point.

The Producer Notes also point to the central importance of format and/or host in BBC1 Factual Entertainment shows. As a dramatic format (hinging on the end 'reveal') and a lively host tending to be what makes a programme 'fun', the implicit emphasis is on entertainment. Although both BBC channels are governed by public service principles, competition for viewers with the commercial channel ITV1 and, latterly, the Sky satellite channels, has urged a populist approach in the BBC1 schedules. It is interesting to note that the Factual Entertainment formats that developed under Documentaries and Contemporary Factual had, by the end of 2005, come to constitute a separate department. Although both are still categorized as dealing in Factual programmes, there is a new Factual Features department that operates separately from the Documentaries department. This name change suggests a weakening of the makeover format's previous links with Popular Documentaries, and a closer association with Features – a category that has always been more indeterminate in its provision of 'information' and 'entertainment'. Examples of traditional Features programming are travel magazines and quiz shows.

Channel 4

In comparison to the BBC, Channel 4 had a clearer organizational divide between Documentaries and Factual Entertainment in 2003, and it was the Features division within the Factual Entertainment department that was responsible for lifestyle and makeover series such as *Property Ladder* and *Location, Location, Location*. Indeed, the Factual Entertainment department was created in 2002 to bring together Features, Daytime, Events (with series such as *Big Brother*) and factual entertainment programmes that had previously been commissioned from the Comedy and Entertainment department. By 2005, the departments had been restructured again and Features was made a separate department from Factual Entertainment. Although not named as such, lifestyle and makeover shows (such as *Ten Years Younger* and *You Are What You Eat*) are commissioned almost entirely by the Features department.

Again, the briefing notes emphasize the importance of presenters and achieving the right balance between information and entertainment. On 'successful C4 Features faces are real experts with on screen charisma, rather than just presenters [...] 20.00 is a very tough slot! Shows need to be entertaining, but they also need to be informative – with "take-out" for the audience' (Channel 4 Producer Notes 2005). Nowhere in any of the Producer Notes for the BBC or Channel 4 were the terms 'makeover' or 'lifestyle' used. This does not, of course, deny the existence of these formats but does add to the difficulties of mapping genre boundaries. What is evident, however, is the centrality of the relationship between information and entertainment in broadcasters' perceptions of all factual entertainment formats and how the balance between the two changes over time and between channels. This is something that we will see reflected in audience perceptions.

Lifestyle Audiences[1]

In the general environment of factual and reality television, audiences most associate lifestyle programmes with other kinds of popular factual genres, such as life experiment programmes (*Faking It*), or reality game shows (*Big Brother*). British audiences use value judgements that are framed according to public and popular divisions, and lifestyle programmes are primarily judged as popular television, and clustered with other popular factual genres. This does not mean to say that lifestyle genres are associated with commercial channels; as we have seen in the previous section, public service broadcasting has championed lifestyle. But it is to say that audiences do not value lifestyle programmes as highly as other more traditional factual genres, such as consumer programmes. For example, 77 per cent of viewers thought that it was important that consumer programmes were shown on television, compared to 18 per cent for lifestyle programmes. Whilst there are connections between consumer-based programmes and lifestyle programmes, as discussed previously, viewers make clear distinctions between programmes with an investigative approach, and those with a more constructed approach to consumer and lifestyle issues. Thus, although one viewer describes lifestyle as 'programmes that are part documentary and part consumer participation' (female, 65+ Socio-Economic Status DE), the majority of viewers see a marked difference between consumer and lifestyle programmes. Before turning to value judgements, and the entertaining and constructed aspects of lifestyle programmes, it is necessary to map the typical lifestyle programme viewer.

The survey used the standard British television industry terms for socio-economic status: ABC1 C2DE. These are based on six categories: AB refers to professional and managerial positions, C1 skilled occupations or junior non-manual workers, C2 refers to skilled manual workers, D semi-skilled manual workers, and E unskilled workers. People who are unemployed or full-time parents and/or homemakers are not classified according to these categories. The survey also used life-stage categories of Pre Family, Family, Post Family, and Inactive. Age, life stage and gender are the most significant factors in frequency of viewing. Viewers in their twenties and thirties, who may be considering having a family, or have children already, are far more likely to be watching lifestyle programmes than older viewers and/or those whose family responsibilities are past, with no dependent children at home. Those viewers who are in retirement or semi-retirement hardly watch lifestyle programmes at all. Women are also more likely to watch lifestyle programmes than men. Of the total sample of 4,516 respondents, 43 per cent regularly or occasionally watched lifestyle, and 50 per cent rarely or never watched the genre. If we break this figure down by gender, 33 per cent of men and 55 per cent of women were regular/occasional viewers. In terms of socioeconomic status, 44 per cent of AB respondents were regular/occasional viewers, compared to 41 per cent for DE respondents. Among 16–24-year-old respondents, 50 per cent were regular/occasional viewers, compared to 36 per cent of 55–64-year-olds. Over half the sample of 25–44-year-olds were regular/occasional viewers of lifestyle. In terms of life stage, 46 per cent of the sample categorised as pre-family were regular/occasional viewers of lifestyle, 58 per cent of those with a family were regular/occasional viewers, and for those post family the figure dropped to 32 per cent.

The statistical data makes no distinction between different types of lifestyle programmes, for example, makeover or gardening shows. The open question in the survey shows that for both older and male viewers there is a higher frequency of viewing for gardening programmes than for makeover shows. Other factors such as household size and the presence of dependent children support the picture that lifestyle programme viewers are more likely to be sharing a household with other people, and/or with dependent children in the home. Newspaper readership profiles support the gender distinction. Readers of the mid market national newspaper *The Daily Mail*, which has a female profile, were slightly more likely to be occasional viewers (30 per cent) than readers of the broadsheet national newspaper *The Telegraph* (22 per cent), which has a more male profile. The majority of newspaper readers, of whatever type of paper, tended not to watch lifestyle programmes (for example, 52 per cent of *Daily Mail* readers, 48 per cent of readers of tabloid newspaper *The Sun*, and 66 per cent of readers of *The Telegraph* did not watch lifestyle programmes). In terms of socio-economic status, there is little difference according to middle-class and working-class groups. People who have a lower income are slightly less likely to watch lifestyle programmes than those with a higher income (55 per cent of people earning approximately £10,000 a year rarely/never watch, compared to 48 per cent of people earning approximately £30,000). The typical lifestyle programme viewer fits with the general pattern for reality TV viewers as a whole (see Hill 2005), although lifestyle programmes usually attract slightly older viewers than other genres such as reality game shows.

An open question in the survey asked respondents to define factual programming as a whole. These illustrative examples show a tendency for younger, and female, viewers to classify general factual programming in relation to lifestyle programmes and a range of popular factual output:

> Anything that isn't labelled as fictional, e.g. lifestyle, game shows, chat shows, travel programmes, *Big Brother* etc. (Female, 25–34, AB)

> Home and garden programmes, e.g. *Gardener's World*, *Changing Rooms*, *Grand Designs*, *Ready Steady Cook*. (Female, 25–34, AB)

> I define any factual programme as not scripted. Programmes such as gardening, cooking, DIY, nature programmes, some chat shows. (Female, 35–44, C1)

The majority of male viewers who did not watch lifestyle programmes were critical of the poor quality and proliferation of such programmes:

> Factual programmes mean mainly daytime and early evening stuff
> to do with doing up gardens, houses, buying and selling houses etc.
> Basically it is all cheap and invariably extremely boring television.
> (Male, 25–34, DE)
>
> Examples of factual television programmes are *Big Brother*, *Wife Swap*,
> *How Clean is Your House*, *Changing Rooms*. These programmes are
> often cheap to produce and are often all over the schedules on each
> channel and rubbish. (Male, 35–44, C1)

For non-viewers, the association of lifestyle programmes with other popular factual output is ammunition for a general criticism of the standards of quality in daytime and evening television. As we shall see, such criticism is connected with attitudes towards the constructed nature of many makeover programmes.

When it comes to talking about lifestyle with friends or family, the same gender and age patterns emerge, so that those who are more likely to be watching tend to also chat about the programmes. For example, 38 per cent of women sometimes talked about lifestyle programmes with others, compared to 20 per cent of men. Similarly, 38 per cent of 25–35-year-olds talked about lifestyle, compared to 16 per cent of respondents aged 65+. However, compared to other factual genres, lifestyle programmes scored low as a talking point, with news, or documentaries, higher on the list of topics to discuss in everyday life (67 per cent of the sample sometimes talked about news). Why this is the case may be connected with the low value accorded to makeover shows, and common perceptions that it is constructed to entertain rather than inform viewers.

The survey compares respondents' personal interest in lifestyle programmes, with their perception of the value of lifestyle programmes on television (respondents were asked 'how important is it that lifestyle is shown on television?' and 'how interested are you personally in lifestyle?'). For the sample as a whole, lifestyle programmes were given a fairly low value status compared to personal interest, which suggests lifestyle programmes were valued for their entertainment elements rather than its perceived importance as a television genre. Of the total sample, only 30 per cent claimed they were personally interested in lifestyle, and 18 per cent claimed it was important that lifestyle was shown on television. The value ratings and personal interest increased for those groups who were likely to watch lifestyle programmes, and decreased for older, and male, groups of viewers. Figure 1 shows that value judgements

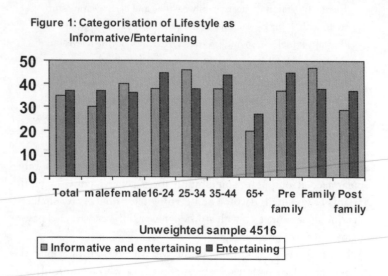

Figure 1: Categorisation of Lifestyle as Informative/Entertaining

Unweighted sample 4516

■ Informative and entertaining ■ Entertaining

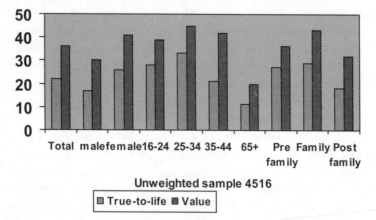

Figure 2: Perception and Value of Lifestyle as True-to-Life

Unweighted sample 4516

■ True-to-life ■ Value

applied to lifestyle programmes are framed according to an information/ entertainment axis. A third of the sample categorized lifestyle programmes as a mixture of information and entertainment, or entertainment only. There was a common categorization of lifestyle programmes, with only minor variations across gender and age divisions, apart from in the 65+ age group. In comparison, a third of the sample thought consumer programmes were informative, and half thought the genre a mixture of both. Given the origins of lifestyle programmes as shows that tell viewers how to do gardening, or DIY (Brunsdon et al. 2001), the definition of lifestyle programmes in Figure 1 shows its development as a genre that provides information within an entertainment frame (Hill 2005).

The issue of learning is one that should be understood in the context of genre expectations. The survey contained three different questions related to learning: general levels of learning (i.e. the number of respondents who claimed they learnt something from watching lifestyle programmes); specific types of learning (respondents could choose from six types); and opinion formation (the number of respondents who claimed lifestyle programmes helped them form opinions about things). We might expect viewers who watch lifestyle programmes to claim they pick up practical tips, for example, 'how to fix a car, how to put up wallpaper, there may be more than one way to do it' (Female, 35–44, C1). However, the reverse is the case. Less than 10 per cent of respondents, across all social groups, claimed they learnt practical things from lifestyle programmes. What viewers claimed to learn about was a general picture of British culture and society which, in relation to lifestyle programmes, suggests learning about cultural patterns or trends in interior design, fashion, or self-improvement. A third of the sample claimed to learn about social issues and general knowledge (35 per cent). Once again, we should bear in mind that the data makes no distinction between different types of lifestyle formats, and we may expect traditional lifestyle programmes such as Gardener's World to be more personally useful to viewers than makeover shows. This finding backs up research conducted by Hill (2005), where viewers rejected the idea of learning from makeover shows. The makeover programme gives viewers a general picture of lifestyle trends, but these are not necessarily trends viewers will follow themselves.

Figure 2 compares respondents' perceptions of the genre as true-to-life, and their attitudes towards the value of the truth claims made within lifestyle programmes (they were asked if they agreed with the statement 'I think lifestyle programmes are true-to-life' and 'how important is it to you that lifestyle programmes are true-to-life?'). It was discovered that viewers did not generally perceive lifestyle programmes as particularly true-to-life. There were minor variations according to gender, age and life stage, but mainly the majority of respondents shared a common understanding of lifestyle programmes, and were somewhat critical of the genre for its constructed nature. In another question, respondents were asked if they thought ordinary people acted up in lifestyle programmes: 54 per cent agreed with the statement and, again, there was little variation according to gender, age or life stage. What the data in Figure 2 indicates is that categorization of lifestyle programmes as a hybrid of information and entertainment leads to expectations that it is constructed in order to make it more entertaining, and this isn't always a good thing. As one female viewer explained: 'I do think that some shows are edited to the programme-makers' own ends to make it more "acted", e.g. *Changing Rooms, Wife Swap, Property Ladder*...'(Female, 25–34, DE).

In summary, the typical lifestyle programme viewer is more likely to be female, in her twenties or thirties, living with other people, and/or with family responsibilities. The content of many lifestyle programmes speak to its core audience, addressing issues such as personal appearance and relationships, interior/exterior design, family care, and showing how these aspects of our lives can be transformed. It is no surprise then that the typical lifestyle programme viewer is at a stage in her life when she is going through major transitions – from dependent to independent living, from full-time education to work, when she is buying a home, starting relationships, having a family, all of which reflect aspects of lifestyle television and all of which suggests that lifestyle programmes speak to viewers' everyday concerns.

But, there are common assumptions about lifestyle programmes (for viewers and non-viewers) that raise issues regarding its socio-cultural and personal value for audiences. The fact that most viewers place little value on lifestyle programmes – learning little about things that personally affect them, and believing it is mainly constructed television where people are performing for the cameras – all points to a general view of lifestyle programmes as light entertainment. This perception of lifestyle programmes is connected to the 'makeover takeover' (Moseley 2000) of the 1990s, where lifestyle programmes moved away from its didactic roots to embrace the spectacle of transformation (Brunsdon et al. 2001). In many ways, audience attitudes towards lifestyle television are connected to women's lifestyle magazines, an inspiration for daytime lifestyle television. When Hermes conducted research on women's magazines, readers described them as 'put downable', meaning they were easy to read and of low cultural value (1995). Lifestyle television is similarly 'put downable', as viewers perceive it as generally entertaining, but having low personal or social value. There is a cultural value to lifestyle programmes in the sense that viewers perceive it is entertaining, and claim to learn about broader cultural trends. Gauntlett's work on lifestyle magazines as providing narrative templates (2002) is useful in thinking of the way viewers are shown patterns of living, and templates for self-improvement. But, if this were the case, we would expect to see viewers placing greater emphasis on using these patterns in their everyday lives, whereas there is actually a reluctance to acknowledge that lifestyle programmes can teach us about how to live our lives. Instead, the research suggests, lifestyle programmes teaches us how other people live their lives, and how television transforms the lives of other people. Therefore, despite the close connection between lifestyle programmes and its target audience, viewers appear to be observing the cultural transformation of lifestyle television rather than British cultural life.

Conclusion

Original makeover shows are predominantly found on public service-orientated channels in Britain and the growth of this genre in recent years has been encouraged within a range of commissioning departments. The absence of the category of lifestyle or makeover programmes in the production context is significant in that the kinds of hybrid formats and international formats that we have come to associate with makeover shows transcend traditional genre labels, and are clearly viewed as part of a wider non-fiction production environment. If producers refer to makeover series as features then this reflects the development of makeover from its origins in daytime magazine slots to its central position as a primetime format. We would argue that the contemporary makeover series is more closely associated with light entertainment rather than factual genres. Its reliance on presenters and formats, and the spectacle of the reveal, has moved the genre away from its information-based roots towards an entertainment frame.

The success of lifestyle programmes on British television is partly explained by its ability to speak to the concerns of its target audience who are themselves going through changes in their lives. One producer describes the makeover as 'takeout' television, where viewers take away tips on interior design, fashion, relationships, parenting and so forth (Channel 4 Producer Notes 2005). But the research simply does not support this view. Whilst the content of makeover series implies viewers take away information, and indeed can be influenced by the lifestyle templates constructed within these programmes, audience research shows that viewers often reject the idea of learning from lifestyle programmes precisely because they perceive it as entertaining and low-quality television.

If anything, lifestyle programmes have taught viewers about the cultural construction of British lifestyle as seen on television – these are TV rooms, TV fashion, and TV makeovers, rather than true-to-life examples of ordinary people and their leisure pursuits. John Hartley's discussion of the uses of television (2000) and its ability to teach people to watch television is appropriate to this analysis, but rather than teaching people to watch more television, the makeover format has taught viewers about the transformation of lifestyle programmes into entertaining primetime television.

Makeover shows take the real life out of lifestyle programming. As with the development of reality TV, the staged reality of makeover ensures that the more entertaining it is, the less real it appears to viewers (Hill 2005). However, just because makeover programmes are staged, it doesn't stop viewers looking for moments of real life within the spectacle of the reveal. Current trends in makeover programmes indicate that these moments of authenticity are less related to lived experiences, and more related to emotional experiences. *Extreme Makeover: Home Edition* is a good example of the makeover as family melodrama. Perhaps makeover programming has moved beyond the genre of lifestyle, and it is time other formats emerge with closer connections to people's lived experiences and cultural and social concerns.

Note

1. The empirical research presented in this article is taken from a project on the reception of factual television in Britain, led by Annette Hill, and funded by two of Ofcom's legacy regulators. Initial research took place during 2003. The research methods included an analysis of media content of a range of factual programmes over a six-month period, and a scheduling and ratings analysis of a range of factual programmes during the same timeframe. Caroline Dover was the research assistant on this part of the project. This analysis formed the basis for a quantitative survey, in association with Ipsos RSL. The survey contained one open question, and seventeen closed questions and was sent to a representative sample of 4,500 people aged 16–65+. Caroline Dover updated the survey of programmes and commissioning structures at the end of 2005.

Chapter Three

'OLD, NEW, BORROWED, BLUE'

Makeover Television in British Primetime

Nigel Morris

Timely academic and journalistic attention to makeover shows, reflecting their prominence in schedules, should not eclipse recognition that perhaps, aside from the programmes, television itself has changed. Rather than seeking significance in what at first appears to be an expression of audiences' tastes and interests within a seemingly free market offering choice, this chapter proposes that makeover programmes in fact demonstrate continuity rather than rupture. While broadcasting's political economy encourages a competition-led tendency towards sensation and excess, it remains 'business as usual', even if the digital era, inevitably and predictably, is altering the mediascape within which commercial rivalry and residual public service principles interact. The emergence of makeover programming manifests not so much a sea change arising out of autonomous social and cultural developments but expansion, combination and reinflection of existing televisual forms. In particular, in the multichannel era, high concept ('water-cooler') programmes have often been transformations of daytime distractions into primetime attractions – routine broadcast events into national Events – aspiring to draw a fascinated and returning gaze rather than a casual glance.

Although most examples here are British, particularities of the United Kingdom's broadcasting history epitomize global issues and trends in the interrelated 'industrial and cultural factors at work in innovation'

(Corner 2004: 291). Policy responses to digital technology have, Ellis (2002) explains, replaced an 'era of scarcity' with 'availability,' whereby broadcasting, formerly 'offer-led' is now 'demand-led' (132). In this competitive system, viewing figures not only record past performance but, for broadcasters, provide 'predictive power': scheduling 'determines the nature and type of programming to be offered to potential audiences' (134). Scheduling, previously 'used to put programmes in order', now '"orders programmes" from the producers' (143). Commissioning editors and overseas purchasers demand established ingredients repackaged and recombined. Among the ingredients central to the overlapping categories of game shows and unscripted reality television which constitute the makeover phenomenon are general rules and conventions familiar from dramatic forms of narrative that makeover programmes, in spreading from daytime, have partly supplanted.

Televisual events

Life comprises successive makeovers, many celebrated or ritualized. Television, rooted in human interest, speech and the everyday, typically focuses on these. Naming ceremonies, starting school or employment, religious initiations, romance, tests, auditions, sexual experimentation, leaving home, military service, graduation, political affiliation, travel, 'outing,' forming and ending relationships, marriage, childbirth, anniversaries, promotion, illness, injury, unemployment, injustice, crime, moving house, separation, divorce, emigration, bereavement, retirement... Willed or imposed, thwarted or achieved, dreaded or yearned for – typical experiences, personally life changing against the backdrop of cyclical and arbitrary social and public events, occupy traditional documentary and docusoap alike.

Television fiction, in common with other fictional forms, likewise hinges on protagonists' ability to alter circumstances or respond appropriately. Narratives entail transitions, sufficiently significant to effect a parallel transition in characters' emotions and behaviour, and a further transition in readers or viewers implicitly 'moved' in some way. Disruption (Todorov 1977) or an inciting incident motivates a quest for new equilibrium, which, under pressure, supposedly exposes 'true' character (McKee 1998: 189, 100–4), often leading to self-knowledge. Stories are worth telling precisely in ratio to the change they represent.

As narrative functions, characters require few individuating qualities. Scholes (1974) hypothesizes a hero given a contract (accepted or rejected), a test (passed or failed) and a judgment, reward or punishment (enjoyed or suffered) (110). While the protagonist, the grammatical subject, is the individual involved and for whom the outcome matters, the role is essentially passive. Countering imposed events, actions are mostly reactions. The protagonist does not advance the narrative unilaterally. Difficulties originate in agents of antagonism, not necessarily characters but any disruption to equilibrium or obstacle between desire and fulfilment, complicating the narrative, raising the stakes, and postponing closure. Accordingly, in *Who Wants to be a Millionaire?* (Celador for ITV, 1998-), increasingly difficult questions and fate's vicissitudes (will a 'Lifeline' help?) threaten progression, the potential makeover from audience member to millionaire. Whereas Chris Tarrant, the presenter of that programme, abets the process, *The Weakest Link* (BBC1/2, 2000-) personifies antagonism in Ann Robinson's sneering put-downs and other contestants' ability to eject a player.

Fifteen minutes of fame, irrespective of the outcome, constitutes a makeover, an elevation from routine existence to temporary celebrity. Participants in extended reality TV contests acknowledge 'voluntary self-imprisonment in a media-created community as a challenge but also a way of confronting or finding themselves,' often by seeking 'a quick route to a new media career' (Biressi and Nunn 2005: 99). But ordinary people on television are interchangeable and dispensable. Their makeover is not permanent, as lack of knowledge, talent or televisual 'charisma' is brutally exposed and hegemony restored as they slip, unnoticed, back into the mundane. Fascination chiefly lies with the antagonist, a permanent feature of the programme's format, whether personified as a formidable and superior judge – as in *The Apprentice* (TalkbackThames/Fremantle for BBC2, 2005-) and *Dragons' Den* (BBC2, 2005-) – or a more abstract correlative of contemporary anxieties structured into the narrative logic, such as the fragility and unpredictability of group loyalty and apparent popularity when competition arises – for example, *Big Brother* (Bazal/Endemol for Channel 4, 2000-) and *The Weakest Link* .

Scholes's model allows numerous permutations of audience positioning. These include involvement as a player, such as participation in a televised lottery; empathy with a protagonist whose life or appearance experts 'make over'; and mastery over participants, occasioning allegiance with the antagonists, as in the elaborated hoax, *Space Cadets* (Endemol for Channel 4, 2005): purportedly cosmonaut training which culminated in a simulated space mission the 'winners' apparently believed was real.

Fluidity and slippage contain critical positioning within the formats' logic. Like fiction, makeovers dramatize ideological, moral and ethical qualms – either defusing them in the knowledge that despite the 'reality' tag it is just TV, with folk judged according to their ability to be 'good sports' by participating; or in certain extreme forms consciously pushing boundaries of taste, acceptability and representability, which consequently are reinforced by their transgression. Vicarious, typically playful, participation simulates mastery over the media-saturated environment, otherwise a postmodern babble of disasters, pandemics, terrorism, crime, global warming, cynicism or political indifference, all seemingly more immediate thanks to surveillance cameras, webcams, camera phones and amateur video. Split identification – between skilled expert or prankster, and makeover recipient, analogous to mythical hero and rescued victim – stages real conflicts between agency and restriction, activity and passivity, control and helplessness.

If every narrative involves a makeover, a narrower definition appears necessary. Yet, as Holmes and Jermyn (2004) argue, 'producing a particular definition of Reality TV' is itself 'complex ... because of the fundamentally hybrid nature of the forms in question' and 'the range of programming' included (2). It is more productive to differentiate the makeover's fluid adaptability and inextricability from the broader reality TV phenomenon and imperatives of programming generally. Rather than a genre or format, the makeover characterizes many hybrid lifestyle, documentary and competition programmes that have provoked controversy through ratings success, consequent visibility in the schedules, dumbing-down accusations, and speculation about what such popularity might mean.

While academic examination of reality TV flourishes, Ellis notes, of leisure and magazine programmes (from which the foregrounded makeover aspect has expanded) that 'This relatively new genre... has been little discussed' (2002: 127, n.14). There are two inter-related reasons for this. One, that they formerly aired almost exclusively on daytime television where many still appear, although particularly interesting is their expansion into mainstream viewing. The other is that commentators only belatedly recognized their centrality to 'shifts in the discourses of gender and their televisual representation' (Moseley 2000: 304). In view of denigrations of mass media for embodying female discourses, back through F. R. Leavis to D. H. Lawrence and earlier, it is unsurprising that the peaktime irruption of daytime formats, previously by definition marginal, coincides with concerns about compromised public service ideals.

The remainder of this chapter discusses hybridity, examines specific characteristics and functions of the makeover category in relation to industry developments, and finally considers the pleasure(s) they offer audiences.

Television hybridity as cultural form

Distinct genres existed from the start of British television. Live plays, ballet, illustrated lectures, classical music, children's puppet shows, sports and other national events comprised the typical 1950s BBC output. Magazine programmes covered various interests, including fashion, make-up and grooming as well as house decorating and repairs, when only one channel existed for everyone, albeit with the Reithian aim of enhancing cultural experience. John (later Lord) Reith, the BBC's first Director-General, had exerted profound influence on public service broadcasting policies since the 1920s. These included a tripartite commitment to entertainment, education and information, and a paternalistic plan to expose audiences to the high culture that most would not otherwise encounter. Independent (commercial) television (ITV) introduced game shows and light entertainment such as *Sunday Night at the London Palladium* (ATV for ITV, 1955-1967, 1973-1974): these - not strictly hybrids but televised stage variety shows - were nevertheless a compendium of entertainments for a wide audience, decidedly populist to attract the biggest possible share for advertisers. The 1960s saw rapid developments in drama as well as current affairs, encouraging important experiments in drama-documentary and documentary drama. Later, the US import, *Miami Vice* (Michael Mann/Universal, 1984-1989), combined police drama with music video and advertising techniques - producing programmes as stylish, expensive looking and (some would say) superficial as the material surrounding them. The 1990s saw docusoaps, reality TV, hybridized drama series such as *Ally McBeal* (David E. Kelley for Fox, 1997-2002) and the kind of makeover programme discussed here, such as those featuring houses and gardens (combining DIY tips, personality glamour, game-show competitions and consumer affairs).

Hybridity is neither new nor intrinsically postmodern (Altman 1999: 145). Nevertheless, television appears increasingly cross generic. This partly results from creative, experimental evolution, which is, in a sense, inevitable - broadcasting is dynamic, never fixed, and always allows new programme categories to emerge and outmoded ones to disappear. But hybridity also responds to ratings. Branston and Stafford (1999) suggest that hybrids help broadcasters create profitable niche audiences (106). This is not entirely convincing; specialization achieves the same, as cable and satellite providers know. However, hybrid programmes on terrestrial television maximize the general, as opposed to a specialist, audience, by combining what might be two or more smaller audiences. This also helps commercial broadcasters maximize revenue by forcing advertising aimed at different audiences into competition for the same slot.

Ellis presents a case study of genre evolution, showing how 'pets 'n' vets' programmes such as *Animal Hospital* (1995–2004) arose by chance to fulfil scheduling demands (2002: 138–42). Scheduling no longer merely involves pulling viewers from a rival programme but attempts to strip them away nightly. BBC1 faced enormous difficulties attracting ITV primetime audiences from police drama *The Bill* (TalkbackThames/Fremantle, 1983–). Both channels regarded as a strong card the 'blue flashing-light show,' exemplified by dramas such as *London's Burning* (LWT for ITV, 1986–2002) and *Casualty* (BBC1, 1986–) and reality TV reconstructions involving emergency services. But the BBC could not devise a challenge to *The Bill*. Unexpectedly, a week-long, stripped series starting on a Bank Holiday Monday, *Animal Hospital Week* (1995), proved popular, and drew viewers from *The Bill*'s 8.00 p.m. Thursday episode. Commissioned as a weekly half-hour in the same slot, it repeated the success. It was not so much the policing factor but its drama that made *The Bill* a hit. *Animal Hospital* shared similar ingredients: uncertainty, suspense, human interest, dedicated professionals battling against the clock, specialist knowledge, suffering, tragic death, courage, heroism, and the added bonuses of sensational horror, miraculous recoveries and, above all, cute fluffy animals.

Such intimate encounters with emotional content equate to 'the moment of revelation,' a factor uniting many popular successes (Moseley 2000: 303). A fleeting event proposes authenticity beyond what the most melodramatic fiction can provide, pure excess that, although it can be facilitated, lies outside programme-makers' direct control. Moseley notes how makeover shows culminate in 'an eagerly awaited yet "surprise" moment of pleasurable spectacle' when ordinary people – often constructed as 'victims' – react to work on their property or personal appearance: 'the private experience and the public display collapse and merge... where emotion, feelings and anger threaten to explode in closeup' (304, 307, 312). *Big Brother*'s premise, says Executive Producer Ruth Wrigley, is that 'nobody can keep up an act all the time in front of the cameras – the world was going to see [participants] as they really were' after prolonged scrutiny (Ritchie 2000: 26). *The Weakest Link* features its 'walk of shame' and interviews failed contestants. Extreme 'survival' challenges such as *I'm a Celebrity Get Me Out of Here!* (Granada for ITV1/2, 2002–) seek to expose a familiar persona's underlying character by setting distasteful tasks. *Pop Idol* (ITV/Thames Television, 2001–2002) continued on digital service ITV2 after contestants' rejection on the main channel, revealing 'true' reactions as if behind the scenes; BBC1's *Fame Academy* (Endemol, 2002) offered a similar continuation on BBC Choice. Taboo smashing – televising death in *The Human Body*'s 'The End of Life' episode (BBC1/TLC, 1998), the dissection of cadavers in *Anatomy for Beginners* (Firefly for Channel 4, 2005) and medical operations outside traditional documentaries' 'discourse of sobriety' (Nichols 1991: 3–4) in *Cosmetic Surgery Live* (Brighter Pictures/Endemol for Five, 2004–) – similarly indicates a desire for authenticity (equated with what was previously hidden), as well as a test, a makeover, for the viewer and indeed broadcasting culture. As Dyer (1997) argues, the unseen – epitomized in a humanist culture by the human personality – presents a problem for visual media (104). The more images proliferate, the less media-savvy sceptics trust them, yet the stronger the need becomes to penetrate beyond them. Plastic surgery pushes this paradox furthest by purporting to recover the 'real' self by constructing artificial features through painful operations on the real body.

Animal Hospital targeted a younger, female demographic and, with its multi-strand narrative and cliffhanger endings, formally resembled the soap opera. Unsurprisingly, subsequent offerings included a series following veterinarians in training, vet dramas, a vet sitcom and a series observing vets starting professional careers, which emphasized personal lives and private thoughts as much as encounters with animals. This Ellis identifies as the genesis of 'the new (and inexpensive) genre of docusoap' (2002: 142).

Hybridity is now foregrounded in the media landscape, although terms like docusoap and celebrity pop-music quiz show maintain generic categories, albeit mixed. There is nothing new in this apparent transgression of boundaries, only in the coverage it receives as a result of the popular press and television outlets' increased mutual dependence on cross-promotion. Television has always operated along generic lines: the BBC has separate departments for different kinds of programming and ITV has regional companies specialized in genres to sell to the network. Smaller independent companies also specialize. Unsurprisingly, the search for novelty within repetition incorporates elements from other genres.

Characteristics and functions of hybrid formats

Broadcasting in many countries has, with proliferating alternatives to terrestrial modes harnessed to a business-oriented neoliberal agenda, tended towards privatization and deregulation (or 're-regulation,' as Barlow et al. insist, emphasizing advantage to commercial players (2005: 30)). Public service broadcasters within multichannel environments justify their continued existence and funding regimes by responding to ratings while diversifying audiences through widening their own range of channels. Hybrid formats on British terrestrial television in part result from new competition (satellite, cable and digital channels, video and computing), as well as the launch of Channel 4 (1982) and Channel Five (1997) and expansion of broadcasting into a 24/7 service. More outlets, for viewers watching less, stimulate novelty and variety alongside trusted formulas. Increased hours provide scope for experimentation; conversely, risk-averse broadcasters buy proven formats.

Fragmentation across multiple channels means that maximizing ratings no longer necessitates pleasing (or, rather, avoiding displeasing) a notional 'general' audience most of the time. 'Lifestyle' channels confirm substantial appetite for specialized programmes about food, house buying, decorating and so on. Thus, relatively freed from universality constraints, British terrestrial broadcasters can nevertheless often claim, through hybridity, to meet more than one of the public service requirements of entertainment, information and education within a single show.

More programmes, plus smaller audiences, drive down costs overall. American imports, part of what *Broadcast* termed a global 'currency' of formats in a multi-directional market (Schreiber 2002: 1), have influenced reality TV in particular. Low production values originated with enormous debts in the 'big three' American corporate networks in the 1980s, and advertiser-driven alterations to audience measurement that further hit revenues badly (Raphael 2004: 121). The amateur video aesthetic, frequently underlining the reality effect, gained acceptance through economic necessity. Moreover, the BBC's legal requirement since the early 1990s to outsource 25 per cent of productions fuelled the spectacular rise of companies, typically non-unionized and reliant on low-paid casualized labour (again reflecting US trends), specializing in particular types of programmes they sell to, or have commissioned by, the BBC and other channel operators, domestically and worldwide.

A prominent independent is Endemol UK Productions, best known for *Big Brother*. They also made some of the BBC's biggest hits of the last decade, including *Ready, Steady, Cook* (1994–), *Changing Rooms* (1996–2004) and *Ground Force* (1996–2004), which have been exported widely and spawned spin-offs and imitators. These combine gameshow and factual formats, fulfilling education and information PSB requirements, with entertainment that is characteristic of soap operas through an open-ended evolution of relationships among a regular cast of characters. Independent production company Bazal (now Endemol UK) called their output 'infotainment'; Endemol's current website describes their programmes as 'factual entertainment'. Endemol also label themselves as 'the UK's largest "non-broadcaster" producer of entertainment formats for the worldwide market.' This reveals a major industry shift: away from the classical formulation that commercial broadcasters deliver audiences to advertisers and the parallel argument that government-run broadcasters deliver the state to audiences. Endemol, and other non-broadcasters such as RDF and Talkback, sell not only programmes to broadcasters but, especially lucratively, formats to programme-makers.

The distinction between genre and format is crucial. Genres cannot be copyrighted. Formats – particular combinations of elements – can. Successful programmes are exported worldwide as locally adaptable franchises, often fulfilling regulatory requirements as domestically produced output (Magder 2004: 147). Distinctive elements are commodities. Production companies cannot copyright the idea of a dealer valuing antiques, or a joiner constructing shelves. They can, though, copyright a game involving teams buying and selling curios or refurbishing property on a fixed budget with expert assistance, and if the format works, earn fortunes from foreign markets. Emphases in makeovers on narrative, conflict, human interest, identification and, increasingly, interactivity put them at the heart of this world trade.

One significant development is delivery across several platforms. Detailed recipes or instructions for repeating a demonstrated process at home nowadays rarely occupy airspace. Viewers instead use Ceefax or digital interactive services, go online or buy the book accompanying the series, which often becomes a bestseller. Endemol UK's parent company has divisions for exploiting rights and brands, and is dedicated to interactive television, e-commerce software and web design. *Big*

Brother indicates Endemol's direction, as the second series utilized nine different media. Not only did *Big Brother 2* attract Channel 4's biggest 2001 audience, it set world records for interactive television voting and mobile text messaging as well as achieving more online hits than any other European entertainment website. Quiz and competition-based programmes feature offshoot contests viewers can join by accessing a web page, interactive digital TV or premium rate telephone number, and the income from calls (except on the BBC) swells the profits. *Who Wants to be a Millionaire?* finances its prizes through calls from potential contestants registering for selection, while one *Big Brother 3* eviction earned telephone income that exceeded the episode's cost (Magder 2004: 150). Contemporary television exemplifies media hybridity as well as genre hybridity as programme-makers seek to harness to their advantage competing entertainment technologies to the extent that – as has already been the case for some time with Hollywood blockbusters – the flagship programme becomes the brand bearer for a franchise of products and experiences. Equally important, interactivity enhances audience awareness and loyalty, increasing the likelihood of return viewing despite the proliferation of distractions.

Endemol, with ventures in over twenty countries, belongs to Telefonica, a telecommunications multinational that acquired British cell-phone operator O_2 for £17.7 billion in late 2005. According to Endemol, 'the majority of the UK group's output now has interactivity at its core.' While 'enhancing content' is promoted as enriching viewers' experiences (www.endemoluk.com/interactive), it is undoubtedly clearing the path towards interactivity not only in the outcome of the programmes, but in gathering personal information and customizing packages of similar programmes for particular households and, as mobile downloading increases, individuals. Advertising will target viewers personally, in connection with selling related to the programme.

This extends from an experiment by Swindon Cable in the 1980s. Britain's first cable station belonged to WH Smith, who owned the Do-It-All DIY supplies chain. Subscribers to its decorating channel could select programmes about specific jobs, guaranteed to start within minutes. The more people requesting a topic, the quicker it came. They could order materials and tools from Do-It-All via the remote control. As well as preceding the programmes with advertisements for related products – paint, for example, might be promoted pending a wallpapering demonstration – the service also offered further programmes pertaining to the later stages of decorating, such as choosing soft furnishings. Despite the liberal market rhetoric of 'choice' cloaking connections between the long, slow rise of DIY/makeover television and consumer marketing technologies, of which Swindon Cable's provision was an early manifestation, clearly Big Brother was watching even then.

Endemol astutely formats programmes so that mass audiences choose them for entertainment, and return regularly, rather than waiting for hyper-enthusiastic decorators or dinner-party hosts to seek them out from an obscure menu. They have, over several years, been building instructional and consumer-based programmes into entertainment with an eye to interactivity, as evidenced by productions advertised in spring 2002 for the Discovery Home and Leisure channel:

> *Tim Brooke Taylor's Golf Clubs* 'sees the "Goodies" star play... some of the UK's best golf courses accompanied by the club professional who gives him tips on how to improve his game.'

> *Boyz in the Wood* features '*Big Brother* winner Craig Phillips and sidekick chippy Rob Butler. The power-drill toting pair construct from scratch desirable items ranging from a table football to a croquet set and a dowry chest giving top tips along the way.'

> *On Site Story* 'follows the epic tale of Keith and his wife Jan building their own dream home – brick by brick.'

The first delivers comedy, local colour and holiday ideas, alongside opportunities for developing sporting technique and possibly booking a hotel, or at least a few lessons, on-line, with the chance of a tie-in book if it sells on to a terrestrial channel. While the second is not obviously a hybrid, the celebrity crossover makes carpentry appear interesting – indeed sexy, a recurrent ploy – and again could promote a glossy book. Thirdly, 'epic' says it all: Keith and Jan's relationship under pressure promises a melodramatic rollercoaster as they interact with a regular cast of neighbours, lorry drivers and sales clerks at the builders' yard. Experts are, no doubt, on hand with advice. But will the tears and tribulations eventually give way to celebrations?

Pleasure

So far we have explored how and why such programmes are packaged. But why are they popular? And what do viewers gain?

Popular they certainly have been. At the end of the 1990s, before digital competition began to bite hard, *Changing Rooms* attracted one of the largest British audiences for the genre, up to 48 per cent of those watching television in its timeslot, amounting to eleven million viewers. Sixteen countries bought the format. *Ground Force*, also on BBC1, similarly reached over eleven million, and pulled in viewers on four continents. *Ready, Steady, Cook* has notched up 1,500 episodes, while its primetime celebrity version regularly made BBC1's top ten. *House Invaders* (Bazal, 1999–2002) and *Garden Invaders* (Bazal, 2001–) have also gained high ratings for the BBC. All were Endemol productions. Prompted by this, other companies have also developed similar formats.

In attempting to understand this popularity, one should at least consider the pleasures offered to audiences by the industry, driven by its own motivations, as well as their ideological implications. Empirical research would be necessary to reveal actual pleasure and sense-making experiences. A useful starting point is Hartley's (2001) examination of daytime TV, originally an American concept defined against the commercial centrality of primetime. After the Second World War there was anxiety about returning women to domesticity. While evening viewing meant relaxation and family entertainment, daytime presented a paradox. Married women were supposed to be *productive*: not sitting around enjoying television. Nevertheless, this benefit of peace and affluence rewarded hard work and sacrifice, and provided a sense of community to counter domestic isolation. Then again, the reason for daytime television – which was not fully instituted in the UK before 1987 – was commercial: to target goods at housewives who, after all, did the shopping. Such goods, however, were not generally luxuries, but related to household labour. Buy them, though, and the promise was that they would provide more leisure time – to be guiltlessly occupied with television.

The ideological work demanded by this awkward equation required an audience who would identify themselves as housewives (despite lively interest in televised Senate Hearings that fanned a moral panic about unwashed dishes and uncooked dinners: Hatch 2002), and so would associate themselves with problems and solutions addressed in commercials. 'Home making and emotionality,' Hartley argues, were primary concerns. Daytime television, he suggests, encouraged American women to:

put their feet up to enjoy soap operas' emotional dilemmas while
relishing the vicissitudes of neighbourliness;

prepare neat culinary and cleansing surprises for the family while
watching help shows;

take note of the hints offered by TV experts to make the household
economy more efficient;

reflect on the politics of the personal with talk shows;

be updated on desirable products and their purposes in commercials
and sponsors' segments;

bring the children back into focus in the afternoon with shows aimed
at pre-schoolers. (2001: 92)

A similar model developed over the last quarter of the twentieth century
in Britain. Hartley's second, third and fifth points are basic elements of
contemporary lifestyle programming. These combine with the emotional
and relational dimension of soap opera: *Changing Rooms'* presenter Carol
Smillie's pregnancy; domesticity; a woman or sensitive man in charge;
how the neighbours will react to foppish Laurence Llewelyn Bowen's
makeover of their dining room; good-natured banter, with underlying
residues of class tension, between builder Handy Andy and capricious
designers. Interviews with participants about tastes and aspirations, and
varying relationships between them – teams comprising married couples,
siblings, mothers and daughters, gay and lesbian partners among other
permutations – further reflect on the politics of the personal, however
informally: Hartley's fourth element.

How aspects of daytime television, targeted at stereotyped housewives,
came to dominate primetime can be partially explained by resurrecting
Dyer's (1977) suggestions about Entertainment and Utopia. Describing
Hollywood musicals as 'Utopian,' Dyer does not claim that they present
viable social models; rather they evoke experiences and feelings related
to generally held ideals. Dyer also identifies three nuanced modes of
'escapism' in television light entertainment (1973). These acknowledge
what audiences seek escape *from* and *to*, and so recuperate an overused,
frequently simplistic and misleading concept by relating it to felt needs
and experiences. Some shows, Dyer suggests, *obliterate* social reality:
magicians suspend normal causality; most comedy involves simply
'having a laugh'; dancing and popular music demonstrate energy and
excitement to expunge tedium and tiredness (examples from Goodwin

1988: 24). Makeover shows similarly obliterate the time and labour of domestic renovations in miraculous 25-minute transformations. Dyer's second mode is *contrast*. The alternative world visited in entertainment tends to operate smoothly. Difficult budgeting contrasts with a designer living room for five hundred quid or a gourmet dinner concocted from random ingredients costing £4.99; the drudgery of cooking contrasts with chefs in high-tech kitchens slicing carrots at lightning speed and exchanging wisecracks while getting a stunning meal on the table in minutes. This leads us into Dyer's third mechanism of *incorporation*: co-option into entertainment of realities that would otherwise sit uneasily with its optimism, so as to suggest that things are not so bad. People have to eat – but isn't it just great fun? The living room needs decorating – regard it as a challenge and an experience rather than a chore and a wasted weekend. *Wife Swap* (RDF for Channel 4, 2004–) raises awkward questions about our own relationships and domestic arrangements, but those awful people make us count our blessings.

Dyer's essay on musicals (1977) posited three 'antidotes' to everyday life: energy, abundance and community. *Energy* counters physical or mental exhaustion. Makeovers supply it through competition and urgency, but also the manner and flair of presenters and experts. It manifests in stylized and rapid editing and camerawork, even complex combinations of ultra-slow camera movements with time-lapse exposures in gardening shows, which routinely feature tilts, pans, crane and tracking shots over plants bursting dramatically into bloom.

Makeover programmes' minimized pre-production – one reason they are competitive – contributes to a feel of spontaneity and liveliness that reinforces such energy. Repeatable formats obviate elaborate scripting. Severely restricted location shooting schedules eliminate studio costs and encourage improvisation. Resultant heavy editing, stylistically reminiscent of action movies and music videos – pacy incidental music is common too – commands attention and recalls advertisements for the consumerist lifestyle that the programmes promote. Computer techniques, including heightened image texture and boxes of typography, resemble print layouts in magazines and tie-in manuals. Moseley points out how the television aesthetic of fashion shows such as *Style Challenge* (BBC1, 1996–1998) resembles fashion magazines (2000: 310); similar cases can be made for gardening, cookery and DIY.

This aesthetic, in turn, relates to *abundance*, which balances the scarcities people feel in their lives and the wider world. Experts and celebrities are endorsements of success. Stylish interiors any householder can potentially create, or dream of one day living in, confirm the rewards of playing the game, accepting aspiration and competition, and the £500 weekend makeover suggests the possibility is closer than people previously realized. Rejecting the taste of redecorated interiors in itself reinforces the luxury of choice. Contestants relaxing over a glass of wine, expensive crane shots over the well-tended foliage of a weed-free garden, or stacks of banknotes ready for disbursement in the *Dragons' Den* reinforce this plenitude, as again does similarity to advertising.

Finally, *community* counteracts social isolation. If people hardly know their neighbours, those on telly busily improve each other's gardens while they are away. If viewers' partners make them a cup of tea only reluctantly, on the box people enthusiastically prepare meals together. If the reason someone is viewing is that they are alone or others in the room have little to say, TV couples, whether contestants or – our other proxies – the regular expert presenters, indulge in light-hearted flirtation while installing a water feature. If the programme addresses viewers as able to achieve similar results, and is interactive so they can join in, this can only increase a sense of belonging.

Building on Dyer's categories suggests why these programmes succeed. Viewers favouring a featured look are fashionable, part of a wider community. Yet the programmes disavow the conformity that predicates them. Viewers who think a recipe looks disgusting or know a better way to prepare it have their individuality reinforced. Abundance, contrast and community especially relate these programmes to their enabling political context. Conservative Prime Minister John Major, in the 1990s, favoured photo opportunities at double-glazing trade shows, symbolizing affluence, consumerist aspiration, security, and retreat into domesticity, after his predecessor Margaret Thatcher notoriously declared, 'There is no such thing as society, only individuals and their families.' Within such an ethos, public service broadcasting ideals receive little government support. Significantly, American daytime programming evolved not simply to sell detergent but to establish a binary divide against which networks convinced regulators of evening broadcasting's 'sophisticated, respectable, and masculine-characterized' social function within a commercial regime (Hilmes 1997, quoted in Hatch 2002: 82). The Thatcher and Reagan-Bush administrations, despite an avowed commitment to family values, opposed regulation in principle, thus permitting a climate for the intimacy, deviancy and horror that Dovey (2000) calls 'freak show' television. Makeover shows affirm and contradict, endorse and resist the confused and conflicting social and political agendas within which the television industry operates and viewers conduct their lives.

Reality TV selectively exploits controversy to attract audiences, yet does so while naturalizing consumerism, inequality and individualism and marginalizing oppositional politics and traditional civic values alike (McChesney 2003: 36). General knowledge cedes to celebrations of conventionality (test yourself against what the nation thinks in quizzes) or to 'useful' knowledge that values different cultural capital: second-guess the bland colours and designs in *House Doctor* (TalkbackThames/ Fremantle for Five, 1998–) and *Property Ladder* (TalkbackThames/ Fremantle for Channel 4, 2001–) that will fetch the highest price rather than express the individuality such programmes paradoxically profess (Palmer 2004). Although often emphasizing team dynamics, programmes promote getting rich by mastering renovation skills or understanding a market; they do not address social or economic problems. Others, ambiguously, reward deceit – *Faking It* (RDF for Channel 4, 2002–) – or success at others' expense, or dramatize resulting ideological conflicts (*The Weakest Link*). While crime shows police the legal margins of deviance, makeover programmes often similarly deploying surveillance technology, encourage a 'them vs. us' dichotomy that constantly reinforces petit bourgeois attitudes, behaviour and taste (Cavender 2004; Palmer 2004); *The Unteachables* (RDF for Channel 4, 2005) – although, like *Jamie's Kitchen* (TalkbackThames/Fremantle for Channel 4, 2002), voicing genuine concerns over British schools – cannily managed both. *Rock School* (RDF for Channel 4, 2005) set the high cultural connotations of an ancient fee-paying academy against heavy metal, yet kept the audience on side by choosing one with a large proportion of lower-income bursary scholars. Class, one of the fundamental differences on which narratives depend, is apparently sidelined, ignored, or overcome by quickly learning to masquerade its signifiers, but this is done in ways that constantly reaffirm them. At the 'reveal,' 'invasion of privacy, covert surveillance, social acceptance/alienation and manipulation' coalesce, no less than in the original cold-war *Candid Camera* (1948–) (Clissold 2004: 40).

Those caveats granted, viewers are encouraged to form opinions on anything from child rearing to the shape of a nose, and may end up defending them while watching. Moreover, the way that programmes negotiate identity permits various positions, both progressive and regressive. The traditional handyman learns how to lay wooden decking on a metal frame – a challenge also to the post-feminist power-tool wielder. Class, and ethnic and sexual diversity, are markedly visible yet never raised as an issue, as still occasionally occurs in soaps (except knowingly and ironically, and perhaps subversively, as in *Queer Eye for the Straight Guy/Girl*: Scout Productions, 2004–2005; UK version for Channel 4, 2005). To the reluctant partner watching a gardening programme under duress, buxom Charlie Dimmock, flinging her hair back like Rita Hayworth in *Gilda* (Charles Vidor, 1946), displays abundant eye-catching features while embodying a tough, energetic role model for Big Strong Girls with dirty nails. If such contradictions attract attention, turning the surrogate family of participants into gossip-column and chat-show celebrities, they reinforce a communal identification that is central to popular culture. Meanwhile, the multichannel ethos of individual choice and self-definition undermines any notion of a single shared culture.

Chapter Four

LIFE
SWAP

Celebrity Expert
as Lifestyle Adviser

Helen Powell and Sylvie Prasad

The British National Television awards of 2005 were significant for their legitimation of the celebrity expert as firmly embedded within television culture. Voted for by the viewing public, the emergence of the category 'Most Popular Expert' not only demonstrates the proliferation and popularity of such figures across the daytime and evening schedule, but also allows for the problematization of their role within contemporary culture. This chapter seeks to explore both how and why this role emerged and the mixed outcomes of the promotion of such expertise. Experts regularly mediate between many aspects of the public world of the market and the private construction of self and home, but is the eventual outcome always that which the terms of the genre intend? Turning to David Chaney's argument (1996), access to lifestyles, an integral feature of late modernity, is made available through vast communication networks which produce images that make styles and experiences familiar on an unprecedented scale. It is within this media environment that the 'celebrity expert' emerges: 'eminent professionals in their field whose talents have been harnessed by television in popular entertainment and lifestyle programmes' (Turberville 2005).

   The first stage in the rise of such programming can be traced back to the 1950s boom in manufacturing and consumption. The emphasis on nation building in the public sphere was underpinned by a return of women, often reluctantly, to the domestic sphere after the Second World War. Homemaking as a necessity was reinforced through advertising. In 1953, the coronation of Queen Elizabeth II was seen as a turning point in a hesitant British public's embrace of the new technology of television. The harnessing of the aspirational values of a post-war society and a new technology that could visually represent a range of different ways of life opened up the possibilities for mobility and transformation. Imported programmes, particularly from the US, were an important means of communicating the home-centred, upwardly mobile, values of a new era. With the advent of commercial television in 1955, the viewer developed an intimate relationship to the new media located at the heart of the home. The vicarious pleasure gained from viewing such programmes was heightened when linked to the possibility that new ways of living might be attainable through the consumption of particular products. DIY programmes were also popular viewing choices in Britain, tapping into the post-war ethos for self-improvement. The form of such programmes was instructional and was presented, whether it be gardening, cooking or carpentry, by an expert in the relevant field.

Moving forward to the 1980s, the emphasis on home ownership in Britain and its expansion under Margaret Thatcher's 'right to buy' campaign was a further stimulus to the investment in all things home-based. However, such programmes took on an additional dynamic at this time as it became recognized that guidance in the construction and maintenance of a lifestyle, in all its facets, could be realized through the medium of television. As Brunsdon remarks, its function becomes one of the elements in 'the more general life styling of 20th century British culture' (2003: 8). From a production perspective, such lifestyle programmes were not only cheap to produce but guaranteed good ratings in a market-driven economy. This combination of demand and economy of production undoubtedly led to the 1990s explosion of the genre across all our television channels 'The new hybrid formats seek to transform instruction into entertainment through the addition of surprise, excitement and suspense' (Brunsdon 2003: 9). Not only is entertainment value created through the interaction of the presenters, experts and participants, such genres also become vehicles by which all involved have the possibility to be transformed into celebrities.

The move from instructional programmes to those which combined entertainment with information is nothing new. Indeed, the blend of education, information and entertainment were the cornerstones of a Reithian vision for public service broadcasting in the UK. Perhaps, more surprisingly, some of these characteristics were familiar in many of the early American-import shows and afforded the viewer pleasure through entertainment but, in presenting a new modern world, offered up the possibility too of transformation. However, in format, the lifestyle programmes of today are far removed from the hobbyist and DIY programmes of 1950s and 60s British television. Makeover TV of the 21st century, combining techniques of 'before' and 'after' shots, the 'reveal' and reactions of those participating, emphasizes a shift to an end result rather than the processes involved. An interesting twist to the narrative that centres on this transformation can be documented through an analysis of programmes such as *What Not to Wear* (BBC) and *How Not to Decorate* (C4). Such programmes take an overtly critical stance towards their audience and begin from the premise that any participant is acting outside the boundaries of 'good taste' and requires 'reform'. Presenters, operating as a team, consistently reinforce each others' judgements in opposition to the views of the participants involved. This enables the celebrity experts to hold the power in defining what constitutes appropriate taste.

The transformative content of these programmes does not operate from a *tabula rasa* as the starting point (for example, the BBC's *Changing Rooms* or *Ground Force*) but rather from the lifestyle faux pas. As the saviours of bad taste, their viewing appeal polysemically derives from a voyeuristically driven audience which simultaneously uses such programmes as vehicles for the assessment of their own sense of taste or simply for the narrative pleasure of watching events unfold and reach resolution, with upset and discord underpinning its flow. The development of the genre's function into that of corrective behaviour includes the UK examples of *DIY SOS* (BBC1), where the public vote on which DIY disaster is to be saved, and *Spendaholics* (BBC3) where the saving of the self from financial ruin is undertaken. Another prime example of the current trend in lifestyle TV is the weekday series *Dial-a-Mum* (ITV1), a makeover programme, so the publicity reads, based on the principle 'mum knows best'. A team of four experts with their own specific skills set out to transform the life of a member of the public. Personal appearance, home decor and diet undergo the usual revamp but, perhaps more uniquely, the inclusion of a psychologist as one of the experts sets this show slightly above the competition. Television experts come alive in such programmes as these, as through demonstrations, that can be recorded and replayed, and later read about in the 'book to accompany the series', they present particular lifestyles as something both accessible and achievable.

The increase in technological development in our society, particularly the rise in electronic media, has, it is suggested (Meyrowitz 1985), impacted upon both the loss of 'social place' and the decline of the expert or specialist. Meyrowitz argues that social roles or positions were linked to particular physical locations and that access to electronic media break down these barriers of 'space' and 'place'. New media forms blur the distinction between the public and private and the exchange of information is no longer tied to particular physical spaces but rather has the effect of merging once discreet communities. The role and function of television has been central to these debates, for the acquisition of knowledge is no longer based on time-honoured skills acquired through family and community, passed down through tradition, but is instead learned on a piecemeal basis and acquired within a more individualistic media-centred environment. For some (Abt and Seesholtz 1994), the loss of real communities cannot be replaced and whilst television in the form of popular programming (soaps, talk shows, reality TV) provides electronic communities, these do not carry the personal and social responsibilities attached to real life. Others (Murdock 1994; Carpignano et al. 1990) offer a more positive view of the role of electronic media in that it is seen as a new 'public sphere'. Adapted from the study by Jürgen Habermas (Calhoun 1992), which examines arenas for public debate, television provides the new cultural space for people to affirm their identities, to be represented, to have reflected the pluralism and diversity of a modern society. Moreover, so the argument goes, it is through popular entertainment programmes that a new 'alternative' public sphere operates. The social construction of public life through news and information programmes, which had hitherto the legitimacy to define the 'real', is undermined and challenged through the performances of audiences and presenters on such shows. Whilst news programmes defer to established experts, more populist shows question this form of knowledge and the status of such experts who usually originate from official political institutions. Such blurring of boundaries through the medium of television not only makes all bodies of knowledge equally accessible but also gives everyone the potential to become 'their own expert'. Whilst Meyrowitz suggests this undermines the status of the expert and single sources of authoritative knowledge, we suggest it has led to the growth of a new kind of 'expert'.

Linda Barker: Celebrity, Brand and Taste-maker

As Chaney (2001) suggests, in a modern society the way in which one is judged by others becomes important and is integral to a sense of identity. Having particular tastes or styles are ways of categorizing people that also carry value judgements (Chaney 2001: 83). If we get it wrong, at the least, we can be held up to ridicule, at the worst, we can be ostracized from the group and lose our sense of belonging. The expert is there to facilitate the decision-making process and narrow the choice, thus lessening the chance of error. The function Linda Barker serves in her role as an expert in *Changing Rooms* is to provide short cuts in the decision-making process and to act as taste-maker for the public (Philips 2005). Her status is endorsed via the TV programmes she presents, by re-enforcement of her credentials as an expert in interior design and as an arbiter of good taste. Interestingly, this is not a taste shared by everyone, but one that has been specifically constructed to appeal to the middle ground, the indefinable ordinary person. So the question posed is, how did Linda Barker move from expert to taste-maker and celebrity?

Barker trained as a Fine Artist before becoming an interior designer. Her television career began on *Home Front* (BBC) in 1994 but she came to prominence in the highly successful makeover show *Changing Rooms* (BBC2 and BBC1). Regular columns in numerous design magazines followed, including *BBC Good Homes* and the *Daily Express Magazine*, extending her coverage in public life. Her endorsements of products are also extensive and an Internet web site allows access to her personal advice on home decorating. Currently, Linda Barker fronts TV commercials for Currys electrical goods and DFS furnishings.

Linda Barker's construction and survival as a celebrity is linked to both her economic use-value and her aspirational-value. This latter term refers to her ability to make our abstract desires concrete. As an expert she offers up the possibility for us to turn our everyday experience in to something unique and distinguished. For, as Chris Rojek suggests, seeking out celebrity is one of the many ways we 'anchor or support our personal life' (2001: 74). She exists in her specific media persona to promote goods and services but as a representation of 'everywoman' her elevation to celebrity status appears to bridge the gap between them (the celebrity) and us (the public). The Barker brand is successfully marketed around her 'everywoman' image and it is through the proliferation of the image that she maintains her celebrity. As one of the regular experts on *Changing Rooms* she is guaranteed media exposure for the duration of the show's run and the cross-marketing of books, products and service spin-offs accelerate her rise to celebrity status – indeed, turning her TV persona into a brand. Celebrities produced through such television programmes differ from Hollywood movie stars and their manufactured public personas in their perceived 'ordinariness' (Marshall 1997). We are looking at people like ourselves, and therefore we assume through this projected familiarity that they can represent our thoughts and desires. As with our faith in popular brands, trust is guaranteed. For those of us with celebrity aspirations they offer, in their 'ordinariness', a role model; the potential, the possibility, for everyone to become a celebrity. However, such assumptions mask the very real efforts individual celebrities, including celebrity experts, put in to the making of their TV appearances. Scratch below the surface and one usually finds a driven soul accompanied by a scaled-down set of agents and PR professionals who, if not totally stage-managing the career, have a hand in its manufacture. In this respect they bear some of the hallmarks of Rojek's (2001) definition of achieved celebrity status without fully making visible the personal drive in their transformation from expert to celebrity.

Yet maintaining the Barker brand, like the marketing of any product in a highly competitive sector, is not without risk. Barker is a celebrity brand with no distinguishing features and this blank canvas is a useful characteristic to highlight, but never over shadow, the products that she promotes. The balancing act between celebrity and maintaining the status of taste-maker is a delicate one as her appearances in *I'm a Celebrity Get Me Out of Here* (ITV1) and adverts for Currys testify. Voted one of the most irritating commercials on television (BBC News 2003), the Currys electrical stores ad made the already ubiquitous Barker, through her endorsement of everyday products, seem as though she lacked the taste and judgement her 'expert' status had hitherto conferred. Interior design is about creating the appearance of illusion, luxury and uniqueness; selling fridges and washing machines isn't.

We need experts to guide and inform us, we need celebrities to embody our dreams and transgressions. Celebrity experts offer us the possibility to bridge the gap between their world and ours. This bridge, however, is illusory. The ideal of transformation portrayed through lifestyle television cannot be replicated in its entirety in everyday life. An outcome of success is never guaranteed. Likewise, if celebrities cross too far into our world the illusion is ruptured and the staged 'ordinariness' becomes just plain ordinary.

The establishment of a recognized role for the celebrity expert within contemporary culture emerged from a series of social changes identifiable within the late 1980s. These trends have been documented by a number of social theorists (Bauman 1988, 1992; Featherstone 1991;Giddens 1991; Beck 1992) who suggest that an inherent feature of late-modernity is the integral role the market plays in the provision of wants and needs. Choice proliferates and is no longer informed predominantly by social status or membership of a particular class but, rather, is based on a fluid and flexible sense of lifestyle. The blurring of boundaries ensues and the social organization of taste by class-differentiated 'habitus' becomes problematic because particular groups can occupy 'contradictory class locations' (Wright 1985; McGuigan 1996). Such choice, however, comes at a price as the act of choosing becomes fraught with anxiety. For if consumption is to be seen to have a value in the defining of the self and, indeed, an aspirational self, and the symbolic value of goods signifies that intent to others, then effective choice within the marketplace requires knowledge and guidance. In this context, the 'expert as celebrity' emerges functioning as both role model and taste-maker. Through mediated interaction they offer up a lifestyle template and practical guidance in its realization. A sense of familiarity and trust is accrued with their audience through a weekly slot on television and via this media exposure the transformation to 'celebrity expert' becomes complete. Television both humanizes and elevates them, and we cling on to their every word as they become, as one critic cynically argues, our 'two-bit spiritual guides' (Bourdieu 1998: 46) in a world where consumption is the new religion. However, the following case study that takes Jamie Oliver as its subject highlights further issues. Here the cause for concern is located not around issues of credibility, as with Linda Barker, but rather with the format of the genre itself. For within the temporal space of often just thirty minutes such programmes seek to both inform and entertain. Whilst this allows for audience participation to take place at multiple levels, and consequently accounts for their popular appeal, for those who search out varying degrees of transformation a second set of problems are inherent.

The Many Faces of Jamie Oliver

Indeed, the aforementioned success of such TV formats is expanded upon by Taylor (2002: 482) who argues, 'lifestyle programmes fasten on to the sense that we are all, insofar as we connect to the backdrop of everyday life, ordinary.' Such programmes make an elision between viewer and purchaser and in so doing 'help interrogate how the changing nature of television has a co-constitutive relationship with the changing nature of the consumer' (Spittle 2002: 58). Through an analysis of Jamie Oliver's public persona we can further position the celebrity expert as a conduit between the viewer and the marketplace. Studying him provides a vehicle though which we can map the cultural impact of one expert-turned-celebrity through a variety of media including television programmes, supermarket advertising and cookery books. Not only does this second case study seek to understand the rise, fall and rise again of Oliver's popularity but, more importantly, it seeks to establish how such expert celebrities serve to mediate between lifestyle on screen and as part of the lived experience. It will also once again highlight the conflict between expectation and realization. For, as Campbell (1989) has argued, one of the key features of being a modern subject is that we have the ability to daydream. That is to say, 'the imaginative elaboration, in a pleasurable direction, of a forthcoming or anticipated real event' (1989: 83). Television programmes of the lifestyle genre may fuel such daydreams but they also help to explain how such programmes can be highly dysfunctional. For the next stage of the daydream is to attach such dreams to actual objects of desire, to experience in reality those pleasures created and enjoyed in the imagination, and it is here that disillusionment often sets in as reality fails to live up to expectation. 'The essential activity of consumption is thus not the actual selection, purchase or use of products, but the imaginative pleasure-seeking to which the product image lends itself, "real" consumption being largely a resultant of this "mentalistic" hedonism' (ibid: 89; emphasis added). Therefore, the consumer projects onto a product the qualitative dimensions conjured up in the daydream but, as Campbell argues, this potential is always greater than the reality (ibid: 89).

However, if we adapt Campbell's analysis to the project of lifestyle construction and our identification with particular celebrities who function as guides along the way, then any 'disillusionment' (ibid: 89) can successfully be managed as we either project onto another object (novelty) or turn to another celebrity expert. It is this cycle of dream/disillusionment/new dream that provides an explanation of ceaseless consumption and the perpetuation of the genre itself.

The paradox of Jamie Oliver, therefore, is that he occupies both the world of the real and the daydream. From his apprenticeship at the *River*

Café, Jamie Oliver initially became known to a mass television audience through the BBC2 television series *The Naked Chef* (beginning in 1999). The format deviated from already-established cookery programmes for, rather than being of a didactic nature, it centred on the lifestyle of the chef and offered up the possibility not just of acquiring new culinary skills but also the adoption of a new lifestyle where good food was at its heart. The sociability of cooking underpinned programme content: from shopping for ingredients and the banter with his suppliers, to the dishing up of the final product for family and friends to share. And, indeed, through this narrative structure an alternative reading of the programme might be constructed, one not necessitated by learning and emulation but, rather, through gaining satisfaction in watching events unfold and reach resolution through the arrival of the guests and the finished product.

As Hollows (2003: 230) argues, 'the power of Jamie as a brand stems from his show's negotiation of the television cookery format to emphasize the importance of lifestyle.' Where Oliver carves out a unique position within the brandscape of the celebrity chef market, however, is that he 'incorporates cooking with a "cool" masculine lifestyle, by disavowing the extent to which both cooking and the construction of lifestyles can be experienced as labour rather than leisure' (Hollows 2003: 231). But it is within the context of Oliver as a brand that the fracturing of the consumer's culinary daydream begins to materialize and the role of celebrity expert becomes problematic. As a successful brand, Oliver's unique selling proposition is that he has tried to position himself as one of the lads with his own 'mockney' lingo, including terms such as 'pukka', and a dress style and home life that many can identify with. But in bringing this expert down to earth and through the creation of a media personality that makes cooking fun and accessible, a noticeable tension arises. From the choice of ingredients to the serving up of the finished product, no mention is given of the years of training Oliver underwent to become a chef. Only in his latest projects *Jamie's Kitchen* and *Jamie's School Dinners* (both C4) is his professionalism foregrounded. Thus whilst this likeable lad might, through his brand, seek to transfer a love of cooking to his consumer audience, in fact the skills he possesses set him apart from that same audience, who, when seeking to emulate him, are often disappointed as they lack one vital ingredient, unavailable in Sainsbury's supermarket, namely expertise. This is a point reiterated by Philips (2005: 221) analysis of television makeover programmes where she argues that 'the television designer's training in design or art school education is never referred to... the personality designer "knows" what is tasteful and stylish without apparently "ever having learnt", their knowledge is presented as "natural" and "innate".' Once again such an argument facilitates in understanding the rupture between the daydream and the reality. For lifestyle programming encourages the mass consumption of a dream, whilst simultaneously generating high audience ratings for the television companies producing them and a boost in sales for retail outlets that are cited during the programme, directly and indirectly. Such shows function to legitimate the acceptability of contemporary trends originated by the celebrity expert but also to perpetuate them and change them when necessary for the future profitability of all concerned. From the viewer's perspective, however, the dream is rarely fully materialized, as the accumulation of cultural capital is always subverted within the context of such programmes and embedded within the persona of the expert (Philips 2005: 221). The programme initiates the dream, the ingredients, and the method, but never the expertise that ultimately denies its realization.

And herein lies another problem of the celebrity expert, for one of the key principles behind the public's acceptance of celebrities is their 'extraordinary ordinariness' (Littler 2003: 5). Celebrities must, in other words, demonstrate a root in the ordinary that we can all identify with. Through successful manipulation of television and its currency within the public sphere, celebrities trade on a fundamental duality of being like us but not exactly, what Rojek terms, 'the public face and the veridical self in celebrity culture' (2001: 192). They position themselves as being of the masses but ultimately they stand apart. And this was borne out in terms of Jamie Oliver's success at the 2005 National Television awards cited earlier. Nominated for three categories, Oliver failed to secure victory in 'The Most Popular Expert on TV' but triumphed in 'The Most Popular Factual Programme' for *Jamie's School Dinners* and received a second 'Special Recognition' award for his work with children and the homeless. This obviously problematizes how the viewing public actually perceive him. For his reward comes not as a popular expert but as a social reformer in respect of a programme that isn't located in the dream worlds of lifestyle creation, but rather in the more grounded reality of school dinners and childhood obesity. Positioning himself not as one of the lads but as a father and a trained chef who has significant cultural capital and expert knowledge, he has gained public credibility in seeking to improve the general health of a nation. Cast in this new role, he is an expert first and a celebrity second. That expertise is now recognized for what it is, something acquired over a long period of time through intense training and an ethic of deferred gratification that no lifestyle programming could ever reproduce, or even try to. Working towards the more realizable goal of adopting a healthier lifestyle rather than the overnight transformation into a kitchen maestro, the television expert can be seen in this case to be reverting to a more fulfilling traditional role, namely that of educator over entertainer.

This chapter has centred on the cult of celebrity, but of a very particular kind. It has been concerned with the way in which television plays a role in constructing media stars whose function is to transfer particular lifestyle knowledges through to the lived experience of ordinary people. Through the specific examples of Linda Barker and Jamie Oliver, it has traced the way in which the celebrity expert emerges in a period of cultural, social and economic change that realizes lifestyle construction as an integral part of modern living. The lifestyle genre on TV subsequently gains popularity not only via the easily available templates it provides but also through the accessibility of the presenter who appears to be 'just like us' – but not quite. For the paradox of celebrity experts is that their appeal derives from a media style that suggests that all is possible. 'No individual agent ought to feel handicapped by the poverty of the imagination... the only job left to be done by the individual himself is to follow the instruction attached to the kit' (Bauman 1988: 63). But what of the skills required in the transference of those instructions to the lived experience? Can they so easily be acquired with only half an hour's viewing on BBC2? Their appeal derives in part from the possibility they suggest of bridging the gap between their world and ours, but this possibility can only ever be illusory. Lifestyles portrayed through television and concomitant media images can never fully translate into the material lived experience; they will always be transformed into something different. And whilst the dream might be followed by disappointment, this is only ever temporary; that is, until a new celebrity expert catches the public's imagination or we learn to adapt our lifestyle desires to a more manageable lived experience. For an integral part of lifestyle construction is the quest for novelty which, coincidentally, is also inherent in the making of television programmes. The future of the genre, it thus seems, remains secure for some time to come.

Chapter Five

MAKE ME
A CELEBRITY

Celebrity Exercise Videos
and the Origins of Makeover Television

Vanessa Russell

Since the late 1960s, home-stereo manufacturers had been trying to develop a cost-efficient, easy-to-use, compact machine that could play pre-packaged visual material similar to LPs and cassettes. Various systems were tried and failed, but the system that gained worldwide acceptance was the Video Home System (VHS). The VHS was launched in 1977 and was a relatively slow but steady hit with its ability to play and record on reel-to-reel tape technology encased inside a sturdy cassette (Hain 2005; High-Tech Productions 2005). For the first time, the general public could control how it viewed television programmes. Home users could buy or rent videotapes of programmes and films, or record programmes from the television to watch in their own time.

Video technology revolutionized community activities. Activities that could once only be done in public could now be done in viewers' homes. Aerobic exercise was one of these activities, and Jane Fonda harnessed the growth of VHS technology to enable people, particularly women, to workout at home and avoid the potential humiliations of exercising in public. It seemed for women that there would be no more embarrassment about joining a gym with its mandatory fat-fold test, no weaering lycra in a room full of strangers, no competitiveness about body shape and no feeling awkward when a move was missed. Unfortunately, many of these humiliations were transferred straight into video format in the form of punitive treatment for beginners, increasingly 'perfect' instructors, competitive body messages and conflicting messages of female docility and strength.

Fonda's exercise programme capitalized on the invasive 'health ethic' that seized western society in the 1980s and continues, intensified, to the present day. 'Healthism,' or the belief that health is the sole responsibility of the individual, blames a 'fat' person for making unhealthy life choices (Lawrence and Germov 1999: 59–60). Healthism does not allow fat to be a rebellion against the health ethic, or a choice, or a metabolic problem, or genetics, or a symptom of the health ethic itself. Fonda's *Workout* brought the health ethic into the home and encouraged society's belief that women's bodies could be remodelled only if they followed the correct exercise programme.

In *Workout*, Fonda's body is proof of her successful remodelling. Fonda was forty-five in 1982, and was using exercise to stave off the effects of middle age. It is natural for an ageing female body to gradually thicken and gain weight, but Fonda began to define herself by working against her body's biology. Fonda's quest for eternal youthfulness was complicated when her exercise video was interpreted by feminists as providing a role model for women by showing feminine strength and empowerment (Kagan and Morse 1988; Dinnerstein and Weitz 2005). Despite Fonda's occasional use of what Myra Dinnerstein and Rose Weitz describe as 'feminist rhetoric' (324), Fonda herself did not make overt feminist declarations. Instead, in her 2005 memoir, *My Life So Far*, Fonda states that she made *Workout* so that she could raise money – seventeen million dollars – for her then-husband, Tom Hayden, and his political activities (Fonda 2005: 392–4).

Fonda's ambivalence towards accepting her position as a feminist role model highlights the contradictions of feminism in the early 1980s. According to feminist historian Roberta Pollack Seid, during this time women moved from focusing on non-gendered clothing to focusing on the body itself (Seid 1989: 244). Bodies were expected to be strong, but thin, and exercise was promoted as a fun and energising way to achieve the new cultural ideal (245). The new ideal was all about health: a healthy body was a fit body, and a fit body was a beautiful body (247). Fonda encapsulated this ideal because her body showed the evidence of long hours spent working out while simultaneously retaining feminine attractiveness.

Research has indicated that being attractive is one of the major motivations of aerobics participants. Pirkko Markula's ethnographic survey of women who regularly attend aerobics classes found that participants were preoccupied with achieving a balance between being strong, 'tight' and 'toned', and being over-muscled, 'bulging' and 'big' (Markula 1995: 441). Women exercised so that their bodies became streamlined, but eased off before their bodies became masculinized. The inherent contradiction in working out is that women want to enhance their femininity by striving to look like lean, athletic boys. Markula attempts to explain this by suggesting that men have power, so women work out until their bodies resemble a non-threatening version of masculinity (442).

The visual presentation of Fonda in *Workout* reinforces her de-feminized figure by its insistent focus on her defiantly unthickened middle. In *Workout*, the camera focuses on Fonda's long-limbed, fat-free body that is sheathed in a skin-tight leotard. Behind her, six similarly sheathed exercisers – four female, two male – follow her moves. The viewer is confronted with the direct gaze of Fonda who looks straight down the camera lens. Fonda literally looks down because the low-angle position of the camera makes her seem larger than life, as if the viewer is a child looking up into an adult's world. The long-shot focuses on Fonda's middle-age-defying torso.

The seductiveness of Fonda's body as an achievable goal meant that, soon after the success of *Workout*, an entire industry of exercise videos appeared. Each featured a heavily groomed celebrity who, with the help of trainers, make-up artists, dieticians, stylists, lighting experts and choreographers, tried to sell the idea that viewers' bodies could be made over into a version of the celebrity's simply by buying and faithfully performing the video workouts. Not everyone was convinced. One aerobics participant in Markula's study commented:

> It kind of makes me mad because I keep hearing that [the instructors]
> stop, put on more make-up and jump another five minutes and then
> come back, wipe off the sweat, and you never see them really ugly. (445)

Despite audience scepticism, from 1988 to 1992, supermodels, actors, and even Barbie, paraded their bodies and instructed viewers on how to achieve their perfection. At the same time, fitness consultants such as Denise Austin and Kathy Smith became the first celebrity exercisers while Richard Simmons, a former fat person, achieved success with his ebullience and use of 'fat' exercisers. Simmons was the first male exerciser to become an exercise-video celebrity, and his global success can be explained in part by his clownish persona that was clearly coded as gay. Simmons's sexuality eased his acceptance into a female-dominated industry and indicated society's preoccupation during the 1980s with gay rights and HIV/AIDS.

Shortly after Simmons's success, celebrities were replaced by fitness professionals who in turn became celebrities. The fitness professionals' bodies were super fit and tanned, with highly developed muscles that were sustained by the gruelling spot training of body sculpting. The idealized standard of beauty was being set at an even higher level. Feminist critic Naomi Wolf interpreted the increasing pressure for women to spend more time working out and sculpting their muscles as evidence that patriarchal society simply wanted to keep women busier so that they could not topple male-dominated culture (Wolf 1991: 187).

By 1995, the exercise-video market was over-saturated and desperately awaiting the arrival of a new craze. In 1998, Billy Blanks produced his *Tae-Bo* series, an energetic, gruelling Thai-boxing-based workout that promoted strength through a community of sweaty, pumped-up bodies. It was the first sustained inclusion of males in what had been a female-dominated market. By 2000, *Tae-Bo* had been superseded by calmer, new-age products. The gentle stretching of the Pilates method and yoga promoted flexibility and meditation as a holistic melding of body and mind. In the mid 2000s, dance-fitness exercise DVDs featured the dance instructors of pop singers such as Britney Spears and Beyoncé Knowles reproducing the dance moves that kept the celebrities in lean, dancer's shape.

An examination of the conventions and codes of celebrity exercise videos shows how the makeover ethic entices viewers into believing that a celebrity's transformation can motivate their own. By using evidence from exercise psychology and ethnographic studies about the effects of exercise videos and aerobics, this article shows how the celebrity instructor's body is used to promote society's impossible ideal image of female beauty.

The word aerobic means 'in the presence of oxygen,' and an aerobic workout uses an increased heart rate to oxygenate the blood and distribute 'oxygen-rich' (Franks et al. 1999: 68) blood to the muscles. An oxygenated body, according to exercise scientists, regulates the metabolism, reduces body fat, lowers blood pressure, maintains bone density, encourages better sleep and improves digestion (McDonald and Hodgdon 1991: 13). The benefits of aerobic exercise are largely unseen and occur inside the body, but the internal benefits of aerobic exercise are rarely advertised either on the packaging or inside celebrity exercise videos.

The focus on the exterior of the body shows the shift in society's thinking that began in the 1920s (Seid 1989; Stearns 1997; Bordo 1993). Industrialization sped up the world and progress was the catchphrase of the time. Anything that hampered progress was marginalized (Seid 1989: 82). The result for women was that they were freed from layers of petticoats and underskirts and instead dressed in slim, figure-hugging clothes. Seid writes about the attitudes of the day: 'The human body – both male and female – was to be as efficient, as effective, as economical, and as beautiful as the sleek new machines, as the rationalized workplace' (83). Significantly, at the same time, the 1920s saw the beginnings the suffragette movement (Bordo 1993; Seid 1989; Wolf 1991). Wolf believes that the sleek, streamlined female body was idealized during this time because the time-consuming and exhausting 'counter image' of extreme thinness was a way to dampen the spirit of equality (Wolf 1991: 17).

The front covers of exercise videos are an immediate entry into the development of the twentieth-century idealization of the thin body. The triumphant female exercise-video instructor, posed on the front cover of an exercise video, has tamed her wild female body and reinforced society's belief that such taming is desirable. The covers show how exercise videos work as a makeover project. In a society where the 'desirable' body is not one that belongs to the everyday woman, the covers of exercise videos show that the celebrity's body is hyper-real, constructed from natural genetics, plastic surgery, eating disorders and/or extreme training.

The professional exercise instructor who becomes a celebrity is usually a former gym instructor or aerobics champion and has submitted his or her body to years of rigorous training, comparable to that of a professional athlete, so that he or she can earn a living by exercising. In comparison, the celebrity instructor – typically female, long and lean – is successful either in film or modelling because of her conformity to the slender ideal that is a reality for only one per cent of the female population (Tebbel 2000: 58). Yet within exercise videos these bodies are presented as normal and achievable. The packaging of exercise videos shows how instructors' bodies promise more than they can deliver so that the viewer finds herself alienated from being motivated to remodel herself.

A physical turning over of the video to read the back cover thwarts the viewer's expectations while simultaneously encouraging them. The copy is written to obscure any scepticism that the viewer may have about attaining the same body as shown on the front, but the tension of expectations remains. After all, ninety-eight per cent of diets fail (Tebbel

2000: 58), but don't all dieters believe they will be part of the two per cent that succeeds? Much of the copy on the exercise video's back cover is written in the 'voice' of the instructor. In the case of the celebrity, the copy has a signature underneath to increase the sense that the celebrity is speaking directly to 'you'. The copy skirts around the issue of how exactly the viewer is going to emulate the instructor by stating that the video will build the viewer up to 'your' peak performance.

For example, Cher's 1991 exercise video, *A New Attitude*, shows how guaranteed transformation is avoided. In the voice of Cher, the copy reads: 'I do this program myself, every day and I know that it works... I know that if you make this commitment to exercise you too will look and feel your best' (Cher 1991). The concession of 'your best' is a heavy modification when compared to the promise of achieving the perfection of the instructor's body. Failure is placed solely on the viewer because it means that the viewer has not 'committed' enough. At this point before even putting an exercise video in the machine, all the viewer has worked hard in committing to (although perhaps not entirely) is the video cover's promise of inclusion into the world of physical fitness, together with a wish to avoid the marginalization of the fat.

On watching the video, the viewer sees the instructor as a mirror to her body. The instructor is an image to copy, both in relation to the aerobics routine and the viewer's body. The instructor often makes this relationship overt. In 1986's *A Week with Raquel*, actor Raquel Welch opens her workout by purring, 'Let me be your mirror image, when I move to the left that means you'll be moving to the right' (Welch 1986).

Elizabeth Kagan and Margaret Morse, in one of the earliest studies of exercise videos in 1988, explore the mirror relationship between viewer and instructor. They argue that the mirrored image of the instructor causes the viewer to identify more with the instructor than with herself. For Kagan and Morse, the viewer is disembodied from the experience of her own movement because she relates to the mirrored reality of the instructor (Kagan and Morse 1988: 171). The viewer's own body is almost forgotten as the viewer tries to attain the look of the instructor. The force of society's desire for the ideal body is ultimately illusory, like a reflection in a mirror.

Like all mirror relationships, the viewer holds the ultimate power of surveillance particularly when it relies on language. While the instructor can only pretend to see into the exerciser's room, the viewer can visually and imaginatively enter the instructor's space. Once the video is released to the public, the instructor is unable to control his or her representations, and the viewer can rebel against the ploys used by the video to make her identify with the instructor. Admittedly, the choices are limited, and mainly consist of fast-forwarding or pressing the mute button (Losano and Risch 2001: 121), but rebellion does open up a foothold where the instructor's dominance can be undermined.

Without exception, the instructors talk to the camera and bolster their imagined audience's egos with encouraging words such as, 'Good job!', 'Great work!', and 'You're looking excellent!' This use of language is called directive discourse, because the speech aims to direct the listener to follow an action. The most ineffectual form of directive discourse happens when the instructors move from general encouragement to pretending that they can see the viewer. Towards the end of his strenuous 1998 *Tae-Bo* workout, instructor Billy Blanks points to the television camera and says: 'Remember, I told you, I'm watching you one hundred per cent of the time; one hundred per cent of the time I'm giving you all my heart, all my love, because I want to see you reach your goal' (Blanks 1998). Blanks has failed to concede that he can only use words to encourage the viewer and can't support or witness the improvements his programme may be making, or any slackening of the viewer's enthusiasm. Language is ineffectual in controlling the body when combined with an unseeing gaze; surveillance only succeeds when the viewer believes that the gaze is constant and real (see Foucault 1975: 195–228).

The viewer can choose to watch or not to watch. Although a person may buy an exercise video, it doesn't mean that she will use it regularly. The viewer may buy the exercise video with good intentions, use it irregularly for some weeks, tire of the routine, and then stash the video in a cupboard. Then there is always the hope that the next video on the market will be more dynamic, more able to encourage will power, involve less work or be more fun. And so the cycle of consumption continues – which is good for the exercise economy, but bad for the viewer who always takes the blame for the failure to be completely made over.

An exercise video can produce one of three images that, together with the illusory mirror and being blamed if a makeover fails, further alienates the viewer. The three alienating effects most commonly used in exercise videos are: the exerciser as a human medical specimen, the marginalized low-impact exerciser and the ridiculed male. The human medical specimen is a female body that is used as a fragmented site to show how the body can be improved; the low-impact body is denigrated for providing a role model for beginner exercisers; while the male is subjected to the ridicule of transgressing into a 'female' sphere.

The human medical specimen is a recurring image in exercise videos. It occurs when an instructor points out the active muscle groups on a prone, mute (and most-often female) body. In the group of videos selected, a younger woman performed the role of 'specimen', and an older – and usually shorter – male played the instructor. The only exception was Cher's A New Attitude, where the instructor was female, but masculinized through her highly developed muscles.

To first take this exception, Cher's A New Attitude features instructor Keli Roberts who herself became a celebrity exerciser shortly after the release of the video. During the third workout, Roberts adjusts one of Cher's poses and stands behind her in a watchful, dominant pose. Roberts then rests her hand on Cher's shoulder and does a few repetitions with her. Throughout this demonstration, Cher is uncharacteristically mute. Similarly, Pilates for Beginners (1999), features instructor Allan Menezes together with two floor-bound exercisers who demonstrate the programme's stretches. Menezes strolls around the two exercisers, one male, one female, and directs them to assume the positions of the routine. Every time he shows the viewer which muscles are being strengthened in the exercise, he walks to the woman and points and touches her body. The female does not respond to his dissections and mechanically continues her stretches.

This mute woman resembles an automaton, a physical specimen of the body who passively displays the exercise's effects. In this way, the body is fragmented into a two-dimensional site where isolated exercise dissects the body into individual parts that can be individually remodelled. Typically, the isolated body parts are called 'problem spots' (Markula 1995: 434). Problem spots are the places where fat naturally gathers on a woman's body: hips, stomach, bottom and thighs. Exercise videos often 'target' specific areas of the body by devoting an entire workout to these particular body parts. Denise Austin has gone so far as to put out an exercise video titled 'Shrink Your Female Fat Zones'.

Similar to the message of Fonda's Workout, the human medical specimen shows how women are working out to transform their bodies into the slim-hipped, narrow boyish shape that society has idealized. Markula's studies of women exercisers find that the women are trying to exercise away the pieces of their body that make them women. 'Logically then,' Markula writes, 'we hate looking like women' (435). The human medical specimen shows how instructors keep prodding and poking, adjusting and correcting the female body, and how women passively accept the intervention.

When being used as a human medical specimen, a woman is not strong, building muscles or becoming fitter. She is a docile woman being instructed to conform to a societal image that is biased towards males. Taken alone this may have only a subliminal impact but, together with the remaining two alienating effects, the human medical specimen works to counter the promotion of a strong, healthy female body and instead promotes society's premise that the only way to attain equality is to become more masculinized.

In contrast, the beginner exerciser has to struggle to master the steps of the programme, and feels inferior when her instructor is too 'perfect'. In aerobic terms, the phrase 'low impact' refers to an exercise routine that reduces the stress that exercise places on the joints (Gudrun 2000: 54). Within exercise videos, the low-impact body eases beginners into aerobics by demonstrating the least stressful method of working out. In video reality, these exercisers are often placed out of shot, dressed in dowdy outfits and rarely speak or express emotion.

Exercise psychologists have found that viewers who are beginning exercise are more likely to believe they can achieve physical improvement if they have an 'inexperienced' exerciser to follow (Fleming and Martin Ginis 2004: 100). These studies have also noted the difficulty in finding exercise videos that use beginner exercisers or instructors who do not fit society's ideal body shape (ibid). Although specific studies have not yet been done about viewer responses to the marginalization of the low-impact exerciser, studies have found that if a beginner exerciser is instructed by what is perceived to be a 'perfect' body, then the beginner's self-esteem significantly suffers as she compares and questions her own ability (Gammage et al. 2004: 180). The viewer believes that she is not coordinated or fit enough to do the exercises, which has a significant effect on her motivation to continue the exercise programme (Fleming and Martin Ginis 2004: 93). From this, the implication is that the beginner exerciser identifies with the low-impact exerciser. If the low-impact exerciser is marginalized, then she loses confidence in her role model and is more inclined to give up exercising altogether.

In exercise videos, disparaging language is occasionally used to deride the low-impact exerciser, which further makes the beginner exerciser feel incapable, unfit and unattractive. The beginner exerciser battles against the contradiction between the instructor's body and the way the instructor treats the low-impact exerciser. The instructor is not performing the low-impact option, and has not achieved fitness by taking 'the easier option' (Halliwell 2001) so any verbal encouragement is largely overridden. This most often occurs in videos where the celebrity is instructed by a fitness professional. Perhaps to exert authority over 'their' video, some celebrities – in particular, Cher and Geri Halliwell – attempt to outperform their instructors by verbally belittling the low-impact exerciser.

A minor, though insidious, example is shown in an exchange between Halliwell and her yoga instructor, Katy Appleton, in 2001's *Geri Yoga*. Appleton tells the audience, 'If you want the gentler option look at Tina [the low-impact exerciser].' Halliwell interrupts her by saying, 'And if you want the hardcore, look at Geri' (Halliwell 2001). Such comments (repeated over and over as the viewer repeats the programme) indoctrinate the viewer and brand the low-impact exerciser with the stigma of underachievement.

The viewer's subsequent feelings of inferiority are most often expressed through what Susan Willis terms 'body rivalry' (Willis 1990: 7). Willis writes that body rivalry is produced in aerobics communities. She writes: 'Women compare, but do not share themselves with others. They see themselves as bodies. They scrutinize their lines and curves and they check out who's wearing the hottest leotard' (ibid). Willis believes that body rivalry is a feature of men's exercise because men are focused on becoming bigger and trying to outperform each other, and the masculine form of body rivalry has been adopted by female exercisers (ibid). To refine Willis's gendered argument, the rivalry in women's exercise can be seen as a result of an appropriated male gaze and consequent masculinization of what has been positioned as a traditionally 'feminine' activity.

The most striking example occurs in Cher's 1991 video, *A New Attitude*, where Cher openly rebukes the low-impact exerciser. No members of her class look even remotely pleased to be exercising, but the low-impact exerciser, Dori Sanchez, looks particularly miserable. Sanchez is often cut out of shot and is dressed in a black leotard with a semi-sheer skirt. She has the fit body of a dancer, but the dress makes her appear dowdier than the others, particularly compared to Cher who is wearing a corset-like Gothic outfit complete with fishnet stockings. A close-up of Sanchez reveals her grimacing until Cher glances at her and says, 'Dori's making me laugh because she's such a sour puss.' The next shot shows Sanchez smiling but, by the end of the strenuous routine, Cher has herself stopped making inappropriate comments and is long-faced and exhausted. Cher's regulatory surveillance denies the community a sense of togetherness, and promotes a group of rival individuals trying to surpass each other. When this occurs, the beginner exerciser cannot compete and feels that the perfection of the instructor's body is even further out of reach (see Fleming and Martin Ginis 2004: 99).

If the low-impact exerciser feels marginalized, then the males in exercise videos are treated as figures of fun. Aerobics has been coded as a female sport because of its non-traditional masculine elements of dance and movement. Tara Brabazon writes that such segregation provides a powerfully feminine space: 'As most of us work in male-dominated environments, aerobics can offer feminine space, a (transitory) movement away from men and masculinity' (2000: 102–3). Jean Grimshaw disputes the assertion that aerobic exercise is a largely female activity and writes that the number of men exercising in aerobics is considerable (1999: 107). She then stereotypes male exercisers and gives them the same bumbling male traits that originally marginalized them:

> Men are ill at ease, inhibited in their movements, and above all stiff and rigid; they often find it very hard to engage in the kinds of co-ordinated or flowing movements which characterize parts of an aerobics class (Grimshaw 1999: 107).

Susan Powter's exercise video, *Burn Fat and Get Fit* (1994), shows how pervasive Grimshaw's stereotype of the awkward male aerobic exerciser is. Powter gained celebrity for being a former fat person whose mantra of 'Stop the Insanity!' urged an end to abuse through extreme dieting. In the video there is one male in the group of three exercisers and he is placed at the rear of the studio, mainly mute and fiercely concentrating. The struggles of female emancipation are reversed as Eric works doubly hard to be accepted into the female community. In a scene similar to the Cher video, Powter verbally prods Eric to enjoy himself. Powter says, 'Come on, Eric, smile – are you having fun?' Eric replies, 'I'm having fun,' and quickly performs a smile. Powter shoots back, 'Come on, shoulders down.' She repeats the verbal bullying later in the video and asks Eric, 'How do you feel?' Eric says, 'Like a million dollars,' to which Powter retorts, 'A million bucks! Where are your hands? Don't tense up.' Immediately after this, Powter wisecracks about Eric, who is performing the low-impact moves: 'Eric gets to use his chair in the whole video, we don't know why.' On careful analysis of the video, Eric stops least often and doesn't complain, but he has committed the crime of transgressing into the female zone.

The three alienating effects in exercise videos show how the marginalizations of those who do not conform to society's ideals of the perfect body have become entrenched within the structure of the videos themselves. Women are docile medical specimens used to demonstrate how muscles work with the aim of making the viewer over into the slim, masculinized body of the instructor. Low-impact exercisers are marginalized by use of outfit, instructor comments and film framing that undermines any sense of inclusion. Men intrude onto a female zone of competitiveness and are ridiculed. The conflict between selling the achievability of the ideal body, and the concession that the ideal body is not actually achievable, is at the heart of celebrity exercise videos.

Makeover television has heeded the most important lesson from celebrity exercise videos: do not alienate the viewer. In makeover television, the viewer is promoted to the position of the achievable body, which circumvents the inherent alienation of exercise videos. Although celebrity exercise videos (and, now, celebrity exercise DVDs) continue to sell, their credibility has been hampered by the celebrities who have been publicly revealed as having undergone repeated plastic surgery or treatment for continuing eating disorders. This crisis of credibility has contributed to the rise of makeover television, in particular shows like *Extreme Makeover* and *The Swan* that use surgical intervention to make over their participants. In effect, these makeover shows screen the interventions that celebrity exercise videos deny.

Visions of swollen, bruised participants working out in the gym while swathed in bandages, chin straps and nose braces after extensive plastic surgery show the viewer a truer story of how to attain the celebrity's ideal body. In this way, makeover television takes the blame off the viewer. Makeover television shows its viewers that it takes more that just working out in front of a television to be made over into society's ideal body.

Chapter Six

DRESSING DOWN

The Chaotic Camcorder Makeover of a Pop Star and Popular Genre

Jennifer Gillan

Rock Star Reality TV – 'documentary as diversion' (Corner 2002) programming that purports to offer insider access to a rock star's 'real' everyday life as it is tracked via surveillance footage – arguably became an official reality TV sub-genre during the second season of *The Osbournes*, the MTV 'Reality star sitcom' (Gillan 2004) featuring Black Sabbath frontman Ozzy Osbourne and his wacky family. The programme was a reality hybrid with its origins in an episode of MTV's *Cribs* and an implied connection to VH1's *Behind the Music* – the latter being the chronicle of a rock band/star's rise, fall and afterlife and the former a music industry celebrity talkshow/tabloid/lifestyle programme along the lines of *Lifestyles of the Rich & Famous*. With its addition of family and anti-family sitcom dynamics to these proven music-television formulae, *The Osbournes* started a sub-genre open to replication. As John Hartley (1999: 119) explains, 'TV was prone to evolution by spin-off. Successful formats were compulsively copied. In this very active semiotic environment, "information" could never be "pure" – it would always be presented via the techniques and generic formats that were regarded as most appealing at the time.'

Once the second season established that *The Osbournes* was more than a one-hit wonder, the assembly line churned out copies. *Nick & Jessica: The Newlyweds* is the 2003–2005 MTV series that almost rivalled ratings for *The Osbournes*, while *Britney & Kevin: Chaotic* is the May–June 2005

UPN miniseries that generated more ridicule than buzz. Although often dismissed as 'Britney-lite', Jessica Simpson offered the more successful reality programme about the transformation of pop princess into ordinary newlywed. Part of the allure of Simpson's show can be attributed to her choice of an appealing leading man. Nick Lachey, a former boy-band star, is both safely suburban and a practical, down-to-earth counterbalance to his ditzy, spoiled wife. It is less important whether Simpson is really a scatterbrained blonde or not than that the straight man/comic relief, husband/wife dynamic has had as successful a sitcom history as the bumbling husband/long-suffering wife format to which *The Osbournes* conformed.

Although Spears tried to offer her story as *Newlyweds: The Prequel*, the general public preferred the original, in part because Britney chose a more lowbrow leading man in Kevin Federline and hence invited comparisons to the reviled trash-TV genre rather than the beloved sitcom. While the bland and middle class Nick and Jessica were perfect for the inane duets on their variety hour, the *Today Show*'s Rockefeller Plaza Christmas-tree lighting, and their 'Tour of Duty', Bob Hope-style USO special, Britney and Kevin, exuding more of a trailer-park trash aura, seem more appropriate as guests on *The Jerry Springer Show*. Kevin's personal life reads like a trash talk-show transcript: he had one illegitimate child and another on the way with Shar Jackson when he abandoned her to go on tour with Britney. The tabloids had a field day with the story and made sure to feature many photographs of Kevin with his mixed-race children. With his easy-to-ridicule white-rapper style (complete with 'do-rag,' cornrows, and extra-large, boxers-baring pants). Kevin's bad reputation isn't helped by the paparazzi images of the formerly stylish Britney looking like one of the bedraggled wives of the men arrested on the reality crimedoc, *Cops*.

Of course, all stars have been subjected to the tabloid use of unflattering pictures to support their outrageous stories. Most stars ignore them, some sue, but Britney talks back. The resulting six-part miniseries, *Britney & Kevin: Chaotic*, can be categorized as star-sanctioned tabloid coverage and rumour control. It is reflective of the recent trend for stars to turn directly to the print and TV tabloid/ entertainment news to respond to or counter the excesses of the star-speculation industry and the paparazzi that perpetuate it. Spears' series offers an extended, personalized version of hosted TV, tabloid/ entertainment news programmes and music-industry docusoaps that offer total 'access' and 'insider' scoops on stars. *Chaotic* promises to deliver on its claims to 'reality' by exposing the pop star as she 'really' is, both 'behind the music' and beneath the make-up. As such it is both a makeover of already-proven reality TV formats and a 'make-under' of a pop star via her personal camcorder footage.

Britney & Kevin: The Makeovers

Spears makes over the original Rock Star Reality TV template by offering her show as a miniseries and using her own camcorder to track her life on tour as well as the evolution of her relationship with Federline from its initial stages to their wedding day. Her use of her own hand-held camera is significant for the programme's claims to 'the real.' As Jon Dovey (2001: 137) explains, 'During the 1990s the low-gauge video image, grainy, underlit and often unsteady, became the pre-eminent televisual signifier of truthfulness.' This essay is less interested in probing the validity of *Chaotic*'s truth claims, than in considering the appeal of its claims to 'the real.'

That appeal is apparent in the favourable DVD reviews on amazon. com (see Spotlight Reviews: *Chaotic*). For many, the rawness of *Chaotic*'s footage contributes to its 'reality effect'. In one posting, 'Todd' explains, 'I thought this show was actually pretty interesting, raw and entertaining. You rarely get a view into a celebrity's REAL life. Most of the time, it seems like they are trying to put on a show in front of the cameras. Since Britney and Kevin shot this one themselves, it had a genuine trueness to it.' 'Chris' elaborates on this idea, arguing that *Chaotic* is not 'typical reality TV': 'are shows like *Newlyweds* and *Big Brother* really reality? Not really, they're glossed-up versions' constructed by 'production editing teams' that add 'background music' and 'special effects'. Other amazon. com reviewers agree that its fuzzy, poorly framed footage made *Chaotic* more 'real' than other reality shows. 'Britney Freak' praises its rawness in comparison to the 'staged' *Newlyweds*: 'M. Chamorro' admits, 'I thought it was going to be boring, you know, the fake "reality" of celebrities. I thought it was going to be another *Newlyweds*... with the rehearsed, obviously written stupid Jessica remarks. Instead, with *Chaotic*, the public got to see home footage of Hollywood's most talked about couple.'

Clearly, twenty-first-century TV audiences are well schooled in reality-TV formats, codes, and structures and have adjusted their viewing strategies accordingly. Aware of the control 'producers have in the editing process' (Andrejevic 2002: 261), they watch critically, but still see 'perpetual surveillance' as the 'antidote to artificial interactions – to "acting"' (ibid.) and camcorder filming as more authentic than professional footage and photographs. These audiences judge characters, says Mark Andrejevic, by their ability to '"be real" – to reveal their interactions and to just be themselves' (261) and take pleasure in perceiving who is or isn't 'acting for the camera'. Viewers have been trained by earlier programming to look for 'the "moment of truth" in a highly constructed and controlled television environment' (Hill 324) as well as for the participants' unintentional disclosure of a 'personal core' (Corner 2002: 261). 'Glamour817'and many others who endorse the DVD, do so because they say it gives 'a glimpse of the real Britney'.

Britney and Kevin also accept what Andrejevic (2002: 265) calls '"the real in reality TV"': that surveillance provides a certain guarantee of authenticity, and that this authenticity becomes a process of self-expression, self-realization, and self-validation.' In *Chaotic*'s embedded interviews, Britney claims that the constant presence of the camera enabled Kevin and her to express themselves, sometimes even forcing them into some 'unwitting disclosures' (Corner 2002: 261). Footage that seems to contradict this romantic trajectory becomes evidence of how they couldn't deal with the intensity of their emotions. Britney insists, 'We used the camera to hide behind.' They got close very quickly by using the camera as an excuse to ask each other personal questions. Britney points out moments in the footage when the camera captured them revealing 'true' feelings that they were verbally denying.

In *Chaotic*'s interview segments, Britney acts as if her miniseries is a documentary offering a 'public-service commentary' about true love. She tells viewers, 'Finding somebody to share your life with... You should embrace that... it really does create miracles.' Josh Wolk of *Entertainment Weekly* got the message that 'the through line of the show was meant to be how Britney met Kevin and the angels sang,' but treated the idea with sarcasm in his EW.com review. The relationship was 'laid out on tape by Brit,' he mocked, 'as if she were assuming that future generations will someday pore over it as an artifact of the Greatest Love of All rather than the short-lived pop culture blip that it is, the romantic equivalent of the Macarena.' He concluded, 'what Britney considers an untouchable love affair has an expiration date stamped all over it. Any time you hear someone describe true love in the exact way that Molly Ringwald did in *Sixteen Candles*, it's fair to assume it won't last.'

That's not what Ruben Garay, the Webmaster of WorldofBritney. com [WoB], assumes in his review of *Chaotic*, a series he characterizes as revealing 'the beauty of unconditional love'. The amateur commentators posting reviews of the DVD on amazon.com also have little trouble with the way the miniseries draws heavily from existing narratives and iconography from the romantic comedy. Spears, who mentions her preference for the genre in a February 2004 posting on her website, has been clearly influenced by *Notting Hill*, the film in which a movie star falls in love with an ordinary guy. *Chaotic*'s final episode also references a different Julia Roberts romantic comedy. In the course of *Notting Hill*, tabloid intervention and half-truths derail the couple's relationship. As it is a 'true love' story about a star who at her core is 'just a girl in love with a boy', the heroine manages to reunite with the ordinary guy and embrace an 'ordinary life' – marriage, pregnancy, and a home with a private park-like garden closed to the paparazzi.

Recycling the plot of *Notting Hill* to cast herself as 'just a girl in love with a boy', Spears unifies the miniseries' commentary interviews and camcorder footage by imposing an overarching romance narrative about Kevin as The One and, thereby, attempts to transform what the tabloids depicted as an ill-conceived fling into a fated meeting of 'true' lovers. *Chaotic* reflects the way that young women, according to Susan Ostrov Weisser (2001: 3), 'often talk of love as courtship (emotion leading to male commitment, marriage, family) in which the values of romantic love are opposed to pornography, cheap sex, promiscuity, and a low valuation of women.' Looked at from a romantic viewpoint, Britney reads Kevin's previous Bad Boy behaviour as a signal that he had just not yet met The One. Even though *Chaotic*'s makeovers are not very revolutionary as they glorify highly conventional aspirations (true love, marriage, motherhood), the fact that the miniseries tackles the familiar terrain of the romance makes it seem more real to some viewers. 'Credibility is maintained' in reality TV, argues Ellis Cashmore (1994: 113), 'by creating characters and contexts that ring true; only the solutions are contrived.' The reviewer, signed on to amazon.com as 'Chad is THE ONE,' concludes: 'This is NOT a reality show, but that's why it's so enjoyable!! This shows Britney meeting and falling in love with Kevin Federline on the European leg of her "Onyx Hotel Tour" last year. This all leads up to their much talked about wedding on September 18, 2004. What you see on this DVD is very rough and unplanned.'

That roughness is what led many other amazon.com reviewers to label *Chaotic* 'embarrassing', 'vulgar', and 'horrific'. Most professional reviewers used similar descriptors in their May 2005 reviews of the *Chaotic* premier. Dubbed as 'TV's non-event of the week' and 'America's crummiest home video' by Tom Shales of *The Washington Post*, *Chaotic* was much maligned in both general and entertainment industry publications. Spears' reality programme, proclaimed to be 'a stinker' by Amy DeLuna of *New York Daily News* and 'stale' by *The Boston Globe*'s Matthew Gilbert, was even voted 'Worst TV Show of the Week' by ParentsTv.org. In *Variety*, Laura Fries concurred with that assessment: 'A self-indulgent, mindless piece of drivel, *Chaotic* is a visual assault of nauseating camera angles.' Describing an episode as a 'solid hour of yammering and mugging into a jiggly camera,' Wolk called Spears' reality show 'career suicide by videocam.' Citing several of the series' most inane moments, Andrew Banks of the *Sunday Mail* wondered if Spears' makeover might have removed too much of the star aura: 'Fans of Britney will see another side of the star, but it may not be one they like.' As Fries put it, 'Instead of cementing Spears' place as an entertainment icon, it reinforces the singer as a comic punch line. One can just imagine the *Saturday Night Live* skit that's sure to come.' In the same month the UPN show premiered, *Saturday Night Live* did just that with its May 2005 parody of a *Chaotic* promo. In March 2005, SNL had already singled out Federline for ridicule in an underwear commercial parody that played on Federline's tabloid reputation and his sloppy style. He became a punchline again in a September 2005 episode of the irreverent animated series *Family Guy*.

Resisting *Chaotic*'s imposed romantic paradigms, the writers for these shows characterized Britney and Kevin in terms of a trash talk show in which the guests become the targets of ridicule and reprimand for their willingness to expose their private lives on national TV (Shattuc 1997; Grindstaff 2004). The ridicule was apparent in most of the professional reviews. In *The Times* (of London), Caitlin Moran called Federline 'a weasel-eyed tracksuited hick' and, in *The New York Times*, Alessandra Stanley said Spears had 'the mind of a child trapped in the body of a blow-up doll.' Wolk branded Spears a 'cigarette-puffing good-time girl who can't wait for her next Federhump,' while Shales described her as a 'smutty-mouthed, pudgy-faced brat.' Both might have always felt this way about Spears, but Pete Paphides, co-author of *The Times* (of London) article, remarked that the miniseries changed for the worse his impression of Spears: 'One of the most famous women in the world has just revealed herself to be a complete hick.' *Variety* declared that *Chaotic*'s depiction of Britney and Kevin 'makes Jessica and Nick look like Mensa candidates.'

Many amateur commentators refer to the show as 'trashy' and/or Britney and Kevin as trailer-park trash. As 'Lisa' puts it, on her Internet

Movie Database (imdb.com) review of *Chaotic*, 'If you're one of those people who slow down to get a better look at traffic accidents or love to watch trashy people on talk shows, this is a must see. Although it is probably the most boring show in the history of reality TV, it is so bad that you can't help but watch it.' In one of the WoB fan forums, 'Amanda' claims to know many former Britney fans who cannot tolerate Spears anymore because Kevin 'turned her into trailer trash'. She is also sceptical of Kevin's motives, referring sarcastically to the 'millions that Kevin made from being Britney's husband'. Others accept that Britney is 'in love', but are doubtful about Kevin. 'Does Kevin sit and talk to the camera at all like Britney has in her own little "Real World Confessions" type thing? No, I didn't think so,' 'R. C.' remarks in an amazon.com review. 'Cristine' describes Kevin as a 'two-timing jobless... loser... one who let this dumb naive rich girl spend lots of money on him so he would stay by her side.' She echoes Shar Jackson's analysis, 'If Britney thinks a leopard can change its spots, she's wrong.' Kevin's ex supposedly made this comment when asked to respond to the rumours that new-dad Kevin was spending his nights going out on the town in the luxury sports car he paid for with the $5 million *Chaotic* pay-cheque Spears gifted to him so he could be financially independent from her. Meanwhile, she stayed home with the baby and worked out so that she would no longer appear in tabloid 'dramatic star weight gain' shots.

One such shot appears on the homepage of DivorceKevin.com as evidence of the detrimental effects Kevin has had on Britney. Created on 21 November 2005 by Jason Cage, a Little Rock, Arkansas radio DJ, the website has provided a forum for people who believe that Kevin is a gold digger. The K-FedUp petition, the centrepiece of DivorceKevin. com, received over twenty thousand signatures by the close of 2005. Cage and his petition signers urge Spears to divorce Federline, referring to him as an unsightly boil, a moocher, and a loser. Dubbing him Federleach and Spenderline, most signers wrote comments along the lines of the following posts: 'For the love of god divorce this man. He is really icky' or, even less charitably, 'You look like crap. Dump him.'

Many Britney fans blame Kevin for debasing their multi-platinum pop star. In a WoB fan forum, 'Amanda' says she would 'like to see her leave his name behind, not become a joke.' She concludes, 'If she gets rid of him soon, I think she can make a huge comeback and leave her trash at the curbside.' Ruben, the site's creator, counters, 'I stopped trashing Kevin, not out of respect for him but out of respect for Britney.' He calls on other fans to do the same: 'Britney is a mess right now, with all the speculations... the last thing she needs is for fans to keep reminding her that she's picked a loser of a husband.' One very public reminder came in the 28 November 2005 issue of *Star* magazine. Of the almost 5,500 readers supposedly polled, almost 90% allegedly said that Kevin was bad for Britney's image, career, and self-esteem. The *Star* headline pleaded, on behalf of its readers, 'Britney, Divorce Kevin Now'!

Dressing Down the Paparazzi

Commenting on the sign on Spears' Malibu compound that reads, 'Surviving Trespassers will be Prosecuted,' *Elle* staff writer Holly Millea (October 2005: 388) remarks, 'Desperate paparazzi times call for desperate star measures, especially when you're a multi-platinum album-selling Grammy winner worth an estimated $123 million.' Although Spears has been on the run from the paparazzi for years, she was thrilled to outsmart them by pulling off a secret wedding a month prior to the official date. *Chaotic*'s final episode functions as a dressing down of the paparazzi by documenting how Britney and Kevin outfoxed the tabloids. As Kevin says in this 'Veil of Secrecy' episode, 'we foiled every single one of them.'

With the programme's teaser line, *Can you handle our truth?*, the couple adopt tabloid rhetoric – we will show you the truth behind the image, the truth that the publicist doesn't want you to see – for their own purposes. *Chaotic* is an intervention in the star-speculation industry – the lucrative business, engaged in by tabloid and entertainment newspapers, magazines, and TV programmes, of selling to the public conjectures about a star's personal life, relationships, and body garnered from mere shreds of evidence. Many misrepresented celebrities have tried to strike back at the tabloids. Cameron Diaz, the film star for whom pop star Justin Timberlake left Spears in 2002, tried a few different talking-back strategies. Once she called *US* directly and asked for the cover to refute break-up rumours. Diaz, chosen as the October 2005 *GQ* cover girl, tried another approach as well – the meta-interview. After the standard *GQ* interview, she participated in an email/phone exchange with the article's author about the finished product so that she could comment on the writer's interpretation of what she had said. The resulting meta-commentary on celebrity interviews and their limitations appeared as a coda to the actual printed interview.

Taking the position of interviewer as well as interviewee, cameraperson as well as subject, Spears goes a step further in *Chaotic*, intervening in her own cultural circulation. Her TV programme engages what Steve Neale (1990) calls the 'intertextual relay' – the industrial, journalistic, and marketing discourses that extend beyond the boundaries of a primary text. The 4 October 2005 letter Spears wrote to fans on the 'Love B: Stream of Consciousness' link on www.britneyspears.com suggests that, prior to making *Chaotic*, she did not feel in control of 'Britney' the brand: 'it's amazing what advisors will push you to do, even if it means taking a naïve, young blonde girl and putting her on the cover of every magazine.' *Chaotic* acknowledges the circulation of authorized and unauthorized representations of 'Britney' (in television industry trade press, viewing guides, tabloids, and star/entertainment print and television news magazines; in advertising campaigns, official publicity releases, promotional materials, and press junkets involving or related to Britney Spears, her CDs, and her branded products). At the same time, the series implies that it will offer a more raw representation of the 'real' Britney. *Chaotic*'s reliance on '"reality" as a promotional marketing tool' reflects the current practice of 'the open and explicit sale of television programming as a representation of "reality"' (Friedman 2002: 7). Its promise of total access contrasts to the authorized celebrity fare typically available: print and TV entertainment magazines that offer brief glimpses of celebrity lives via coverage pieced together from publicity materials, red-carpet appearances, and behind-the-scenes film/TV/music-video footage. The miniseries format enabled Spears to offer her own more sustained commentary on her personal life.

Such an intervention seems particularly important to female stars as they are more often positioned as the object of the gaze, with no control about how images and stories offer fragmented glimpses of their bodies and lives. Joshua Gamson (1994) confirms that the 'paid specialists [that] surround the celebrities to increase and protect their market value,' package women like Britney Spears as an 'objectified body and commodified sexuality' to appeal to the 'male gaze,' while 'simultaneously building and using the performer's "attention-getting power"'(61, 2). *Chaotic* is Spears' attempt to take charge of her own circulation and represent herself as a 'whole person'. When she is not the bearer of the camera's gaze, Spears only allows herself to be looked at by a controlled group – Federline, selected friends, employees, and concert camerapersons, and, for her post-marriage commentary/ interview, a UPN camera set up as if it were a Barbara Walters-style interviewer. The difference, of course, is that nobody is asking her or Kevin, sometimes seated next to her on a couch, 'the tough questions'. Although the same is true of the way the 'cast' of The Osbournes are 'interviewed', the editors in that reality programme could then balance any seemingly rehearsed comment with a contradictory piece of the extensive 24/7 surveillance footage they had amassed. Because Spears is more explicitly the subject and the editor of the footage, her interviews come across as more staged and likely contributed to some readings of the show and its narrative as inauthentic. Still, the fact that Spears gets to wield the camera and edit and manipulate the footage for her own purposes is significant. Chaotic represents a mode of star empowerment in which the star gets to talk back and respond to paparazzi in a court of public opinion rather than a court of law – the usual, but unsatisfying mode of response to tabloid dissemination of misinformation.

The glamorous and sexy Britney who launched a thousand cover stories was a media production, Chaotic contends. Disturbed by the way her sexy images were circulated and allowed to develop lives of their own, Spears claims she is no longer interested in putting herself on display. In her October 2005 website letter, she says she is tired of being 'the Icon everyone says she is.' 'My prerogative right now,' she declares, 'is to just chill & let all the other overexposed blondes on the cover of US Weekly be your entertainment.' Her reality TV show affords the pop star a chance to present her dressed-down self to the world.

As its star as well as its principal creator, executive producer, and chief cameraperson, Spears uses Chaotic to orchestrate her 'make under', filming herself in her 'everyday life' without her professional hair and make-up. She then offers concert footage of herself as she is before, after, and during the process of being transformed from a surprisingly ordinary twenty-two year old into a startling sexy and permanently Lolita-esque performer. The juxtaposition of the different footage establishes Chaotic as a 'make under' show. Fans applauded Spears' willingness to show herself 'made under' and to document how she undergoes the glamorizing process prior to a public appearance. By repeating this commodified celebrity transformation scene several times throughout the programme, Spears assures her fans that she doesn't even look like the 'Britney' publicity shots without a whole team of 'artists'. As 'Glamour817' explains, 'This isn't a glamorous, glossy compilation of "Britney" and her life... this was more of a homemade, rough-draft video.' Not everyone liked the dressed-down Britney. To make this point, the homepage of DivorceKevin.com uses a 'Before' and an 'After' picture to demonstrate the detrimental reverse makeover that Britney has undergone since meeting Kevin. In a discussion thread on his WoB site, Ruben tells another fan that laments the loss of the glamour girl, 'the Britney that you used to know is OVER.' Was the 'real Britney' ever like the cover girl, he wonders, or was that a creation of 'countless make-up artists and stylists'.

The toning down of Spears' perfected public image into a flawed, but ultimately more 'real', private one plays into *Chaotic*'s claims to authenticity. It shares similarities to gamedocs 'in which contestants are often de-glamorised and "in the raw" when filmed through the unflattering aesthetic of Reality TV, and this facilitates the program's claim to realism' (Holmes 2004: 116). 'Britney Freak' attributes the 'realness' of the *Chaotic* programme to Spears' un-styled hair and make-up – an indicator for many of the other fan/reviewers as well of Spears' willingness to show people 'her real side'. Yet, like other TV programmes, *Chaotic* 'strives to convince us that its words and images reproduce our own experience or that of people like us' and invites us 'to forget that a story is being constructed' (Taylor 1991: 38). As David Carr of *The New York Times* says, 'there is something both gory and glorious in seeing Ms. Spears in her unalloyed state with mussed hair and a bad sweat suit – more Smurf than sex goddess.' On amazon.com, 'Miranda' implies that this is the 'real' person beneath the image: 'Britney is such a dork and she knows it and it is so cool to see a celebrity acting like this.' She adds, 'who wants to watch someone with their nose in the air doing tons of things that we could all never dream about doing. It is funny and cool to see someone acting real like that.'

Chaotic offers meta-commentary on Richard Dyer's famous formulation of the interplay between stardom as the combination of manufacture and the talent/specialness (Dyer 1986) and the star as living both an ordinary life and a glamorous lifestyle (see Ellis 1992: 95). Reflective of the way reality TV emphasizes 'the virtues of a particular combination of "ordinariness" and "specialness"' (Holmes 2004), *Chaotic*'s message is that despite the talent and lifestyle that make her a star, Spears' hobbies, attitude, and behaviour make her refreshingly ordinary. It worked for 'Rarr', another amazon.com reviewer: 'This is the most honest reality TV show you will ever see. Britney and Kevin share some of their most private moments with the public and keep you laughing non-stop. Whether it's Britney sliding over a table or singing out of the window to random people – you will be entertained.' Her ordinariness is also supposed to be conveyed in moments in which she is making faces at the camera, sliding across a hard wood floor, taking Kevin on a tour of her fabulous hotel suite and acting awestruck as if she has never gotten used to the perks of stardom. Dyer (1986: 6) explains, 'even though we understand the celebrity image to be a sign construction, we often value those that appear to be "being themselves".' Addressing other 'true fans' who know the 'real Britney', 'Seige2000' offered the following amazon.com review: 'It really shows Britney Spears as a real person who is funny, outgoing, and truly loves her friends and family. The show got a lot of flack because Britney isn't prim and proper but isn't that what we have always loved about Britney? Not to mention, when Britney & Kevin finally get married it's really a great and emotional moment!' Although more cynical about the supposedly romantic aspects of the series, especially given that Britney flew Kevin '(practically kicking and screaming) to England to be with her' five days after they met, Linda Stasi of *The New York Post* praised Spears' willingness to expose herself: '[she] isn't hiding any of it. Not the sex. Not the loneliness. Not the need. Not the craving.'

The 'Reveal': A New Britney (or Brand?)

In addition to its make under of her over-produced image, *Chaotic* is also Spears' attempt to take some risks by allowing herself to be under-protected both in terms of her personal life and her career. In her song 'Overprotected', Spears addresses the problem of being a teen star whose personal and professional decisions are handled by others. In the song, and in *Chaotic*, Britney frames her makeover as a move toward independence, a rebellion against overly controlling parents and their stand-ins. After 14 years of being carefully managed by others, Spears chose to assert her freedom by curtailing it at 22 through marriage and step-motherhood, followed by motherhood a year later.

Spears equates motherhood with independence in the *Elle* interview (Millea 2005: 294): 'Having a child and getting married, it's gonna help me not be influenced so much, or manipulated, which can happen in a huge way… it's a sticky thing because you love these people. The sad thing is that it's usually the ones closest to you. And you have to completely separate yourself.' Previously, she just longed to 'please people and become what they want[ed] to see,' she explains, 'it was always because I was always overprotected' (ibid.). Spears casts doubt on her 'independent woman' claim by describing her pregnancy as if it were a way to outfox her parents. She admits that her mother was 'taken aback' by news of the pregnancy: 'I think she thought I was probably going to wait a little bit…

but those weren't the plans of Britney' (Millea 2005: 394). Her parents are the absent presence in *Chaotic*. No longer a closely chaperoned teen star, Spears invites a virtual stranger instead of her mother on tour with her. When Spears' parents do finally appear in the final episode, their displeasure is evident. The moment a few hours before the wedding, when her father refuses to acknowledge that Britney is actually marrying Kevin, seems like one of those moments of 'truth' in the 'highly constructed and controlled television environment' (Hill 2002: 234).

Chaotic also offers another rupture in Spears' intended narrative. In the camcorder footage used for episode one, taken when Spears' head of security did not know that Kevin would be a permanent fixture or that there would be a reality TV show, he is caught on film harassing Kevin and calling him a 'punk'. Mo explains in the after-the-fact interview, 'There was nothing I liked about Kevin when I first met him' - not the way he walked, talked, or dressed. Mo falls into line with the governing narrative, assuring viewers that Kevin is great and his initial reaction came out over protectiveness. Spears includes his comment, 'I thought, "this guy's here for a free ride",' so that Mo can admit that he had misjudged Kevin. Even with the retraction, the initial response is a rupture in Spears' carefully orchestrated 'true love' story. That he understands he needs to reframe his earlier response in terms of the 'Overprotected' theme suggests much about the performative element of the format; similar to other reality TV participants, he knows what the show's creator wants and delivers (Grindstaff 166). With each of the 'talking heads' sticking closely to the message – the star is new and improved and it's all because she found The One and is having his baby – the docusoap functions like a PR campaign.

The miniseries manages to blend personal revelation, celebrity news and 'Britney' brand advertising. Ostensibly, the camcorder show ends with Britney and Kevin's secret wedding, the event that symbolises their ability to one-up the paparazzi. At that point in the narrative, Kevin's makeover is complete and the disreputable baseball cap- and do-rag-wearing Bad Boy has been gelled and blow-dried into a presentable Armani-wearing celebrity companion, husband and father-to-be. A self-promoted primetime celebrity 'Reveal', *Chaotic* also allows Spears to reveal some satellite brands (Britney's Husband and Baby). In the ultimate convergence of new 'Britney' products, the morning after Spears produced a baby boy, her new fragrance Fantasy was released. When fans logged on to www.britneyspears.com to find out about the baby the morning he was born, they learned about the release of the fragrance. Carr notes cynically in *The New York Times* that the 'baby made its global premiere as a telltale bump clutched by Ms. Spears' in the "Someday".' video. Perhaps the 'real Britney' *Chaotic* is offering is just another iteration of the brand.

The makeover of the Britney brand was a necessary one given Spears' new status as a pregnant pop singer. The fans that grew up with Britney – following her from Mouseketeer to Pop Princess to Teen Temptress to Modern Bride – welcomed her newest incarnation. 'Kris', along with many others, posted congratulatory notes after the baby's birth on the <www.britneyspears.com> message board: 'I have seen your life come full circle,' she wrote. Some of the well-wishers shared their experiences as young mothers and others wrote romantically about someday also becoming mothers. WoB.com soon added its own internal link, WoBmomma, a linked website for Britney fans who are mothers.

In the 'Someday' video, a pregnant Spears asserts that her life 'has come full circle' and implies that in the process she underwent a makeover of the soul as well as the body. Her former flesh-baring costuming and frenzied gyrations on a stage crowded with back-up dancers are replaced in the new video with a solitary, fabric-draped Spears evoking an ethereal calmness that is reflected in the singer's lyrical, costuming and staging choices. The image recalls Madonna's Kaballah makeover, her post-sexploitation stage in which she added new-age and eastern signifiers, a makeover that came in her thirties after a tabloid-headlining first marriage and a few other misguided relationships. Spears, who at 22 released her greatest hits album *My Prerogative*, seems in a rush to claim a reinvention, making the transformation seem forced, and leaving us to wonder whether the 'real Britney' *Chaotic* supposedly unveils is just another performance.

Although the miniseries encourages its viewers to 'hang on to the reality of the star's authentic self' (Dyer 1998: 10), it also raises the question of whether her identity and the viewers' own identities are essentially performative. By blurring public and private lives, stardom gives the illusion of intimacy, Dyer reminds us. While *Chaotic* removes the distancing aura of the star, it does not remove the distance; viewers get some intimate details from Spears' life, but are hardly more intimate with her. The promised 'truth' of the promos proves only to be a teaser. *Chaotic*'s 'reveal' of a married and pregnant Britney whose curves are directed toward nurturing rather than seduction was definitely disappointing for the viewers who were less interested in Spears' 'unwitting disclosure of personal core' (Corner 2002: 261) than they were in an unwitting or, better yet, a knowing exposure of something more than Britney's core muscles. The star did expose herself, but only that she was an ordinary teen beneath the Lolita image, a juvenile girl who preferred mugging for the camera to exhibiting her body for it.

As *The Osbournes* demonstrated, the deglamorization produced by reality-TV surveillance footage can also be demystification. This process worked to Ozzy Osbourne's advantage as it enabled the heavy-metal icon most famous for biting the head off a bat to extend his appeal beyond his niche audience. If Ozzy's reality programme demonstrates that he is less dysfunctional than he looks, Britney's exposes that she is less in control of her raw sexuality than she seems. She is more like an ordinary teenager than the fantasy girl her many salacious cover photos implied. The 'reveal' exposes the singer, famous for a sexy schoolgirl video, to be a silly schoolgirl with a head full of romantic fantasies. She is less every man's fantasy girl than a girl caught up in a fantasy about meeting the man who is The One. The 'reveal' is troubling as it exposes how invested in the idea of romantic love young women still are. While Britney seems to intend *Chaotic* to be read as a synonym for the wild and crazy life that sometimes prevents you from noticing the important things (i.e. how fulfilled you will be by love, marriage, and the baby carriage), it seems more indicative of the muddled decision-making of the romantically influenced young woman. Carr (2005) remarks that there is 'something telling and even melancholic' about the representation of 'true love' in *Chaotic*, particularly the way 'these two young people need the presence of a camera – and millions of viewers – to get to know each other.' He is struck that Federline slipped in 'a montage he said he made without Ms. Spears' knowledge. "I put this together, baby," he said into the camera while choking up, "to show you how much I care".' Carr's comments point to how reality TV must negotiate the tension between bearing 'witness to what took place in front of the camera' and presenting a 'reality' that has been staged and/or manipulated for the camera. *Chaotic* seems mostly to bear witness to Britney and Kevin's romantic fantasy.

By pitching the programme as 'our truth', Britney and Kevin put the issue of mediated truth on the discursive agenda of the miniseries. *Chaotic* plays out issues surrounding the mediation of identity which, in turn, speak to broader discourses concerning selfhood and individualism. Given its disclosure of Britney's 'mediated theatrical play with identity' (Kellner 1992: 142), the interview commentary sections' implication that the 'self' can be produced and reproduced at will, and the programme's more general 'performance of the real' (Roscoe 2001: 485), *Chaotic* acknowledges the contingent and partial nature of truth. Despite its emphasis on the value of discovering an 'authentic self' beneath the performance, it exposes such a discovery to be more fantasy than actuality. All that is revealed by Spears is that identity itself is chaotic. It's not her truth the audience can't handle, it's her fantasy.

Chapter Seven

FAKING IT

and the Transformation of Personal Identity

Joanne Morreale

Reality television programmes have now infiltrated virtually every area of the medium, and they occupy a significant portion of the televisual terrain. Like other television genres, reality programmes reproduce themselves by hijacking pre-existent forms: cop shows, dramas, soap operas, sitcoms, game shows, and self-improvement shows. Their rapid proliferation has irrevocably altered our mediascape and, to the extent that our interactions with mass-mediated cultural forms shape our identities, they are in the process of altering us. One of the most recent developments in reality programming has been the makeover show, where participants are offered everything from redecorated apartments to redesigned bodies. Here I consider the hybrid makeover, game, and reality show *Faking It* as a cultural form that intensifies the well-established relationship between commodification and personal identity. *Faking It* provides a televisual Petri dish in which to observe the contemporary production of the self as commodity-sign, inscribed by markers of class and identity. Most importantly, it is indicative of a cultural shift from the notion of *having* a product to *being* a product as a route to personal fulfilment.

Faking It (itself an ironic name for a so-called reality programme) began airing in the UK on Channel 4/BBC in 2000, and reruns appeared in the States on BBC America. After *Faking It* won Europe's top entertainment award at the Montreux International Television Festival in 2002, the US-based Learning Channel bought the programme. The American version went on the air in March 2003, and production ended in 2005. The BBC version of *Faking It* has been sold around the world, and either has or soon will appear in Canada, Australia, Denmark, Norway, Sweden, and South Africa. Domestic versions are currently in próduction in Germany, the Netherlands, Belgium and Brazil.

While there are some stylistic and thematic differences between the English and American versions, here I will bracket them and focus on the more significant commonalities. The same production company, RDF Media, made both British and American versions, and Stephen Lambert was executive producer of both, and thus the similarities are more extreme than might otherwise be the case. Both versions are premised on the idea that, given a coterie of specialist trainers for one month, an ordinary person can transform him or herself well enough to fool a panel of experts. According to The Learning Channel's casting call (28 September 2004):

> *Faking It* is a transformational battle against the odds. It tells the story of what happens when real people take up the challenge of converting themselves into someone entirely different. Our hero/heroine is plucked from their daily lives and given four weeks to master a skill well enough to fool a group of expert judges. During the month of intensive training, top practitioners, famous in their field, mentor the faker and try their best to help them succeed.
> In the final test at the end of the month, the faker must not only demonstrate the skill required, but they must look, act, and talk the part as well. At the heart of the show is the journey the faker takes into an unknown world and the relationships that develop between the faker and their mentors.

Participants don't just learn the skills associated with a particular profession, but they must also adopt the appropriate personas. Much of *Faking It* involves class passing, most typically upward – a carpenter becomes an interior designer, a punk singer becomes a classical music conductor, a housepainter become a conceptual artist, or a fast food vendor becomes a chef. Both the English and American versions have episodes entirely devoted to social class; in the former, a chemist's assistant from the North of England becomes an 'aristocrat' while, in the latter, an organic farmer from Nebraska becomes a 'posh' socialite.

There are also programmes that revolve around gender; for example, in both the English and American programmes a naval officer and a drag racer, respectively, become drag queens or, in the USA, an androgynous Harvard graduate becomes a cheerleader.

Faking It's premise is that these new selves will offer fulfilment, that transformation is commensurate with improvement. In this way, *Faking It* reaffirms the therapeutic ethos that marked the rise of twentieth-century consumer culture and has continued to define the contemporary milieu (see Jackson Lears 1983). Stated briefly, the therapeutic ethos replaced the Protestant ethic of salvation through self-denial. It emerged in Europe and the United States in the late 1800s as the result of a confluence of factors: urbanization, new technological developments, the rise of the market economy, the growing authority of science and medicine, and the decline of religious institutions. The therapeutic ethos promises self-fulfilment through consumption, through *having* rather than *being*, and thus explains the constant quest for products that bring physical, emotional, or spiritual health.

Most importantly, *Faking It* refigures the therapeutic ethos by promising fulfilment through *becoming* a commodity rather than *having* one. Identity is presented as a lifestyle choice, and its fabrication is inextricably linked to practices of consumption. *Faking It* replays the process of socialization whereby people assemble disparate parts – behavioural 'bytes' – to project a coherent self-image. In the language of advertising, participants try on 'new and improved' selves that they can parlay into social capital. Not only do they adopt clothing and hairstyles, they incorporate qualities, attitudes, behaviours, gestures, movements, and skills, to the extent that they erase the distinction between identity and image. By the culmination of the process, they have become the self that they are taught to enact. *Faking It* implies that identity and social class, like Judith Butler's take on gender, is inherently performative, an 'incessant and repeated action' which exists only as it's played out in continuous enactments (Butler 1990: 112). Although these categories appear natural, they are only manifest by doing, by reproducing the signifiers of class, social identity, and gender that we consciously and unconsciously learn from others. Butler writes, 'Such acts, gestures, enactments, generally construed, are *performative* in the sense that the essence or identity that they otherwise purport to express are *fabrications* manufactured and sustained through corporeal signs and other discursive means' (136). *Faking It* thus condenses, speeds up and makes overt the performative genesis of identity.

Faking It puts on display the processes of fabrication whereby the self is created. It popularizes the idea that identity is created through social performance; it highlights that identity is a game one plays, the product of role-playing and rehearsal of already fabricated images. Paradoxically, however, *Faking It* both frees and shores up the self. The self may be fluid and mobile, but it is still constrained by the capitalist ideology of individualism: with will-power, determination, and role models (and the right hair and clothes), people can re-incarnate themselves as particular social types. Indeed, part of the appeal of *Faking It*, and similar makeover reality shows, may be that they simultaneously subvert and support hegemonic beliefs; while they undermine the precepts of social order and hierarchy, they bolster the ideologies of individualism and the possibility of success.

Faking It's frame as reality rather than fiction accords it an assumed veracity. Indeed, it bills itself as a documentary rather than a reality show, which provides another layer of legitimacy. Yet, every episode follows the same formula, and even the jury at Montreaux commended it for its drama rather than realism. According to one jury member, 'It treats the reality genre with complete sympathy for the participants and combines great storytelling with compelling drama and emotions, and is truly groundbreaking' (Turner 2003). The particular situations and experiences viewers see are also confined to what plays well on television. The professions selected are visually compelling: chef, ballet dancer, horse racer, cheerleader, aristocrat, drag queen. Dramatic music underscores important scenes, and the camerawork and editing are highly stylized throughout the programme. Time-lapse photography frequently represents an activity that took several hours in just a few minutes (and thus signals that transformation is virtually instantaneous). As in all ostensibly non-fiction films, situations are occasionally set up for the camera's benefit, and it is common knowledge that scenes on reality programmes are often scripted for dramatic effect. While the filming of the entire show takes place over the course of three weeks to a month, viewers see less than an hour's worth of footage. The highly contrived result is filtered, packaged and marketed as 'reality'.

Within the context of the narrative, coaches and a mentor encourage participants to take on the identity of the kind of person involved in a particular profession. The coaches become role models who teach participants the ritualized sets of behaviours, rules, norms and expectations that correspond to a particular stereotype of a social class and occupation. Participants are always uprooted from their homes and taken to unfamiliar places; the process is referred to as 'lifestyle immersion'. They live with either their coach or mentor, and the intense relationship that develops is typically what motivates the participant (the motivation can either be positive or negative; sometimes participants want to succeed in order to 'show them' rather than to please them). Although not all of the relationships go smoothly, there does seem to be a hint of the 'Stockholm effect', a psychological term used to account for the fact that hostages kept in isolation from other people will often begin to identify with the aims of their captors. While the participants are not exactly hostages, and the coaches are hardly captors, the exclusivity and intensity of the relationship does seem to facilitate the process of transformation.

Viewers see signs of the often-painful labour that is involved in this personal transformation; these signs serve as visual markers of authenticity that demonstrate that the participant is truly suffering on the path to self-fulfilment. Both the participants and coaches independently provide a video diary where they express their feelings to the camera. In the case of the participants, these 'authentic' moments of personal revelation reinforce the therapeutic idea that self-reflection and self-knowledge, made possible by participating in *Faking It*, makes transformation possible. Bratich (in this volume) suggests that personal growth through self-knowledge is a recurrent theme in reality shows, as is the notion that resistance to transformation is a character defect. In *Faking It*, the possibility of the participants' resistance serves as the dramatic crux of every episode. There is typically a moment of crisis where the participant falters and the coaches voice their concerns on-camera. The coaches and/or mentor then have a motivational talk with the participant, where they stress that he or she needs to try harder and to believe in her/himself (another recurrent theme). Paradoxically, the participants succeed in re-asserting themselves only after submitting to the disciplinary control of these 'authorities'.

It is also significant that participants on *Faking It* are *filmed* as they learn their new identities. Being seen is an important aspect of identity formation, and serves as a pivotal moment in *Faking It*. Every episode includes both a makeover and a shopping spree where coaches help participants choose appropriate clothing and accessories. A mirror then serves as a metaphor for the participants' transformation. They are always shown gazing at their new selves, freshly coiffed and dressed in clothes that mark their new social positions. The Lacanian drama of the mirror stage is played out for viewers. Viewers watch as the mirror marks the moment of (mis)recognition, when participants see themselves as whole and complete, as the actualization of potential. Andy, originally a drag-car racer, says it best when he gazes at himself made-up as a drag queen for the first time, 'I looked in the mirror and I saw that I had become Portia – not me' ('Drag Racer to Drag Queen', 2003). Viewers watching the scene are similarly subject to a moment of (mis)recognition as they see the mock transformation become 'real'.

Online questionnaires where people can apply to be on the show make clear that the producers seek participants who are 'in a rut', 'have never realized their dreams', and 'have never stepped outside their safety zone' (and those are just the first three questions). Participants thus begin from a position of lack and inadequacy, and it is only when they see their completed images in the mirror, which are, not coincidentally, attained through the purchase of products, that their transformation can take place. They present the illusion of a unified self who is 'better' than what was there before. As one online fan wrote to Lesley, a Harvard graduate who became a cheerleader for the Atlanta Falcons, 'If your mirror isn't showing you how special you are, then get a new mirror. The one you have must be broken' (The Learning Channel website, *Faking It* forum).

Viewers are again reminded of the importance of being seen at the conclusion of every programme, when the coaches and mentors watch the candidate perform for the panel of experts from a surveillance station located off-site. As Mark Andrejevic (2004) notes, the naturalization of surveillance is an important ideological component of reality programmes. Participants do not win monetary prizes; everything rests upon a final performance where a panel of judges tries to guess who the impostor is in a group of supposed professionals. Participants succeed if their new identities are validated by the judges and, less obviously, by viewers watching them on television. The stakes are raised as these 'others' who judge the participants are considered experts – who ostensibly should know the real from the fake. Even when the participant fails to fool all of the experts, the coaches are inevitably proud of the performance (participants rarely fail to fool at least one judge, perhaps a testament to how little the so-called experts know). Transformation is attainable, given the participant's continued motivation and effort (i.e. willingness to play the game). As in life, success is judged by the performative skill of impression management. It doesn't matter how much the participants know; what matters is how well they can act like they know what they are doing.

Faking It is a modern version of the television game show *What's My Line?* (1950-1967), and it is instructive to compare the two. Like *Faking It*, the participants on *What's My Line?* were ordinary people selected for having somewhat unusual occupations. But *What's My Line?* centred on a panel of minor celebrities who tried to pose clever and amusing questions, while the participants, often guided by the advice of the host/mentor, would simply answer yes or no. The game primarily relied on language cues, and the goal was to find the 'correct' answer. If the panel failed to guess, the contestant would win a small monetary prize. *Faking It* shifts the focus onto the contestants, in accord with reality television's preoccupation with amateurs (who work for free). The candidate's occupation is here a starting point from which to make some kind of qualitative shift – a dancer to a show-jumper, or a beer expert to a sommelier, or a telephone operator to a television producer.

While *What's My Line?* was tied to the logic of representation, *Faking It* is better understood in relation to the simulacrum. The participants on *Faking It* simulate rather than represent their professions and identities. According to Brian Massumi (1987: 2):

> A common definition of a simulacrum is a copy of a copy whose relation to the model has become so attenuated that it can no longer properly be said to be a copy. It stands on its own as a copy, without a model... The simulacrum is less a copy twice removed than a phenomenon of a different nature altogether. It undermines the very distinction between copy and model... The thrust of the process is not to become an equivalent of the "model" but to turn against it and its world in order to open a new space for the simulacrum's own mad proliferation.

What's My Line? was an attempt to faithfully represent the real. But 'experts' on *Faking It* are not asked to select who is real, but to identify who is not real. Who is the least convincing simulator of a drag queen, interior designer or polo player? It is not surprising that judges rarely get it completely right or wrong. In a thirty-day crash course, *Faking It* participants learn to copy their models, who are themselves 'copies'. As Erving Goffman (1979: 1-9) notes, ordinary behaviour is highly ritualized; people act out and live social ideals, presenting stereotypical images of themselves to others. What we know of an aristocrat, dancer, carpenter, or drag queen is already a fabrication. *Faking It* is thus a hyper-ritualized representation of a representation. The new personas that are created, whether they demonstrate gender or class mobility, all indicate the desire to fulfil oneself by becoming the imaginary other, the idealized image that is somehow more complete.

In the English episode called 'Lady Lisa' (2000), for example, a chemist's assistant is taught to become an aristocrat. She had a voice coach, etiquette and deportment coach, and an upper-class male mentor who was a Society Editor at *The Daily Mail*. Lisa had lessons on how to walk, how to talk, use upper-class table manners, and introduce appropriate conversational topics; furthermore, make-up, a new hairstyle, and new clothing altered her appearance. Lisa was encouraged to 'educate' herself by visiting art galleries in the little free time she had. Her guides clearly meant for viewers to see her as a latter-day Pygmalion. The deportment coach even remarked to the camera soon after meeting her, 'I'm dying to tidy her hair, get her some make-up. Everything needs to be chiselled, the edges sorted out' ('Lady Lisa', 2000).

The mentors and coaches, while at times approaching parody, provide a condensed version of the way we learn class, identity and gender through instruction, emulation and practice. Throughout, there is a tension between the coaches, who try to shape the participants, and the participants who must respond to their advice. As Bratich (in this volume) writes in regard to all reality television, 'Individuals, through their bodies and minds, are fragmented and then recomposed as flexible and open-ended, ready to absorb command mechanisms as if they were their own.' Thus Lisa rehearses words until she enunciates just like her coach ('Lady Lisa', 2000), and Lesley, a Harvard graduate, is taught to smile and 'adopt the proper attitude' for a cheerleader ('Ivy League to Big League', 2003). Andy the drag queen learns the difficult art of how to walk not like a woman, but with the deliberate excesses of a man playing a woman ('Drag Racer to Drag Queen', 2003). But the purpose of their mimicry is not to become indistinguishable from their teachers; the simulacrum does not bear a simple relationship of resemblance to the model. Instead, imitating their role models allows participants to differentiate and alter themselves. Their mimicry affords them an advantage in the game, whether that is *Faking It* or the world outside. It is through mimicry that they redefine their value as commodity-signs. Brian Massumi's description of mimicry in the animal kingdom serves as a useful analogy:

Resemblance is a beginning masking the advent of a whole new
vital dimension. This even applies to mimicry in nature. An insect
that mimics a leaf does so not to meld with the vegetable state of its
surrounding milieu, but to re-enter the predatory realm of animal
warfare on a new footing (1987: 2).

There were several participants who clearly used what they learned to
'put themselves on a new footing.' Paul O'Hare, initially a housepainter,
became a conceptual artist ('Faking It Changed My Life', 2002). Lisa
Dickinson-Grey, the ultimate game player, revealed that she was an actress
who saw the programme as a good opportunity to improve her diction and
get an agent (which she did) (ibid.). Matt Davies, an insurance man who
'faked it' as a stuntman, left his job and began training to become a scuba
diving instructor ('Faking It Changed My Life', Part 2, 2004). In line with
the ideological project of the programme, even those participants who
didn't profoundly alter their lives presented their experience as a means
of personal growth and transformation. Chris Sweeney, who moved
from punk rocker to classical conductor, asserted, 'My life had to change.
Faking It came along at the right time and gave me the push I needed.
I was at school. People never thought I'd amount to anything. Now I'm
determined to go and be someone' ('Faking It Changed My Life', 2002).
Lucy Craig, who went from ferry stewardess to racing-yacht skipper, said,
'Now I need to use my new-found confidence to fulfil my potential. I
have always been held back by a fear of failure before, but I have broken
free of that' (ibid.). David Keith, radiographer to fashion photographer,
declared, 'My attitude toward people changed. I became much more
open to people, much more friendly. I had to fit in visually and that
meant getting a new sense of style' (ibid.). All of these published accounts
coincide with the stated objectives of the show's creators. According to
executive producer Stephen Lambert, 'This is a programme of hope
which shows how people are capable of extraordinary things given the
right support and encouragement. Many of the people featured have
found their lives changed forever by the experience' (Sherwin 2003: 11).
According to Joy Press in the *Village Voice* (2003: 48), '*Faking It* ultimately
suggests something both inspirational and unsettling: that we lack any
essential character, and our personalities and life paths are merely by-
products of the opportunities presented to us.' Like the happy consumers
in television commercials, participants advertise the possibility of self-
fulfilment, premised on the tacit acknowledgement that identity is open,

transient, up for grabs. You don't like your identity? Change it! No guilt, no worries, no repercussions – just do it!

Faking It exhibits a kind of staged performativity that obliterates the line between reality and fabrication. Participants play themselves learning to play a new version of themselves. For example, Sian Evans, an initially reserved cellist who became an extroverted disc jockey, noted, 'I started to feel a bit confused about who I was, which part of me was faking it and which was real.' She later began to work as a disc jockey on weekends ('Faking It Changed My Life', 2002). On one level, the performances are clearly not real; the participants can quit the game and drop their roles at a whim (though not one ever did). At one point, Lisa broke down and was subsequently allowed an unplanned trip home for the weekend. 'I'll always be a Yorkshire lass', she sobbed, though was it Lisa the actress or Lisa the Yorkshire lass who addressed the camera? ('Lady Lisa', 2000). Lesley the cheerleader-in-training ripped out the hair extensions that were supposed to make her look more feminine and refused to wear make-up to one of her coaching sessions ('From Ivy League to Big League', 2003). Lesley was one of the most resistant and least altered of all the participants. As a Harvard graduate and yoga teacher, she was clearly slumming it in the marketplace of new and improved identities.

But while participants were aware of playing a game, its duration was the real time of their lives. At one point, Lisa's coach criticized her by saying, 'you have to have an awareness that when you laugh, when you're more emotionally up, that's when the accent can reappear' ('Lady Lisa', 2000). And, despite Lesley the cheerleader's efforts to remain detached, she could not contain her excitement when she saw her face magnified on the giant screen after her cheerleading tryout ('From Ivy League to Big League', 2003). Through the staged performances of ordinary people in live situations, the line between reality and fabrication disappears.

Faking It is all about the simulation rather than the representation of class and identity. Simulation thus produces the real, which is to say the hyper real where images are no longer anchored by representation. *Faking It* is thus a way that the culture speaks to itself and renders tacit knowledge explicit. It makes visible the ways that identity is created through rehearsal and performance of already fabricated images. It naturalizes the idea that identity is fluid and mobile, a commodity sign that we circulate in an endless attempt to make meaning. *Faking It* confirms that there is no coherent core, no deep interior behind the surface appearance of a social self. As Kenneth Gergen (1992) writes, 'Slowly we are losing confidence that there is a coherent, identifiable substance behind the mask. The harder we look, the more difficult it is to find "anyone at home".'

Our becoming, our transformational potential becomes confined to image consumption and production. Only our resources limit our existence. According to MW Smith, author of *Reading Simulacra* (2001: 9), 'If you sport a Gold Visa you can even define your gender if you wish – at the local gender market, buy an organ transplant package including dual hair removal and hormone shots, complete with lipstick and make-up for the final touches. In the capitalist and consumerist axiomatic of Barbara Kruger, "I buy, therefore I am".' In the logic of capital, if commodities provide the source of our identities, we are endlessly required to buy and buy again in the quest for self-fulfilment.

Reality television continues to self-replicate, just as the boundary between public and private, subject and object, reality and fabrication, representation and simulation continues to dissipate. MTV's *Made* helps teenagers with low self-esteem become varsity football players, cheerleaders, or surfers. *Extreme Makeover*, *I Want a Celebrity Face*, and *The Swan* completely alter the physical appearance of participants. Fox's *Renovate My Family* was promoted as a 'life improvement show that each week spotlighted a family that would, with the help of makeover professionals, restore and redecorate their lives.' In each one-hour-long episode, a group of professionals attempts to remake a family from 'home to wardrobe to much more personal and psychological aspects beyond possessions and appearance' (Rogers 2004).

Here we see a magnification of the problem of the commodified self in the thrall of the therapeutic ethos. Initially the therapeutic ethos was promoted as a means to heal the wounds inflicted by a newly impersonal, bureaucratic, urbanized society, but it quickly became a means of social control, used to help people adjust to a developing corporate system. Lears writes that the same factors that led to the emergence of the therapeutic ethos in the late nineteenth century also fostered widespread feelings of anomie, a sense of 'unreality', and a longing for the intense, authentic, experience of 'real life'. He states, 'As early as 1909, cultural commentators were lamenting the "Era of Pre-digestion", which had rendered vigorous, firsthand experience obsolete' (1983: 7). If anything, mediated, mechanized, and secondary experiences are even more predominant today. It is not uncommon to come across a passage such as the following:

Just as millions live on top of the San Andreas Fault, we all walk
private and societal surfaces, full of cracks and structural breaks, that
when pressed, release in us that intense and profound need for a
sense of belonging, for a sense of the 'real'. Unfortunately, millions
of Americans feel that our remote government/corporations and
fractured neighbourhoods seem no longer able to nurture this need.
How do we then live with the realization that society, as we have
constructed it, does not satisfy our hunger for the 'real'? (Dorfman
2002)

Yearnings for 'authentic' experience may partly account for the appeal
of reality television. While appearing to satisfy our desire for 'reality',
Faking It puts on display the processes of fabrication whereby the real is
created. Ostensibly a representation of the real, reality television offers
yet another second-hand experience. Now people are offered a pre-
packaged, mass-mediated version of self-fulfilment. In the event that they
feel rootless, fragmented, and disengaged, they – and soon their family
– are provided with a pre-fabricated identity that comes pre-validated by
a cadre of so-called experts. While reality shows such as *Faking It* and its
follow-ups acknowledge the fluidity of identity, they do so only to freeze
it into pre-established moulds.

Chapter Eight

SELF-MADE WOMEN

Cosmetic Surgery Shows and the Construction of Female Psychopathology

Elizabeth Atwood Gailey

The ritualized distortion and objectification of the female body as an instrument of social control is far from a novel phenomenon. As Foucault observed, 'nothing is more material, physical, corporeal than the exercise of power' (1990: 57). Yet the recent proliferation of reality television (RT) programming – and shows focusing on cosmetic surgery 'makeovers' in particular – lend new meaning to the notion of the body as inscribed with social significance. Shows such as *Extreme Makeover*, *Plastic Surgery: Before & After*, and *Dr. 90210* depict female bodies as they are probed, painted, suctioned, carved with surgical instruments, and stuffed with foreign objects. Like pornography, these images are compelling not only in their claims to authenticity, but also in their appeal to the taboo and voyeuristic, to the fantasy of 'complete access to all that is hidden' (Deery 2004, following Baudrillard 1988).

Among the most important challenges facing popular-culture scholars studying the trajectories of gendered body regimes is the increasing sophistication of cyber-technological genres that create virtual, interpersonal, intimate, and voyeuristically shared worlds with viewers. Although cosmetic surgery RT stops short of the level of inhabitation that Morse (1998) describes in *Virtualities: Television, Media Art, and Cyberculture*, the proliferation of this genre represents a significant elaboration of televisual colonization of the consciousness of female

viewers. Given the promise of such shows 'to restore direct access to the
fullness of the real' (Andrejevic 2004: 201), it is vital that we investigate
both the image worlds they create and the specific ways in which they
operate as institutions of cultural management.

This chapter takes up this challenge by focusing on the porous
membrane through which female bodies and subjectivities are constructed
and pathologized in remarkably congruent ways across the reality
spectrum. Acknowledging that, in the post-modern era, viewers relate
to television as a collectivity rather than as isolated 'shows', I map out
some of the ideological affinities between extreme makeover RT and other
televisual spaces in which coercive new body regimes are constructed
through mutually reinforcing dialogic exchange. Additionally, I discuss
specific meaning-making features of cosmetic surgery RT, including rituals
of confession and transformation. Recent scholarship suggests that post-
capitalist economic shifts have created the need for new types of gendered
identities and subjectivities. This chapter hopes to illuminate some of the
most critical of these as they emerge in newly popular cultural forms.

For this project, I watched and analysed a broad sample of cosmetic
surgery RT, including *The Swan*, *Extreme Makeover*, and MTV's *I Want
a Famous Face*. However, I focused primarily on two shows, which have
remained in almost constant rotation on cable television over the past
several years. These include seasons 2004–2005 of the E! Channel's *Dr.
90210* and seasons 2003–2005 of the Discovery Channel's *Plastic Surgery:
Before & After* series.

Extreme Makeover RT: Ideological and Structural Affinities

Like a virus that has colonized nearly every space in the televisual
landscape, reality television is a self-replicating system that works by
appropriating pre-existing structures and 'authenticating' them through
the conventions of the documentary form. This explains why genres
ranging from game and talk shows to 'true crime' and soap operas
possess recognizable affinities with cosmetic surgery RT. Programmes like
Dr. 90210 and The Discovery Channel's *Plastic Surgery* series represent
a hybrid RT genre that borrows structural and thematic elements from
both fiction and non-fiction television. Fictional dramas like *ER*, *Nip/
Tuck*, and *CSI* share obvious commonalities with extreme makeover RT,
most notably the valorization of medical practitioners and technologies,
as well as hyper-real portrayals of violated bodies. But cosmetic surgery
reality programming principally borrows from and builds on other reality

formats. Chief among these are game docs like *Fear Factor*, as well as what might be called 'misogynist TV', discussed later in this chapter.

At first glance, *Fear Factor* seems an odd choice in terms of its compatibility with cosmetic surgery shows. Yet both trade on fetishization of bodily taboos and voyeuristic fascination with rituals of physical suffering and boundary crossing. Images of *Fear Factor* contestants crawling with spiders, struggling to escape rats and snakes, or ingesting buffalo testicles and cow-bile smoothies – all for monetary gain – are not that incongruous with either the repulsively graphic scenes of surgery on extreme makeover shows or with their portrayals of 'brave' women risking life and limb – quite literally – for the promise of status elevation and enhanced economic opportunity.

Beyond the 'extreme' aesthetics of both shows, female bodies on *Fear Factor* also mirror the 'desired bodies' carved out of human flesh on extreme makeover RT. *Fear Factor*'s female contestants, selected less for athletic prowess than for their large breasts, 'six-pack' stomachs, and 'I'm-game-for-anything' attitudes, are the relentless objects of the camera's gaze, which pans over their breasts, buttocks, and legs in a way that leaves little doubt as to the true nature of the 'competition'. It is essentially this same feminine ideal that is the ritual focus of subjects' 'after' photos on cosmetic surgery RT.

A particularly hyper-feminine version of this fetishized body ideal (in this case, huge breasts, tiny waists, and baby-like facial features) is also clearly on display on 'misogynist TV', a genre that includes *Howard Stern*, *The Man Show*, segments of *Comedy Central*, and RT programmes such as *Girls Gone Wild*, *Joe Millionaire*, *The Bachelor*, *Outback Jack*, and, most recently, *The Girls Next Door*. This last show, the newest variation of 'harem-themed' reality programming, casts a voyeuristic lens on Hugh Hefner and his three blonde 'girlfriends', who live together in a sort of post-feminist, soft-porn sisterhood at the Playboy Mansion. In its conceit of a single, octogenarian 'sugar daddy' surrounded by a bevy of adoring, sexually ready and knowledgeable 'playmates' in their twenties, *The Girls Next Door* recalls several features of cosmetic surgery makeover shows. An obvious example is the portrayal in both shows of women with porn-star cleavages bonding over the success of their breast augmentation surgeries. In one episode of *Plastic Surgery: Before & After*, in fact, a group of women in a restaurant become so excited about their implants that they impulsively lift their shirts to show them off for the camera, something even the women on *The Girls Next Door* might consider unseemly.

As this example suggests, both misogynist TV and cosmetic surgery reality programming present female subjectivities within predictably narrow, psychopathological boundaries. Women are either portrayed as material objects – little more than a collection of (often cartoonishly) formulaic body parts – or, equally limiting and pathological – as self-exploitative, entrepreneurial agents who are more than willing to use their bodies to 'get ahead'. Aside from their overtly sexist agendas and implications, these portrayals, examined from a political-economy perspective, feed into the organizational and epistemological logics of the global marketplace, through which women are urged to reformulate themselves as 'low-need,' self-managed subjects 'liberated' from reliance on government or corporate support (Hochschild 1994).

Certain interactions between physicians such as Dr Rey – the charismatic star of *Dr. 90210* – and his attractive female patients also reflect the sensibilities of misogynist TV. Like Hefner (or Howard Stern, for that matter), Dr Rey functions as a male-fantasy stand-in whose female patients disrobe for him in front of the camera, as he touches their body parts and critiques their 'flaws.' During post-surgical follow-ups, as a counterpoint to this professional critique, he lavishes praise upon the liposuctioned, tummy-tucked, augmented, and plumped-up bodies that offer themselves for his inspection. Admiring his own workmanship, he gushes, 'They're so perky!', 'You're so sexy!', 'You look hot!' The following exchange between Dr Rey and a 22-year-old breast implant patient who arrived for her post-operative check-up helps demonstrate this peculiarly sexualized form of address:

> Dr Rey: How are you? You look beautiful. You look beautiful. Let me take a look at them. They look hot! You are healing really, really fast. I don't know how that can be!
>
> Heather: I am really happy with them. And I got them soft...
>
> Dr Rey: You look beautiful! Beautiful!
>
> Heather: Thank you.
>
> Dr Rey: You look awesome! Put your shirt on, let me see what they look like with your shirt on. Oh my gosh! You look crazy girl! You look crazy! You look awesome! You look great! Wear your bra. You did a great job. You were a great patient. You never complained. You did a great job. Keep up the hard work and I will see you soon.

Here, Dr Rey's flattery not only rhetorically reinforces Heather's transformation from ordinary to 'awesome', but rewards her pliability both as a patient and a woman.

Female patients like Heather generally appear to appreciate such sexualized address from their doctors. However, this is not always the case. In an episode of *Dr. 90210* entitled 'Addicted to Plastic Surgery', Dr Rey greets a patient in the recovery room as she awakens from a particularly brutal bout of surgery. Leaning over her, he thrusts a mirror in front of her swollen, bandaged face. 'You're *sexy!*' he yells. Before turning her head away, she grants him a look of such absolute agony and incredulity that it temporarily disrupts the show's narrative fidelity. It is a darkly humorous moment – one so stunningly contradictory and yet totally rational within its own distorted logics – that it exposes a crack in the thin veneer of medical respectability cloaking the practice of cosmetic surgery, revealing some of its most fundamental contradictions. The first is that having and retaining a 'hot' body requires the intervention of highly trained surgeons employing an arsenal of high-tech weaponry. And second, women desiring liberation through the acquisition of 'sexy' new bodies must first submit themselves to intense rituals of physical violation, often followed by an intensely painful period of recovery.

The Perfectionist Project and Pathological Motherhood

So far, I have discussed some of the more overt examples of the construction across the televisual spectrum of highly regulated, pathological female bodies and subjectivities. I turn now to the subtler realm of television devoted to 'everyday' gender socialization where extreme makeover shows have forged perhaps their most successful ideological partnerships. The ultimate in 'female socialization TV,' of course, is the line-up of (often back-to-back) daytime shows featured on Personal TLC, including *A Dating Story, A Wedding Story, A Baby Story, A Personal Story,* and *A Makeover Story*.

As a televisual how-to manual on 'doing gender,' Personal TLC lays out a prescriptive trajectory for teenagers and young adult females into which extreme makeover RT fits with eerie precision (Maher 2004). Formerly known as The Learning Channel, TLC begins its instructional project with tutorials on how to attract a man (*A Dating Story* and *A Makeover Story*), how to retain him (*A Wedding Story*), and how to complete the fantasy of heteronormative domesticity (*A Baby Story*) (ibid.). Continuing this pedagogical project are *Dr. 90210* and the *Plastic Surgery* series, which not only promote traditional heteronormative sex roles for young single women, but coach mothers in the art of rehabilitating themselves as sexualized subjects post-childbirth.

Like Personal TLC, extreme makeover RT appears to cater primarily to female viewers in their early 20s to mid 30s. One of the surprises of this study, in fact, is that it is relatively young women, rather than those 50 and over, whom these shows feature most prominently. What this suggests, ironically, is that although contemporary gender regimes continue to uphold marriage and motherhood as the ultimate measures of true womanhood, the newest standards – which mandate that women continue to perform sexual viability well into their late 30s or even 40s – *render motherhood itself pathological*. In undergoing tummy tucks, liposuctions, breast lifts and breast augmentations, young mothers portrayed on extreme makeover shows seek to recover, as it were, the sexually ripe bodies of their teens and early 20s. Cosmetic surgery shows do more than simply portray this desire as justified; they imply that reclaiming the 'blown out' body parts sacrificed to childbirth is a routine aspect of responsible women's self-management and care. Mothers completing the cycle of childbirth must 'get back into the game' by resurrecting their former bodies – or, better yet, by acquiring the 'new and improved' models made possible by modern medical technology.

This was the theme of a *Plastic Surgery* profile of Christy, a slender 43-year-old who looked a decade younger. The segment opened with video footage of her jogging to the backbeat of electronic music, a scene designed to set up the oft-repeated caution that 'no amount of exercise will work' to erase the scars of motherhood inscribed on women's bodies. In line with the formulaic production and editing conventions of makeover RT, Christy confesses her hopes and fears about her approaching surgery (a rhetorical strategy used both to build suspense and to communicate the 'naturalness' of patients' anxieties). She plans to undergo what her doctor refers to as a 'mommy makeover', which includes breast augmentation surgery (featuring cutesy-sounding 'gummy-bear' implants), along with a tummy tuck and liposuction to remove both fat and sagging skin common after childbirth. The following excerpt exemplifies the way in which the 'perfectionist project' is sold to mothers on these shows as compensation for childbirth and 'good' parenting:

> Christy: I want to be pretty, and I don't think there's anything wrong with that. And I think this is my time...
>
> Narrator: But Christy's had three children, and it's going to take more than exercise to get the perfect body. She's decided to have

plastic surgery.

Christy: I love my children, and I know I have my scars from that. I want to call them my battle scars.

Narrator: She'd also like larger breasts.

Christy: I have to say I'm dissatisfied with the size of them. They were actually fuller before I had my first child. After I breast-fed him for about a year, the fullness had just gone away.

After graphic visuals of her surgery – accompanied by a blow-by-blow account of the procedures involved – she appears seven weeks later arriving at her doctor's office. Her story is notable for what is left out – namely, even the most casual reference to the pain and discomfort of her ordeal. Glowing and fully restored to health, she bounces into his office, expressing delight with her new body. After praising her 'beautiful' breasts and asking if she's been 'shopping for bras yet' (a common trope signifying both transformation and the intersection of shopping and gender performance), he exclaims, 'Wow, look at this *skinny* waist!' And indeed, she *does* have a skinny waist – as well as the body of a voluptuous 18-year-old. Toward the end of the vignette, she vamps like Marilyn Monroe, shaking her breasts and twirling seductively before a group of 'old friends from high school', who applaud and whistle appreciatively. Finally, facing the camera, she delivers the lesson viewers are meant to take away: 'I put so much into being a good mother for my children. And it was time to give back something to myself. And this was my gift to me.' To the backbeat of swelling electronic music, a screen appears with her revolving 'before' and 'after' photos accompanied by facts about her 'mommy makeover', including duration (3.5 hours), recovery time (3–4 weeks), and cost ($25,000–$30,000).

Here, the underlying advertising agenda of cosmetic surgery RT asserts itself most blatantly. After exposure to what is essentially a 15-minute infomercial, female viewers are provided price and other purchasing details at the 'point of sale,' including cosmetic surgery's USP (unique selling proposition): the erasure of time and motherhood from their bodies so as to rehabilitate them as sexually viable subjects. It should come as no surprise that cosmetic surgeons – including the doctor profiled in this segment – post video clips of the *Plastic Surgery* series on their web sites as 'educational' tools for potential clients (Marina Plastic Surgery Associates 2005).

Meanwhile, viewers tuning into an episode on TLC's *Personal Story* the same year would have seen a strikingly similar narrative in an episode featuring Ana, a mother in her late 30s, who expresses despair about the negative impact of pregnancy and breastfeeding on her breast size. '*I guess you could say she's sacrificed her body to have children*,' her friend remarks. Later, Ana's doctor delivers this tutorial on pregnancy's polluting effects on women's bodies: 'Tummy tucks or abdominoplasties are very common in all women, especially women who have had multiple pregnancies. You look at women who have had four children – their abdomens usually look worse than if they'd had two. But we see women who've only had one, and they have blown-out abdomens.' A 'blown-out abdomen', as it turns out, simply refers to a body bearing the normal marks of pregnancy. Redefined as pathological, it now requires medical 'treatment': adominoplasty.

Another *Plastic Surgery* episode entitled 'Back Where We Belong' featured three mothers with middle- or even lower-middle-class backgrounds. Each is described by the male narrator as a 'loving' mother, an evaluation supported by video footage of them interacting happily with their offspring. Amid confessions about weight gain and the loss of their 'true' selves over the years, snapshots reflecting their more energetic, slimmer, sexier, younger pasts appear. Invariably, their pregnancies – rather than diet, inactivity, or the passage of time – are blamed for the unacceptable state of their bodies. And once again the point is emphasized that 'no amount of exercise and dieting' could eradicate their rolls of fat, sagging, stretch-marked flesh or shrunken, 'unwomanly' breasts. This, of course, leaves only surgery as an option. Ignoring the inevitability of ageing and natural life-cycle changes, the quest to go 'back where we belong' was presented not only as unquestioningly valid, but as deeply sympathetic.

Paradoxically, the formulaic vignettes featured in both extreme makeover RT and Personal TLC – of women playing with their children, preparing meals for their families, strolling with their partners at sunset – serve simultaneously as signifiers of 'normalcy' *and* of 'transcendence', of 'everydayness' *and* of 'perfection'. This contradiction makes sense, given that normalization of the 'perfectionist project' is precisely the product sold to female viewers of both RT genres (perfect coupling, perfect wedding, perfect childbirth, perfect body = perfect happiness). Meanwhile, normalization of plastic surgery is proceeding apace. Between 1992 and 2004, breast augmentation alone increased by more than 700 per cent in the United States (Levy 2005), prompting Haiken (2000: 83) to describe it as 'one of the fastest-growing medical practices in the world.'

The 'Real Me, Only Better': Transformation and the 'Self-Made' Woman

In extreme makeover RT's construction of the feminine, the idea of undergoing surgery to obtain bigger, 'perkier' breasts, thinner thighs, or nipped-and-tucked stomachs is sold to viewers in two somewhat contradictory ways. On the one hand, cosmetic surgery is portrayed as just another in a series of logical, self-management practices – not unlike everyday grooming rituals – carried out by average women. At the same time, however, the practice is also swathed in familiar narratives of spiritual transformation and empowerment. It is the combination of these that no doubt proves most compelling for female viewers of these shows.

Transformation occupies a privileged space in commercial culture precisely because of its relative scarcity in actual day-to-day life. As the dramatic engine driving RT fare ranging from channels such as HGTV and QVC to shows like *Oprah* and *Queer Eye for the Straight Guy*, it is, as Bratich notes elsewhere in this volume, 'the very essence of reality TV itself.' Most commonly linked to products and regimes related to domestic and body aesthetics, 'transformation TV' sells 'desirable fictions of plenitude, pleasure and power' to mostly female consumers (Everett 2004: 159–160). Cosmetic surgery shows, however, do more than simply trade in the discourses of transformation. What they promise are *extreme* transformations. Elsewhere in this volume, Akass and McCabe argue that plastic surgery shows are essentially fairy tales 'about looking and being seen'. But in the mythic narratives of *Dr. 90210* and the *Plastic Surgery* series, the fairy tale expands beyond the desire to gaze and be gazed upon. Presenting the surgical invasion of healthy bodies within the framework of female courage, self-nurturance, sacrifice, and social salvation, these shows restore the humiliated to self-confidence, the lonely and rejected to emotional and sexual connection, and the erstwhile house-bound to active lives replete with mountain bikes and jet skis – all in less than an hour and with minimal attention to the pain or complications of major surgery.

Of course, before subjects undergo their extreme transformations, they must endure extreme rituals of humiliation and sacrifice, beginning with confessional narratives and – most crucially – public exposure of their (pathological) bodies. Often introduced to viewers wearing nothing but bras and thong underwear, with on-screen text and voiceover narration outlining the multiple procedures they 'require', female subjects are rendered abject – little more than a collection of (repugnant) body parts. As Spitzack (1991) writes, social disciplining of the body is first achieved 'by fragmenting it into isolated parts – face, hair, legs, breasts – and then redefining those parts as inherently flawed and pathological' (cited in Woodstock 2001: 425). Bulging and drooping, sagging and fleshy, especially in the unflattering light of obligatory 'before' shots, their bodies are metaphors for 'sinful' excess, loss of control, and deviance from endlessly defined and redefined beauty regimes. Resistance is possible, of course. But non-conformance, even to increasingly bizarre standards of female attractiveness, is inevitably translated into sexual undesirability and ultimately deviance.

Construction of female deviance takes a variety of forms on cosmetic surgery shows. For example, according to one online source, nearly two-thirds of women in the world wear size A- or B-cup bras ('Who Needs Breast Implants?', www.007b.com/who_needs_breast_implants.php). Yet on these programmes, small and medium breasts are constructed as deviant: 'flat', 'boyish', 'underdeveloped', 'undersized'. Other imagined flaws, such as millimetre differences in the size of a subject's right and left breasts, also assume ominous dimensions. An example of what Lears (2004) calls 'the narcissism of minor differences' (28), this obsessive focus on perceived body 'irregularities' promotes the 'cultural production of women's psychopathology' (Blackman 2004: 220).

Most vulnerable to social censure for 'deviance,' of course, are large women, who embody the 'too muchness' of female materiality (Bordo 1993). For their transgressions, heavy females not only risk loss of 'cultural viability', but something akin to 'social death' itself (Fraser 2001: 122). Their 'fleshy rolls', as Murray (2004) observes, present 'a parody of female sexuality, a distortion of contemporary paradigms of feminine beauty and desirability' (237). Signifying moral and aesthetic failure, fat women are expected not only to disavow their flesh, but also to surrender their identities as sexual beings (ibid.).

Not surprisingly, given the tyranny of these disciplining regimes, expressions of disdain for fat bodies are a signature element of cosmetic surgery RT. Even the (mostly male) surgeons on these shows appear repulsed by fat female patients. That doctors should find these women unattractive is not surprising, given their dual roles as appearance police and merchandisers of female insecurity and pathology. Yet their pointed comments, combined with graphic video footage of oozing, excessive flesh, expose the deeply anti-female thrust of these shows.

Scenes highlighting surgical removal of thick, glistening slabs of female fat are, in fact, the 'money shot' of extreme makeover RT. At once voyeuristic, sadistic, and grotesquely titillating, these scenes represent the most powerful indictment of the (desexualized) female body in television history. In a 2005 episode of *Dr. 90210*, for example, a doctor operates on Jenny, a 24-year-old undergoing what he irreverently refers to as the 'blue plate special' – a tummy tuck, breast augmentation and lift, liposuction, and hip contouring. As he labours over her body in surgery, he comments on its thick layers of fat and complains about the extra work and time required to carve through it. After wrestling with a particularly capacious section of fat, he lifts it out and holds it up for the camera's inspection. 'To give you an idea of how big this piece is,' he says, spreading the bloody slab across the expanse of his chest, 'This is just one half of what we're going to take off!' Later, the camera returns to the scene of carnage, resting its lurid gaze on a foot-high basin overflowing with fat and tissue extracted from the woman's corpus.

Such ritualistically brutal scenes, along with humiliating, near-nude shots of 'overweight' female subjects undergoing inspection by their doctors and discussed on camera by 'concerned' relatives and friends, are generally accompanied by confessional vignettes in which the subjects themselves both conflate notions of 'body' and 'self' and insist that their *embodied* selves mask their '*true*' selves. 'When I look in the mirror, I don't see the 'real' me,' they complain. The confessional, of course, is a staple of the reality genre, originating with *Real World* and *Big Brother*, but also a hallmark of talk shows, which function, as Lowney (1999) argues, to construct Otherness and deviance.

Conclusion: The Circular Logics of Doing Gender

The notion that cosmetic surgery has the power to change 'life and everything around it' – a belief expressed by 30-year-old Shifa prior to her breast augmentation surgery on an episode of *Dr. 90210* – is the transformational myth at the centre of extreme makeover RT. It is, of course, a dream grounded in the circular logics of gender discipline and performance. The 'back story' omitted from cosmetic surgery RT involves the relentless campaign of oppressive images of ideal femininity to which women are subjected almost from birth. If female subjects fail to meet society's rigid standards of beauty, thinness, youth, or 'hotness', they are redefined as dysfunctional and their bodies sites of pathology. In the hopes of 'liberating' themselves, they intensify their self-disciplinary and rehabilitative efforts by splitting off and disavowing the 'too muchness' or 'too littleness' of their material selves. Unwilling or unable to acknowledge the social context in which they do so, they invariably describe surgical intervention as *intra*personally motivated ('I'm not doing this for anyone else. It's just something I want to do for myself'). Yet they inadvertently reveal their *inter*personal motivations in stories relating social stigma, sexual dysfunction, and embarrassment resulting from others' reactions to their 'deviant' bodies.

Emerging from the ritualized ordeal of surgery, they are, paradoxically, both liberated from and reinscribed with their own subordination. Having shaken, at least temporarily, the stigma of Otherness, they present themselves as advertising icons for freedom and happiness. Yet theirs is a liberation requiring utter submission to social authority. After all, the underlying mythos of plastic surgery RT is not only that the ageing process is preventable and that women's roles as sexual subjects may be extended almost indefinitely, but that *women* bear the responsibility when this (patriarchal) fantasy breaks down.

Female actors on extreme makeover shows actually do undergo transformation. Far from journeyers in a magical realm, however, they are controlled subjects who undergo the most extreme of disciplining regimes so they may emerge as fully docile, disciplined subjects. As such, they are 'up for grabs', literally opened up and made pliable in preparation for colonization by any number of authoritative agents (see Bratich's insightful discussion of this topic in this volume).

As this chapter shows, constructions on extreme makeover RT that objectify and pathologize women are echoed and mutually reinforced across a broad range of televisual space. Most disturbing, the females portrayed in the examples discussed here are more narrowly constructed than popular-culture portrayals prior to the women's movement of the 1960s and 1970s. Either women are completely denied subjectivity through objectification or presented as 'liberated', risk-taking 'entrepreneurs' whose knowledge of the trade-value of their bodies provides a powerful model of self-motivation and self-awareness for viewer-subjects. Performing perhaps the ultimate act of the 'self-made' subject, women who undergo cosmetic surgery on these shows not only personify the exercise of political power through women's bodies, but reveal themselves as paragons of the neo-liberal doctrines of self-help and self-sufficiency. They are, in every way, then, 'self-made women,' products of the hegemonic alliance of patriarchy and global capitalism.

Chapter Nine

A PERFECT LIE

Visual (Dis)Pleasures and Policing Femininity in Nip/Tuck

Kim Akass and Janet McCabe

Make me beautiful...
Make me...
Perfect soul.
Perfect mind.
Perfect face.
... A perfect lie.

Tell me what you don't like about yourself: Introduction

Superficially, at least, plastic surgery on *Nip/Tuck* (FX, 2003–) makes over women into images of feminine perfection. In the pilot, Christian Troy (Julian McMahon) enjoys a night of wanton sexual passion with Kimber Henry (Kelly Carlson). Next morning their post-coital conversation turns to the body beautiful. Kimber, a model by profession, imagines that she is a perfect specimen of feminine beauty. Think again, Kimber. Not so. Meticulously scrutinized by one of Miami's top plastic surgeons, she is quickly disabused of any such notion. His discerning medical gaze reveals that at best she is a size eight – and no way is she twenty-one-years old. She is twenty-six but would be perfect with 'a little bit of work'. Shaken to her very core by his candid professional assessment, Kimber is utterly entranced. She stares at him in wide-eyed anticipation, holding on to his every last word. She could not be more mesmerized if he had declared his undying love. What can she say? She is powerless to resist his detailed critique of her physical flaws.

Kimber stands motionless in front of the mirror, giving up her docile body to Christian's medical gaze that will change her – and our – perception of it. Drawing over her compliant form with scarlet lipstick, he leaves few features untouched. Hardly any part of her body escapes his scrupulous surgical assessment. Starting with forehead ('needs botox'), eyes ('a light peel... one eye is half a millimetre higher than the other'), nose ('flat boxer'), breasts ('one size bigger... a "C"') and stomach ('abdominal liposuction'), each feature is subject to adjustment and alteration. Using a cosmetic usually meant to enhance surface glamour, to make a woman appear more beautiful, his artwork literally turns the female body into a grotesque spectacle. But his authoritative gaze detailing feminine imperfection also confirms what feminism has long told us – that woman *is* body. Anaesthesia further renders it obedient, when the male surgeon will physically break, bend, staple and stretch the immobile body into a disciplined one that adheres to prevailing ideals of feminine beauty. Voilà. By the end of the pilot, Kimber is indeed a ten. Her new surgically enhanced look is now perfectly proportioned with a boob job to die for. Her ascension to the ideal is complete. What more could she ask?

But is this not a matter of perception? What we (and Kimber) may see as visually pleasing, Christian sees as flawed. She looks aghast when she sees herself through his eyes: 'Am I really this ugly? I was homecoming queen.' Representing a classic American image of feminine success and normalcy only to be told that her perception of beauty is false devastates her – and shocks the viewer. But there is more to this than meets the eye. On the surface at least with her peroxide-blonde hair and enticing sexuality she evokes the archetypal fifties sex-kitten, Marilyn Monroe. Kimber foregrounds her to-be-looked-at-ness in ways similar to those discussed by Laura Mulvey in her critique of the visual pleasures of classical Hollywood cinema (1989). But rather than being held in the male gaze, contemplated as erotic object, she is subject to unremitting scrutiny, constant discussion and endless deliberation. Rather than desired, she is deconstructed. The male hero may still hold her in his gaze but she no longer beguiles him as she has done his cinematic counterpart. Here, in a televisual world where disclosure and intimacy are narrative requirements, our hero talks about the female body in ways rarely heard on the big screen. What we are suggesting is that the cable series *Nip/*

Tuck makes over Hollywood visual pleasures to reveal a new politics of the look as seen on TV; and in so doing exposes – and makes strange – the way the normalizing gaze that polices femininity and disciplines the female body works within American (visual) culture.

Visual frontiers: From territorial conquest to cutting-edge surgery

Feminists have long found compelling Michel Foucault's insights into how our modern age 'discovered' the body as an object and target of infinitesimal power. 'It is easy enough to find signs of the attention,' writes Foucault, '... paid to the body – to the body that is manipulated, shaped, trained, which obeys, responds, becomes skilful and increases its forces' (1991: 136). According to him, the body does not simply exist but is in the grip of stringent networks of discursive power that impose on it restrictions, rules and requirements. This power is not something certain groups or individuals *possess*. Nevertheless, it *produces* and normalizes bodies – in a calculated management of its movements, gestures, attitudes, and behaviours – to serve as well as make sense of specific historical formulations of dominance and subordination. Uninterrupted and constant subtle coercion act upon the body rendering it obedient and, in turn, useful to the prevailing social order.

Understanding female anatomy has long been subject to regimes of social power that seek to scrutinize it, dissect it and modify it. But looking at how this gendered body functions for the American political anatomy has repercussions for the politics of looking and status of the observer. Obstetrics, for example, became established in America at the very moment the Republic came into being. 'Discovering' and mastering the female reproductive system coincides with the conception of the nation, the mapping of uncharted land and the management of territorial (often violent) expansion with the push westward. America pioneered modern surgery in this field, which literally found women's bodies at the medical frontier – 'ovariotomy, hysterectomy and the repair of the vesico-vaginal fistula' (Barker-Benfield 2002: 82). Obstetrics expanded into gynaecology during the mid nineteenth century, at a time when the nation was divided by the American Civil War (1861–1865) and racial schism, and profound anxieties were starting to grow around mass immigration and the first calls for female suffrage. In the midst of these developments, the female reproductive system and the vicissitudes of the menstrual cycle (with male doctors often experimenting on impoverished immigrant women or Black female slaves without anaesthetics) became an object of meticulous empirical inquiry and a locus of scientific knowledge to reveal a society 'of surveillance' (Foucault 1991: 217). Cutting into female genitalia opened up the woman's body to knowledge, and in the process of these ocular inspections the woman and her body in a sense became *visible*.

The woman's body finds itself at the forefront of medical advancement as our society becomes once again obsessed with self-transformation, this time related to a preoccupation with the body beautiful – slenderness, diet, anti-ageing and cosmetic enhancement. Plastic surgery, according to Susan Bordo, 'is now a $1.75-billion-a-year industry in the United States' (2003: 25). New industries and technologies are built to re-fashion, cosmetically modify and physically sculpt the body, 'insuring the [latest] production of self-monitoring and self-disciplining "docile bodies" sensitive to any departure from social norms and habituated to self-improvement and self-transformation in the service of those norms' (186). Obsession with body-management and surface appearance encloses the modern body in new regimes of discursive power related to globalization, the mass media and consumer-capitalism, whereby we are subtly coerced as never before to self-monitor and incessantly self-scrutinize the minutiae of our bodies so that no blemish goes unseen and no detail is overlooked. Ceaseless preoccupation with physical self-improvement functions as one of the most dominant normalizing mechanisms in our culture. More often than not, the female body is subject to endless confession, in which we must admit to ourselves and anyone else as often as possible everything about our bodies that violates cultural norms – abnormalities in physiognomy, shape and size. Transforming dissatisfaction into (consumer) aspiration culturally manages an insatiable female desire. Not only will we own up to our bodies contravening the cultural ideal but also we will actively seek at the same time to do something about it with repeated visits to the cosmetic counter, the beauty therapist – and even the plastic surgeon.

The contemporary age may not have initiated the homogenization of a feminine ideal; but, rather, it hastened it, altered its scale and disseminated it through new forms of media technology and business practice. In any case, an ideal image of the body beautiful produced in and by American culture functions as a model 'against which the self continually measures, judges, "disciplines," and "corrects" itself' (25). *Nip/Tuck* in the pilot *normalizes* a particular model of feminine beauty – that is, the Caucasian, Anglo-Saxoned-featured, slender and youthful, toned feminine body best represented by both Kimber and Julia McNamara (Joely Richardson).

Hollywood cinema has long regulated versions of this archetype from Jean Harlow to Cameron Diaz, functioning at different historical moments and made useful to the prevailing ideology in terms of disseminating and policing ideas of femininity and the feminine form. Here the female body enters into the machinery of American visual culture that will break it down, adjust it, modify it and give it representation. While Hollywood works hard to conceal the process, *Nip/Tuck* openly acknowledges and graphically reveals how the female body is coerced and self-corrected into the ideal. But because the series is so entangled in the very representational strategies that produce the ideal in the first place, *Nip/Tuck* can never seriously question that this is something worth pursuing.

The ideal made to appear natural is introduced at the very beginning when Christian delivers his meticulous assessment of Kimber's flaws. What emerges here is the fact that the ideal is culturally produced and requires a great attention to detail. His perception is so finely honed as to recognize even the smallest deviation. Nothing escapes it. Most shocking perhaps is his ability to detect her Irish origins from merely glancing at her nose. He advises eliminating this trace of difference along with the other physical imperfections he has identified. Made visible here is the way the ideal body is ascribed the authority of professionals (plastic surgeons), institutions (the medical practice) and state laws (medical licences), and such authority elevates certain bodies to a level of cultural value and prestige that guarantees their identification with the ideal.

Season Three finds Jewish mother Marian Berg (Valerie Landsberg) bringing her daughter, Madison (Hallee Hirsh), in for a consultation ('Madison Berg', 3.10). Like a bar mitzvah for the Jewish child as rite of passage, Madison has long known that rhinoplasty will signal her entrance into mainstream American femininity. The McNamara/ Troy practice provides the 'Sweet Sixteen' package for this very special occasion. Shaving a little off the nose will replace her decidedly 'ethnic' look with a much more delicate WASP-ish version. Whereas the mother, who went through a similar procedure years before, has clearly met resistance from her daughter it is only when Christian shows her the evidence of their handiwork on a fellow classmate that Madison changes her mind. Never realizing that her peer was Jewish, she willingly agrees to the surgery. Effacement of ethnic difference is time and again less about the denial of culture and racial self-hatred than a pleasure of, and desire for, assimilation into the cultural ideal. Passing here is about being seen as 'natural' by the normalizing gaze, as about an (in)visibility predicated on a culturally sanctioned denial of any ethnic or racial difference contravening the norm. Whereas in classical Hollywood the exotic visual other is mastered and made non-threatening, turned into a fetish in the gaze, in fact, here it becomes subject to an incessantly talkative one. Beguiled by the to-be-looked-at-ness of the female, the gaze brought to television cannot stop talking about what it sees, persistently dissecting, relentlessly scrutinizing, continually investigating bodies that do not easily conform to American cultural ideals.

Another example of the politics of looking and the body beautiful can be found back in Season Two when Manya Mobika (Aisha Tyler), a Somalian model, consults McNamara/Troy about the possibilities of reconstructive surgery to reverse the effects of a cultural ideal ('Manya Mobika', 2.3). The complicated and intimate nature of her problem intrigues Sean McNamara (Dylan Walsh) and Christian when she tells them that she was the 'victim' of genital mutilation as a child. Informing the doctors that this is standard practice in her country for a woman to be considered 'perfect', she says: 'Over ninety per cent have it done. It is a Fatwa. One of the ten obligations a woman must adhere to in order to achieve perfection.' What she wants is for them to reconstruct her clitoris so that she will know the same sexual pleasure as the American models she works with. But it is soon revealed that there is more at stake than how one culture's disfigurement is another's purification.

Performing female circumcision and the routine of plastic surgery are highly ritualized forms of power enacted upon the female body to normalize it while justifying the right to do so. Within Somalian culture, this procedure makes docile the female form, removing sexual urges, regulating fecundity and rendering the body culturally acceptable. Here in America, medical intervention calls into question the way culture acts on the female body in the clinical analysis it makes of it and how it is defined as mutilated. Christian may decry Somalian men who 'have to neuter their women to get a hard on,' but does he not gain pleasure (quite literally, in fact) from exercising power that watches, monitors and acts on that same body? By telling his colleagues that he can 'cure' his patient because he has 'been inside so much pussy that he should know how to make her come', Christian reveals an alternative cultural imperialism and patriarchal dominance over the body. The surgeons perform vaginal reconstruction using pioneering surgical techniques to enhance their medical reputation, their work carried out in a context in which the supremacy and importance of American cultural ideals dictating the way the 'correct' woman's body *should* look go unquestioned. The way the male surgeons peer between her legs, the perpetual examinations, and their insistent observations of the architecture of her vagina, constructs and dominates the female body in the process of 'knowing' it. *Nip/Tuck* takes pleasure in exercising a power over the bodies it keeps watch over, making them adhere to cultural codes and monitoring their enforcement. But there is further pleasure in resisting and defying that powerful normalizing gaze. Narrating back the experience of being the patient, exposing subjected and concealed knowledge at the very moment another kind of knowledge is being constructed, the series engages in a perpetual game of power and pleasure.

Key to this circular play of power and pleasure is the normalizing gaze, one that functions as a mechanism for defining, monitoring and questioning how and what one is looking at. Despite Sean reproaching Christian for forgetting the person at the end of the vagina, and despite their exhortations that female clients tell them what they do not like about themselves, the surgeons' privileged observatory position places the client in a stark visual field of concentrated and unremitting surveillance. Wrenching out confessions takes place in a sterile environment where we, like Sean and Christian, have no choice but to look. The use of tight claustrophobic close-ups, blocks of contrasting colours, surfaces that shimmer but lack any real depth of field – or what the show's creator, Ryan Murphy, calls 'chrome-noir' – means that the gaze is never allowed to penetrate beneath the image. Instead, the façade is subject to perpetual and endless scrutiny, to continual and unremitting looking. If, as Foucault tells us, we have entered 'an age of the infinite examination and of compulsory objectification' (1991: 189), then *Nip/Tuck* literally makes visible the ways we come to see and understand our bodies, and what we can and should do to discipline them. Nothing can stand up to such intense levels of inspection. Even our perfect Kimber finds herself back on the table having microsuction on her stomach just so she can fit into a size '0' wedding dress ('Madison Berg', 3.10). She wants to look beautiful; and she takes delight in self-disciplining her body into one deserving approval from the normalizing gaze. Week after week this ritual of visual (dis)pleasure is repeated in the consulting room, in the operating theatre and in recovery where the body is subject to an incessant normalizing gaze that pulls us in, holds us there, and cannot stop looking and talking about what it sees.

'Make me look like I'm in my prime – make me desirable again': Ageing and the ocular uncanny

Bodies are taken charge of by a (tele)visual (dis)pleasure that aims to allow them no obscurity, no reprieve. Candidly revealing and graphically highlighting the cultural expectations of what women should look like make for an often-uncomfortable visual encounter. Inviting an audience to voyeuristically fixate on self-transformation, homogenization and physical perfection positions *Nip/Tuck* within the reality TV makeover craze. Christian and Sean's weekly invitation to 'tell us what you don't like about yourself' is positively avuncular when compared to *The Swan*'s confessionals involving emotionally distraught women incessantly admitting to years of self-hatred, itemizing every imperfection, every blemish that contravenes the culturally produced feminine ideal. We may recoil from *Nip/Tuck*'s ability to focus on the smallest and most insignificant physical imperfection but are we not at the same time complicit with our culture's pervasive obsession in endlessly judging and policing the female body by bringing into discourse what we see as violation? Over thirty years after feminist activists stormed the 1969 'Miss America' pageant, and even as feminism raised our consciousness to understand how 'the most mundane, "trivial" aspects of women's bodily existence were in fact significant elements in the social construction of an oppressive feminine norm' (Bordo 2003: 18), women remain firmly inculcated in *wanting* to embody normalizing ideals of beauty; and compulsively talk of the pursuit of the ideal, now using the language of liberation and post-feminist empowerment.

Nowhere is this more evident on *Nip/Tuck* than in the demand for anti-ageing surgery where clients become entangled in America's obsession with youth and ideas of the 'useful' female body. Not too surprising for a country that has historically prided itself on being a young and virile nation that the ageing body has no place within the political anatomy and must be somehow repressed and/or denied. The idea of the fecund female body has lingered long within the American cultural imagination, from the innocent Puritan to the young prairie wife starting life anew in virgin territories, to the contemporary valorization of the youthful slender model that invites us to buy products to affect similar benefits. It has already been noted on the DVD commentary to Season One that 47 per cent of all cosmetic procedures performed in America are related to reversing the signs of ageing; and, in turn, the plastic surgery industry has established new norms for what the older woman should look like

– 'achievable only through continual cosmetic surgery – in which the surface of the female body ceases to age physically as the body grows chronologically old' (Bordo 2003: 26).

Nip/Tuck is implicated and deeply entangled in this discourse, as the ageing process troubles the idea of the beautiful, attractive and sublime female body that the series works so hard to promote as the desirable norm. Feelings of dread inspired by the visibly ageing body provoke a crisis for the normalizing gaze. It triggers a visual moment of uncertainty – or what we shall call the 'ocular uncanny' – when something that our culture knows about only too well, but works so hard to repress, returns. Nowadays our culture may feel it has a measure of control over the body's ageing processes – good diet, regular exercise, cosmetics and anti-ageing products, medicines and medical procedures – but nevertheless our concerns over the body's eventual decay can never be entirely dispelled. As soon as we *actually* see what our culture works so hard to deny and forget we experience the uncanny. Given that we are imbibed in and through the normalizing gaze means that, however we may resist or attempt to defy it, its crisis is ours. In *Nip/Tuck* this ocular uncanny manifests itself when the gaze stops talking, when something not easily definable interrupts speech, and causes a momentary shudder in the text and in the observer – the protagonist, the viewer.

Nip/Tuck depends heavily for its effect on dramatic departures from reality that take viewers into the realm of the fantastic. In its ludicrous storylines, unbelievably superficial characterizations, heightened *mise en scène* and histrionic dialogue, *Nip/Tuck* focuses so much on surface appearance that even the most familiar suddenly looks strange and beyond speech. Within this fantastic televisual world, pleasure is invaded by a feeling of unease, which allows the viewer no easy escape, and no respite, while bringing to light and questioning the normalizing gaze that inculcates us into accepting what it sees as 'truth'. Nowhere for us is this momentary ocular shudder more evident than when ageing interrupts the talkative gaze – an unease involving being seen and unseen, visibility and invisibility, self-perception and self-monitoring.

First under the knife in Season Two is Dr Erica Noughton (Vanessa Redgrave). Erica is Julia's mother and has come to town specifically to ask her son-in-law to perform a face-lift. Anaesthetics render her docile and literally deprive her of language; but given that she is a successful and internationally renowned Freudian child psychologist it is hardly surprising that the sight of Erica's inert body is *unheimlich*. So uncanny is the sight of her inanimate body that it causes Sean and Christian a momentary shudder. Familiar to both, its docility arouses repressed thoughts in the men. Most unnerving is Christian imagining Julia on the table in place of her mother: the Wicked Stepmother morphed into Snow White. Responding to Christian's remark on the uncanny likeness between the women, Sean confesses he feels the same, loses his nerve and is unable to continue. Christian must perform the surgery instead. Christian's hallucinatory exchange of mother and daughter may be inspired by his own confusion over sleeping with the mother while desiring the daughter whom he had slept with many years ago, but the visual trickery also betrays a textual unease and wish fulfilment. Defying logic by replacing Erica's anaesthetized ageing body with Julia's animated youthful one, the *mise en scène* conveys the text's own barely contained hysteria over what ageing does to the body. Our culture may feel it has surmounted its dread of ageing by bringing the corporeal body back to youth and incessantly explaining how this can be achieved through various lotions and potions, and even cosmetic surgery; but what *Nip/Tuck* does in this moment of uncanny-ness involving 'doubling, dividing and interchanging of the self' (Freud 1987: 356) between mother and daughter, when both surgeons lose the power of speech in the gaze, plays out what can never quite be enclosed within the logical reasoning of the talkative normalizing gaze.

Only on the operating table do we ever get taken beneath the surface image. Cutting around Erica's hairline enables Christian to pull taut the face, and weaving thread through needles lifts the skin to accentuate the cheekbones. If in reality shows like *Extreme Makeover* and *The Swan* the blood and gore are concealed with the focus on the 'Reveal,' with the talkative gaze narrating this trajectory at every stage, then what gets exposed in *Nip/Tuck* is what is normally kept out of sight. Seeing the full horror of the surgical procedures, without speech but choreographed through an elaborate *mise en scène* and musical accompaniment, makes visible what the text of the makeover show works so hard to repress. We are positioned to identify with the female struggle to bring her body back into cultural line. Nowhere do makeover shows ever question that this is the right strategy to undertake but instead subtly coerce us to see self-transformation as logical and absolutely necessary. Whereas sharing the intense and unremitting medical gaze that has pathologized and 'cured' the ageing body in *Nip/Tuck* results in another moment of ocular uncanny. Our aroused feelings of self-disgust and (dis)pleasure are less at the sight of what the female body must physically endure but at our all too late realization of our own complicit-ness with the pervasive power and pleasure of the normalizing look that compels women to desire beauty and youth at any cost.

Recalling Hollywood's codes and conventions of visual pleasure, and reminiscent of glossy fashion and lifestyle magazines, the *mise en scène* of *Nip/Tuck* also plays with surface image and takes indulgent delight in the silent object of the gaze. *Nip/Tuck* in fact manipulates the image by playing by the old rules while acknowledging the deception it creates. But this is no easy matter. Take, for example, the way the production techniques convey Erica's new and invigorated look. Shot in soft-focus, backlit to eliminate unsightly shadows, made-up to look luminous, Erica looks glamorous and wrinkle-free through technological trickery long used to make women appear flawless. There is a 'flat-ness' to her facial features, her skin looks radiant, and no blemish or unsightly liver spots can be detected. But positioned alongside her daughter, her beauty suddenly becomes strikingly artificial. Of course, Julia is no more natural than her mother, as both women are constructed within the visual representational strategies of *Nip/Tuck* that do not merely transform but normalize the female body to prevailing ideals defining and regulating feminine beauty. Calling attention to the artifice – although conforming to what the normalizing gaze tells us women of her age should aspire to look like – does not necessarily mean to critique but to introduce unease around the familial doppelgänger. Televisual alchemy may have surmounted the ageing process, but in the momentary shudder created by mother and daughter looking the same but different, cinematic convention pitched against televisual, the visual technology designed specifically to enhance the image of the feminine ideal is drawn attention to and in the process made strange. The more the text attempts to conceal the age difference, and to blur the physical disparities between mother and daughter, the more it reveals the struggle involved in representational values over the reproduction of various assumptions and beliefs of the normalizing gaze that define what the ideal should look like in the first place.

One of the icons of plastic surgery in America is Joan Rivers. She has long made a living from stand-up routines that incessantly lampoon the way American culture sees the ageing female body as a grotesque sight. Cackling from the margins of culture, gender and ethnicity, nothing on this subject is beyond the vernacular of Rivers. Consulting McNamara/ Troy about future cosmetic surgery, and in answer to their customary question 'tell me what you don't like about yourself', Rivers treats us to a fine example of her acerbic wit when she replies, 'Are you kidding me? Everything. My body's dropping so fast my gynaecologist needs a hard hat' ('Joan Rivers', 2.13). Her efforts to hold back the years have become part of her star persona and the source of much of her camp vaudevillian humour. Not surprisingly, she turns up on *Nip/Tuck*. What is surprising is her request that Christian and Sean perform a 'complete makeover' restoring her 'natural' appearance. Her reasoning? Her career needs a jumpstart and she longs to resurrect her old jokes about the monstrous nature of the ageing female body.

But reversing the surgery is no easy matter, for it goes against the conventional wisdom of the normalizing gaze as well as the advice of her doctors. Christian and Sean digitally construct what she would look like without surgery. This aberrant sequence within the logic of *Nip/Tuck* suspends narrative verisimilitude, producing humour as well as provoking momentary unease at the same time. On one level she verbalizes the uncanny shudder we feel on seeing the computer-generated image of her aged double. Why would she want to reverse the fairy-tale self-transformation and return to the crone we – and Christian and Sean – ask? On another level – humour aside – the CGI returns to us that which the surgeons and visual pleasures have worked so hard to repress. Visual trickery, usually at the service of the self-transformation narrative where convention dictates the ageing body is returned to youth, here acts as a disciplinary mechanism to bring Rivers to her senses and back into cultural line. And we find ourselves again conspiring with the normalizing gaze policing the female body, shocked by what we see and desirous that she do the right thing and not have the surgery. Reversing the same principle of the reality makeover show, our gaze is trained to judge and police the female form, and approve of women self-correcting their bodies to the prevailing cultural norm.

We end this chapter where we began, with Kimber Henry. Her new and improved body beautiful fails to deliver her hoped for Prince Charming. Instead, she drifts from one man's bed to another, moves from modelling into pornography, thereby swapping one form of objectification for another – and acquires a slight cocaine habit along the way. Has Christian's handiwork brought her to this? Her fate seems to verify everything Andrea Dworkin (1981) said about male possession of the female body. But in a post-feminist fairy-tale twist, Kimber emerges from the self-transformative experience with an improved sense of self and a great money-spinning idea for exploiting our (sexual) obsession with the feminine ideal. Season Two finds her back at the offices of McNamara/Troy ('Kimber Henry', 2.10). Not for herself this time – but for her newly designed latex-rubber 'Kimber' doll whose vagina she feels is a little 'too generic'. Her detailed awareness of how the reconstructed female orifice, and with its new suction function gives complete sexual satisfaction to the user, opens up female anatomy to knowledge. Taking charge of the discourse on what constitutes the ideal finds her 'intensifying areas, electrifying surfaces' (Foucault 1998: 44) and further wrapping the sexual female body in the pervasiveness of a normalizing gaze that allows it no escape from endless scrutiny and ocular inspection. Contemporary feminists like Ariel Levy (2005) may struggle to account for why women claim that being sexually provocative and promiscuous is liberating, but does Kimber not find her voice when talking about modifying and homogenizing the sexual feminine ideal for profit? It should be no surprise that the idea for the ultimate docile female body comes from her – the woman 'most sensitive to any departure from social norms and habituated to self-improvement and self-transformation in the service of those norms' (Bordo 2003: 186).

Eliminating the imperfect real for the perfect and consumable simulacra may be empowering for Kimber, but in appropriating the language of the talkative gaze she unsettles those, like Christian and Sean, who define the normative gaze. Darkly brooding yet deeply flawed, Christian passes on the challenge; but his more moral and politically correct partner, Sean, agrees to perform the 'cutting edge' procedure. Later he avails himself of the newly installed suction function in a night of onanistic pleasure – and then shame. At the height of passion the televisual alchemy intervenes when the silent inanimate doll morphs into the animated living and breathing Kimber. Visual uncertainty aroused by an inanimate object flickering to life temporarily unnerves the normalizing gaze that Sean embodies. Attraction and evasions trace around the body and encircle the politics of looking. Pleasure in having control gives way to uncertainty; and the pervasive normalizing gaze finds itself invaded, questioned, defied and challenged by that which it works hard to keep watch over.

Nip/Tuck is a modern-day fairy tale, a morality tale about looking and being seen. It is as uncanny as anything that E. T. A. Hoffmann could have written. What *Nip/Tuck* does so disturbingly, pleasurably and shockingly is to dissect the '*perpetual spirals of power and pleasure*' (Foucault

1998: 45) of the normalizing gaze, not only in how looking and the look operate in the text, but also in how we, the viewers, are deeply entangled and implicated. The drama series *Nip/Tuck* at first glance critiques our culture's obsession with body image and its self-transformation while constructing the female as grotesque and making visible a rampant misogynistic gaze policing it. But in peeling back the various textual layers, as well as delving into our own pleasurable discomfort, the series reveals our deeply entangled investment in the discursive strategies that police and regulate contemporary femininity and the ideal female body through the normalizing gaze. We may feel that we have power over what we see and how we look – and this is precisely what the normalizing gaze wants us to think – but what makes *Nip/Tuck* so pleasurably uncomfortable to watch is the way it deals with, and makes known, the effects of a visual power that we no longer perceive constraining us.

Chapter Ten

THE GENTLE ART OF MANSCAPING

Lessons in Hetero-Masculinity from the Queer Eye Guys

Joanna L. Di Mattia

'Think of it as a wilderness. In the beginning, there are trees and forests and wild weeds everywhere. And then civilization comes along and somebody says, "I'm going to separate these flowers from the rest." All of a sudden, rather than this unruly growth, you have a landscaped world' (Kyan Douglas, *Queer Eye for the Straight Guy*).

You, Only Better

On the eve of his long-delayed wedding dinner (episode 32), straight guy Chris Lim declares his heartfelt thanks to the Fab 5, the team of makeover experts at the centre of *Queer Eye for the Straight Guy*. Chris tells them, 'You've really shown me what it *means* to be a man.' The irony of his observation is not lost on the Fab 5 or their audience. The Fab 5 are 'out' gay men in a social and political climate that continues to promote the idea that gay men are neither normal nor 'real' men but fairies, faggots and queens. That this straight guy has learned what it means to be a man from bodies considered deviant and even *un-American* suggests a crisis in the policing of boundaries between homosexuality and heterosexuality. *What it means to be a man* – an elusive, unstable ideology at the best of times – is challenged further here, and problematized by interventions into this hegemonic discourse by homosexual men.

This chapter offers a feminist critique of *Queer Eye for the Straight Guy* that explores its place in the continuing narrative of American masculinity. Of particular interest is the increasingly unstable route via which hegemonic modes of masculinity are socialized and represented in the wider culture. *Queer Eye for the Straight Guy* derails a traditional narrative of heterosexual potency and dominance and disturbs the site of homosocial male bonding, so often a key locale for the making of men. Throughout the Bush era, while under increasing pressure to offer an ideologically conservative product, popular culture has re-positioned itself as a space that contests the dominant story of American masculinity. It is my position, here, that gay men play a vital role in shaping these stories in the post-9/11 era, despite the fact that debates about national identity repeatedly marginalize their voices. The Fab 5 trespass across the icons and narratives of hetero-masculinity and, in doing so, redefine them. By derailing these masculine conventions, the show interrogates the question of 'what it means to be a man.' This chapter understands masculinity as contingent, contested, and socially policed, and the male body as a vulnerable and insecure site for the validation of male power and privilege. Despite the current breadth of critical commentary on *Queer Eye*, little accounts for the destabilization of hegemonic masculinity and heteronormativity that it involves. Within feminist or queer studies frameworks, these manoeuvres must be positively applauded. Through this destabilization, *Queer Eye* disrupts the idea that gay men are not 'real men' and know nothing about authentic masculinity.

Despite calls for the increased 'visibility' of gay men and lesbians on American television, American popular culture remains concerned with reinforcing the interests of heteronormative masculinity. Since its debut on US cable network Bravo in July 2003, *Queer Eye for the Straight Guy* has been the subject of both praise and criticism from the gay and lesbian community and those concerned with matters of gay and lesbian representation more generally. *Queer Eye for the Straight Guy* has introduced five stylish gay men into the public imagination – Ted Allen (food and wine connoisseur), Thom Filicia (design doctor), Carson Kressley (fashion savant), Kyan Douglas (grooming guru), and Jai Rodriguez (culture vulture) – who possess the necessary skills to transform boys into men. But the Fab 5 provide lessons in more than how to look, cook, dress, behave, and live *better*, and there is more than just external '*tjuzing*' at work here (Carson's term for 'putting on the finishing touches'). The Fab 5's mission of 'manscaping' the world, one straight guy at a time, aims to provide straight men with the tools to be better boyfriends or husbands in nearly every area but the bedroom.

In the context of personal and social change, this chapter looks critically at the socio-cultural meaning of what is being 'made over' when gay men and straight men interact on *Queer Eye for the Straight Guy*. I explore the importance of homosocial bonding to these interactions, the life lessons and journey from boy to man that each straight guy embarks upon, and the reproduction of heterosexual coupling. I maintain that the show is an important cultural product that deconstructs and dethrones hetero-masculine norms. The show's weekly strategy offers the *possibility* of reading the straight guy's masculinity as something other than resolutely heterosexual. After a little '*tjuzing*', the conventional foundations of hegemonic masculinity are displaced. Every week, *Queer Eye for the Straight Guy* unveils straight men ignorant in the modes of appropriately heterosexual masculinity. The show can be said to engage with conventional stereotypes of gay men as naturally stylish, but it also subverts these. *Queer Eye for the Straight Guy* suggests that in a time of continuing upheaval to the power and privilege of hegemonic masculinity (defined as heterosexual here), it is gay men showing straight men how to do hetero-masculinity correctly. As a result, in addition to altering patterns of consumption, *Queer Eye* has 'made over' ways of thinking about masculinity, at a time in American social history where the demonization of gay men is routine.

The post-9/11 era poses significant challenges to definitions of hegemonic masculinity in America, where what it means to be an American male (and, in turn, an American) are in a constant state of flux, unable to be stabilized by old mythologies. In election year 2004, this 'crisis' was evident in the Bush administration's 'sex crusade' against all things defined as 'deviant' in the area of gender identity, sexuality, and sexual practice. This 'sex crusade' encompasses pushes for abstinence-only sex education, continued attacks on reproductive rights, and the stalled constitutional amendment to ban gay marriage. I define this 'sex crusade' as a series of real and rhetorical strategies compelled by the need to strengthen conventional, heroic, 'man on top' gender roles (within a heteronormative framework) at a time concerned with the weakened status of a mythological, national masculine corpus in the post-9/11 era. This concern with defining 'normal' masculinity as heterosexual, monogamous, and married, is indicative of a continuing process of rearticulating and renegotiating ideologies of not only masculinity but also citizenship and nationhood.

As Dana Heller argues in her introduction to *The Selling of 9/11: How a National Tragedy Became a Commodity*, the post-9/11 era is characterized as a time of continuous refashioning of national identity and nationhood (2005: 3). In this context, the question of what it means to be an American is more urgent than ever before. While Bush's policies condemn those defined as socially deviant, a new brand of American hero is normalized in the wider culture. Heller explains that, 'the post-9/11 working-class hero represented a nostalgic cultural longing for normalcy and simplicity in the face of new extraordinary complexities and uncertainties' (11). For Heller, the refashioning of American cultural and national identity post-9/11 is focused specifically on the resuscitation of 'masculine confidence' evident in the proliferation of images of 'heterosexual masculinity' as America's 'best line of defense' (14). Through the recurring, iconic image of the firefighter (resolutely masculine *and* heterosexual), a discourse of heroic masculinity is reinvigorated, thus 'reaffirming faith in masculinity and by extension in the nation itself' (13–14).

Paradoxically, in Bush's America, this desire for 'normalcy' is juxtaposed with the increased visibility of gay issues in the political realm and gay men's bodies in popular cultural narratives. This contradictory landscape which negotiates gay visibility is, as Heller suggests, one in which Americans are mythologized into a 'heterogenous bloc' devoid of difference (13). I would suggest, however, that while gay men and women become more visible in this 'accepting' cultural climate of collective loss and grief, this visibility coexists within a cultural climate of fear, revealed through concern with securing the homeland from both external and *internal* threats – from what is different, not 'normal', and, in turn, 'un-American'. Heller notes that popular-culture texts (like *Queer Eye*), play a pivotal role in 'the commercial commemoration and reimagining of national identity and heroism in the wake of 9/11, a process by which myths of the past are being rewritten to accommodate new possibilities' (2005: 15). Heller's argument suggests an inclusive status for non-hegemonic masculinities in the dominant story of American national identity. In a landscape hungry for heroes, *Queer Eye for the Straight Guy* provides a provocative intervention into this script, and potentially expands the meaning of masculinity in the post-9/11 era while challenging its often limiting proscriptive roles.

The Fab 5 are imagined as *superheroes* armed with an arsenal of tools specific to their individual talents: shopping bags, hairdryer, paint brush, whisk, and CDs. The Fab 5's transgression into this heteronormative iconography has significant outcomes for understandings of both discourses of heroism and masculinity. As homo-heroes, the gay Fab 5 challenge a discourse of American heroism that remains, for the most part, the province of the heterosexual male. Representations of gay men on American television, from *Will and Grace* to *Queer as Folk* and *Six Feet Under*, occupy a vital position in the negotiation of this paradoxical terrain in which the visibility of gay men and women is carefully policed and regulated. As a makeover show, *Queer Eye for the Straight Guy* plays a role in shaping the citizenry and defining what is 'normal'. With this ironic intervention in mind it is vital to ask, then, what exactly is being "made over" on *Queer Eye for the Straight Guy?* I would suggest that not only is the heterosexual male citizenry 'reshaped', but so, too, are social perceptions of gay men and their role in the contours that define hegemonic masculinity.

Importantly, the Fab 5's super heroic manscaping takes place at the nexus of 'Gay Street' and 'Straight Street' – a potentially disruptive, destabilizing space where it all 'comes out' the right way in the end. This nexus is, however, by its very nature, a place of constant instability and change. The Fab 5 explain that the transformation they produce is not a 'makeover' but a 'make better'. On the show itself, and reinforced in their book, *The Fab 5's Guide to Looking Better, Cooking Better, Dressing Better, Behaving Better and Living Better*, and on the Bravo website, the 'make better' is not designed to turn the straight guy into someone else (i.e. a gay guy). Rather, the goal is to take what he has and improve on it and, importantly, provide him with tools needed for future maintenance of that look and lifestyle. By employing the 'before' and 'after' tropes of the makeover genre, what we see on *Queer Eye* is *what* exactly 'maketh' the man in Bush's America. *Queer Eye for the Straight Guy* is a cultural product that challenges the imperative of an essentialized masculinity and highlights the performative nature of gender identity. On *Queer Eye* it isn't only the straight man's corpus that is transformed through its interaction with the gay corpus, but the socio-cultural ideology attached to those bodies, the spaces they occupy, and how they are interconnected.

'What's Gay About this Situation?'

Hegemonic masculinity is produced in opposition to women and non-hegemonic men. The articulation of heteronormative masculinity is repeatedly undermined and threatened by the existence of intimate, non-sexual bonds between men. Such a homosocial structure is central to the expression of masculinity on *Queer Eye for the Straight Guy*. Sharon Bird argues that the refusal of intimacy between men, or emotional detachment in male-bonding activities, is vital to enable a stable boundary between the heterosexual and the homoerotic in these male-to-male identifications (1996: 121–2). This boundary is always under pressure of collapsing when men appear to be 'too close'. The visibility of gay men is both dependent on the codes of hegemonic masculinity and a constant reminder of the potential to make these codes over when the borders between masculine and feminine, straight and queer, become slippery and unstable. Nowhere is this potential for remodelling masculinity more evident than in the presentation of the manscaping site as a distinctly homosocial one, in which a group of men come together to learn about masculinity from each other.

The Fab 5's brotherly bond defines the character of the manscaping or homosocial space in which the straight guy finds himself. Mark Gallagher suggests that the show emphasizes the 'pleasure' of having buddies (2004: 224). The dynamic five succeed in its mission because they share a vision, an ethos, and a 'sameness' defined by their homosexuality. The potential destabilization of this homosocial union by a homoerotic current is nullified by the already publicly declared gay status of each member of the Fab 5. Things become less secure, however, when a straight man enters this grouping. Each episode features displays of 'non-sexual' hugging and emotional outpourings of gratitude that open a space for slippage between two different identities. And while the straight guy's heterosexuality remains intact by the conclusion of the show, and no real sexual boundaries between hetero- and homosexuality have been tainted, there is clearly a shift in the straight guy's perception of himself and his new gay buddies. As I detail below, for example, John Verdi (in episode eight) is visibly stunned to discover his similarity to the gay Fab 5.

As noted above, the manscaping arena is a 'men only' space that reinforces manhood in men through the bonds they form with each other. Specifically, homosocial bonds are formed because of an *interest* in masculinity – a desire to learn what it means to be a man and to have that manhood legitimized by other men. In his study, *When Men Meet: Homosexuality and Modernity*, Henning Bech explores the fine line between male homosexual attraction and men's homosocial attraction to 'masculinity' itself. Bech suggests that all male-bonding activities are 'sustained by the same broader phenomenon: the interest between men in what men can do with one another' (1987: 49). But while homosociality offers a space in which men can learn from each other what masculinity means, it is this *interest* in other men that destabilizes the heteronormativity these bonds seek to produce. In turn, they reveal the insecure foundations on which male bonds and masculinity are constructed. Bech argues that men look at each other because 'in the very decision to be a man there is a relation to another man (concretely or as a category); the decision implies a certain and interested social relation' (51). This dynamic is explained from the view of 'one who isn't man enough, who wants to be more of a man... Between the poles a *comparison*: I am not as he; and a *wish*, a *longing*, a *desire*: I want to be like him' (ibid.).

Queer Eye for the Straight Guy actively illuminates Bech's contention that men have always learned about masculinity in the company of other men, and that this *interest* stems from a feeling of inadequacy. Moreover, *Queer Eye for the Straight Guy* highlights the 'slipperiness' of the borders between the homosocial and the homoerotic. Men's interest in other men is essential in learning what it means to be a man but, inevitably, these male-only, 'closeted' spaces produce identifications that are inconsistent with the homosocial order's heterosexual imperative. With an *interest* in masculinity and a longing to be 'more of a man' as its focal point, *Queer Eye for the Straight Guy* asks the question: how is what you learn about being a man affected by who's giving the lessons?

In the Introduction to their book, the Fab 5 note the 'misreading' that their 'make-betters' might potentially trigger. They write: 'Women know who's gay and who isn't, and gay men *definitely* know. If tomorrow morning you shave correctly and wear a shirt that's actually your size, gay men aren't all of a sudden going to start palming your ass on the sidewalks' (2004: 12). In addition, they are quick to point out that, 'A queer "eye" doesn't mean a queer look' (12). On *Queer Eye for the Straight Guy*'s first episode, Carson takes the first straight guy, Brian 'Butch' Schepel, shopping and asks him, provocatively, 'have you ever had a man undress you before?' When Carson suggests that Butch rolls up his sleeves, Butch notes that he 'prefers them straight'. Carson quips, 'So do I'. From the beginning, the couture change room is established as a transgressive homosocial space in which the lines between straight bodies and gay bodies are easily blurred. It is also a primary location for Carson's sexual innuendoes, a space that is less group-oriented, and more focused on the 'coupling' of a queer guy with a straight guy. Although the change room, like the bathroom and the day spa, are spaces that contain little real risk to the sexual identity of either Carson or whoever's shirt he happens to be tucking in, they are locations in which our thinking about bodies and gender identity is challenged. Such destabilizing acts indicate that post-9/11 anxieties about the potency and security of heterosexual masculinity remain, as they always have been, embedded in fears of the feminine and queer; and, further, that such acts inevitably force us to reconsider hegemonic masculinity's loaded relationship to both.

Episode eight reveals the complex negotiation of this terrain, where the security of hegemonic masculinity is disrupted by new ways of thinking about and seeing masculinity and the male body. The straight guy *du jour* is Port Authority Officer John Verdi, who lives on Staten Island with his girlfriend of three years, Ayana. From the moment John opens the door of his house to see five gay men standing, waiting to swoop, he is visibly troubled by their bodies. His first comment is to exclaim, 'Are you fucking kidding me?' John is particularly uncomfortable with being touched by the Fab 5. Jaap Kooijman suggests that 'it is this uneasiness, which demonstrates the instability of the allegedly rigid distinction between gay and straight' (2005: 106).

This rigid distinction is disrupted by how much John needs the lessons in masculinity the Fab 5 offer. John wants to learn to be more romantic, but doesn't know what this involves. When Jai explains to John that the longer couples are together the more they tend to become like roommates, he is positioned as an expert in heterosexual relations (although his advice can also apply to gay couples). John's anxiety about gay men is repositioned as an anxiety about trying new things and a realization that he needs to change. As a female friend notes, John 'dresses like he is in high school'. When John comments on Ayana's 'boobage' in the top Carson chose for her, Carson quips that 'he's such a romantic,' suggesting that a complete overhaul might be impossible here. Despite John's discomfort with his closeness to the Fab 5, he is *interested* in what they can teach him about being 'sexy' and more romantic. His initial discomfort is diffused by his dependence on the Fab 5 as purveyors of superior knowledge about what makes a man attractive. While their knowledge is represented in the service of hetero-masculinity – that is, they show John how to be sexy *for* Ayana – this expertise, nevertheless, emanates from their position as gay men who also know a thing or two about what makes a man sexy.

Things get interesting later in the episode when Kyan takes John to get an airbrush tan. John is anxious about standing in disposable underwear, alongside a gay man. Sensing his discomfort, Kyan exaggerates the threat of their half-naked proximity, asking the woman spraying them with tan if she can do something to make John's penis look bigger. This is the final straw for John, who is agitated by the fact that Kyan is looking at him *below* the belly button. Kyan wants to know, 'What's gay about this situation?' to which John tellingly reveals that it is the mere closeness of their bodies, not the threat of actual sexual contact, that potentially destabilizes his own hetero-masculinity. While Kylo-Patrick Hart suggests that 'it becomes instantly evident that it will take some work for this subject to realize that gay men do not threaten his sexuality or identity as a macho straight guy' (2004: 249), I would argue that the Fab 5 *do* threaten and challenge the stability of John's macho straight guy persona. The destabilization of categories requires a redefinition of those categories. This imperative is clear when Ted has to rename quiche, 'vegetable torta', and dress it up in more heterosexual terms, referencing the popular humour book *Real Men Don't Eat Quiche* (1982) which celebrates an ethic of masculinity that is both regressive and pathological in its insistence on all things macho. Ted finds himself explaining that, 'It's not quiche. It's an Italian quiche. It's a manly quiche. It's a quiche with balls,' in order to convince John to prepare it for his picnic with Ayana. This process of renaming and remodelling is indicative of the need to reinstate borders between hetero- and homo-masculinities in a space where these have become less secure.

While these anxieties are always present, they are quelled with quick wit and incredulity on the part of the Fab 5. The possibility of looking for too long or identifying too closely is contained and managed through an idealization of the most positive aspects of the homosocial bond and the subordination of its conventional tropes. If male bonding is posited on insecurity, rivalry, and the sexual exchange of women to negotiate the 'problem' of men's closeness, the bonds forged on *Queer Eye* work against this approach, promoting a sense of togetherness based on the men's shared manhood, not their difference centred on sexuality. Here, masculinity is not articulated around the passivity, invisibility, and exchangeability of female bodies. Because the Fab 5 are gay men, women don't figure as objects of sexual exchange used by men to strengthen their manhood. Rather, a union with *one* woman is actively positioned as the ultimate goal in the manscaping journey. And by the end of his time with the Fab 5, John Verdi is more comfortable touching and hugging gay men and John relates to them as other men, first and foremost. While such a reading reinforces the view that gay visibility is tolerated so long as gay men 'play down' their differences to the straight populous (and I would indeed argue for the problematic nature of such representations and visibility), my reading of *Queer Eye for the Straight Guy* is in the context of the ruptures it produces in the narrative of hegemonic masculinity.

Becoming Butch

Queer Eye for the Straight Guy's first episode institutes its formula: the Fab 5 help a straight guy to look and feel better and in doing this learn something about appropriate hetero-masculinity. It is an episode that raises key questions around the reproduction of this identity and the often-ambiguous effects of the Fab 5's interventions into the hegemonic order. Episode one's unreconstructed wild man, Brian 'Butch' Schepel, hasn't cut his hair in nine years, wears overalls and work boots even when he *isn't* working, and lives in a chaotic apartment in New York's East Village. What is immediately striking about the Fab 5's first 'make better' project is his name – Butch – that has meaning for both those familiar with its use in the gay lexicon, and those aware of its hyper-masculine connotations.

As the show's initial image of a straight man in crisis, Butch's name is incongruous with his inadequate manhood and presents a dilemma the show quickly sets about to resolve. While Butch appears manly in a rough, unpolished way, he is also depicted as a man in need of softening or feminization in order to move ahead in his life. In 'gayspeak', however, as a term that denotes the masculine lesbian, butch suggests an inauthentic attempt to access male privilege. Either way, as a man, Butch Schepel is found lacking. In the *Queer Eye* universe, where the meanings attached to hegemonic masculinity are in a constant state of flux, *becoming Butch* is equivalent to attaining the elusive title: 'real man'.

Entering Butch's apartment, both Thom and Jai are dumbfounded by the sight of his bed: a narrow, 'prison-like' affair, where neither queer guy can imagine Butch performing the act that defines him as heterosexual. Thom notes that, 'this apartment's a real chick magnet.' As part of his journey from boy to man, the Fab 5's mission is to get Butch ready for his first art exhibition. By the show's end, the Fab 5 have unveiled the real man lurking within the previously unmanicured corpus. The connection is clear: as long as Butch remains an overall-wearing, long-haired boy, he will never be a man, and therefore never fulfil his dreams of artistic success. Butch's transformation, as the show's archetypal beginning, is indicative of the *Queer Eye* motto: 'We're not here to change you. We're here to make you better.' The theme of rebirth and remodelling this man into a new 'concept', as Thom describes it, permeates Butch's encounters with each member of the Fab 5. Taking him to the hairdresser to remove Butch's shaggy ponytail, Kyan declares that this haircut inducts Butch into a new phase of his life. He calls it, 'the rebirth of the artist.' Later, Carson reinforces this notion of change by calling him, 'the artist formerly known as Butch.'

Importantly, when his manscaping is complete, Butch is suddenly highly attractive to women. All around the gallery, women cannot take their eyes from his improvements. From the Fab 5 loft, Carson notes the 'roaring approval of the crowd' and in particular that the 'girls are going crazy.' More concerned with the potency and viability of Butch's remodelled hetero-masculinity, the Fab 5 take turns commenting on his attractiveness. Jai notes that Butch's good friend and portrait model, Laurel, is clearly 'into' Butch. Carson observes that Butch's new manliness is unsettling the manhood of the other men in the room: 'The guys look kinda angry... like they're a bit jealous.' Through a process of feminization that destabilizes heteronormativity, Butch has become an icon of masculinity. Butch's evident superiority is emphasized by Laurel's repeated requests to her own long-haired boyfriend to try and be a bit more like Butch, and perhaps get a haircut, new clothes, and a tan. Butch's remodelling is complete here, at the point where he becomes a viable sexual being in a heterosexual dating arena. Thom tellingly observes of Laurel's attentiveness: 'She so wants to sleep with him, she can barely see *straight*'.

While there is an emphasis throughout *Queer Eye for the Straight Guy* on reassuring the straight guys that they are being 'made better' and not made gay, episode one highlights the potential disruption of the security of hetero-masculinity that occurs when homosexual men visibly intervene and redefine it. But perhaps seeing these transformations as simply making a straight guy better belies the fact that the Fab 5 have indeed changed not only him, but also effected a change in the way their audience, like Butch's adoring public, sees and thinks about homosexuality's relationship to straight masculinity in the post-9/11 era. There is a distinct process of looking, admiring, and identifying at work here, where Butch's manhood, as that of the representative straight guy, is displayed for approval not only by the gay Fab 5 but also for all of us located within the heterosexual matrix.

Life Lessons

A key step in becoming skilled in the norms of hetero-masculinity requires that the straight guy learn how to be more romantic. With the aid of the Fab 5, straight men across America (and beyond) are learning the art of wooing women. The special events that function as catalysts for the manscaping makeover are those that mark a transition from boyhood to manhood. This journey is conceptualized as a journey from immature frat-boy, to committed, responsible man, that is often visualized by the Fab 5 literally picking up underwear strewn across the straight guy's floor (a recurring feature of the 'frat-boy' home). These boys in need of masculinizing are positioned as deviant, not only in appearance, but also in habits, and these bad habits get in the way of romance. Their bathrooms are uniformly filthy, their kitchens unsanitary and littered with pizza boxes and beer bottles, their closets filled with clothing that is either the wrong size or made of the wrong fabric. They spend too much time on the couch, and not enough time on themselves or their girlfriends/wives. The change they seek is a serious and functional one – lessons not only in cooking, cleaning, and dressing, but also in *living*.

The necessity of coupling with a female is the impetus for a shift from this particularly regressive model of masculinity towards a more competent and successful performance of heterosexual manhood. As a result, heterosexual milestones feature heavily in these episodes: dates, the planning of a special dinner or party for a girlfriend or wife, the alteration of a home to make space for a woman to move in, or the meeting of a girlfriend's parents for the first time. Throughout the episode, the straight guys agree to this manscaping in order to become better boyfriends or husbands. In episode six, for example, a freshly groomed Vincent makes his public singing debut with a sentimental love song he has written for his wife: 'I'm So in Love with You.' In episode four, a shaved and shorn Josh takes dancing lessons so he and his girlfriend can spend time doing something she enjoys. These milestones are deftly handled by the Fab 5, who are well versed in the language of heterosexual mating rituals – like the rest of us, gay men have had no choice but to imbibe these rituals via popular culture images.

But these lessons are not without their hiccups. *Queer Eye for the Straight Guy* cameraman, Andrew Lane (episode five), is described as an infantile Drew Carey lookalike, struggling to enter manhood. When the Fab 5 invade his domain, Andrew is living with his brother, and has been, in his words, 'hanging out' with his girlfriend, Diana, for four months. Because his 'man-pad' is in a constant state of disorder, Andrew spends most of his time at Diana's place. The Fab 5's mission is to send

Andrew on a 'big-boy date' to show Diana that he wants to be a better boyfriend. As part of the 'make better' process, Ted takes Andrew for a test run at the New York restaurant where he will later have dinner with Diana. Ted wants Andrew to become familiar with the wine list, so that he doesn't spend the better part of the date deciding what to drink. But more than this, Ted suggests that Andrew's proficiency with the wine list will allow him more time to gaze 'soulfully' into Diana's eyes. When Andrew exhibits some difficulty breaking lobster claws, he explains to Ted that he is afraid of 'looking weak'. Andrew's remodelling is fraught with instability over the definition of what is or isn't manly behaviour because he is contrasted with a gay man competent in the cracking of a lobster claw. Unlike Andrew, Ted shows no signs of weakness and no fear of appearing as such.

A competent performance of heterosexuality, and one that is ready for romance, is also located in the maintenance of an appropriately masculine body. Kyan subjects the hirsute Andrew to both an eyebrow and back wax, and when they return to his newly renovated abode, Kyan continues the grooming/remodelling process. He trims Andrew's nose hair and 'manscapes' Andrew's chest hair. As Kyan explains, this will both 'tame' his manhood, and also make it more defined. Here, the 'manscaping' metaphor is rendered tangible, as the contradiction on which hetero-masculinity is built. To make these straight men better requires a careful negotiation of conventional notions of masculinity with more 'metrosexual' sensibilities around care of the self. Although these are never explicitly couched as homosexual, the fact that these corporeal transitions are enabled by and performed by homosexual men nevertheless permits an unstable signification to emerge. Although Andrew, on his journey from boy to man, is encouraged to become more comfortable in his own skin, and therefore more successful at hetero-masculinity, he is also convinced to abandon all the things (including his chest hair) that have previously defined him as male.

In addition to dates, asking a girlfriend to move in is reconfigured as the straight guy learning to 'make over' his life to 'make room' for a woman. In episode three, long-haired Tom is a thirty-year-old straight guy who acts like a boy. The Fab 5's mission, and Ted's in particular, is to teach Tom to prepare a romantic dinner, over which he will ask his girlfriend, Lisa, to move in with him. As the website synopsis explains: 'Tom is a guy who has grown older but forgot to grow up.' After gentle lessons in grooming, dressing, and cooking, and some serious redecoration, the transformation is completed by the empty closet put aside for Lisa's things that indicates the opening of a tangible space for her in his life. When Tom asks Lisa to live with him in this remasculinized space, she eagerly says yes. Similarly, Ross (episode 14) is resisting the changes necessary to fully incorporate a woman into his home. Although his girlfriend, Teresa, has already moved in, there is little evidence of her feminine presence or her personality within the apartment's walls. The Fab 5 teach Ross some valuable lessons in compromise, which includes taking Teresa salsa dancing, despite the fact that he remains a macho Marine at heart. By simply following the lesson plan laid out by the Fab 5 in how to be a better boyfriend and in turn a better man, both Tom and Ross are successful in taking that next step on the road to heterosexual union: cohabitation.

For Alan (episode 11), following the instructions laid out by the Fab 5 proves a more difficult task. His mission is to throw a cocktail party so his parents can meet his girlfriend Katie's parents for the first time. When the Fab 5 leave Alan to his own devices, his nerves get the better of him and he breaks the retro glassware that Ted has bought him. As both sets of parents arrive, Alan fumbles with the cocktail recipes, and makes the mixed drinks too strong. But because Alan has been schooled in the ways of gentlemanly masculinity, he is able to rescue what might have been a potential disaster, offering a toast to Katie and to their parents. Gustavus Stadler suggests that in the teaching of these life lessons in hetero-masculinity, heterosexuality is repeatedly made *abject*, and that it is the Fab 5's presence that 'jolts the guy into realizing his own straight sexuality in its fullest, most socially supported form' (2005: 109). I would add, here, that without the help of the gay Fab 5, straight guys like Andrew, Tom, Ross, and Alan remain coded as deviant heterosexuals. The real subversion is that the Fab 5 are playing a part in the reproduction and reconfiguration of hetero-masculine norms, rarely attributed to non-hegemonic masculinities.

Here Come the Brides

The most significant of heterosexual milestones, undoubtedly, involves the marriage proposal and wedding ceremony itself. In one of *Queer Eye for the Straight Guy*'s most extravagant, popular, and memorable makeovers, John Bargeman (episode seven) is provided with all the necessary accoutrements to produce a classic, hyper-romantic marriage proposal to his lovely girlfriend, Tina. Despite a lack of initial expertise, John does everything necessary to create a perfect romantic evening.

And the Fab 5 provide the material necessary to accomplish this with both their individual skills and their superior knowledge of romantic codes and conventions. Here, this knowledge is gleaned from Hollywood narratives – *Casablanca* and Cary Grant movies – and reinterpreted by the gay Fab 5 for the consumption of a deficient straight guy. As Carson tells him, 'You have had the best training, if you screw this up, it's not our fault.'

John and Tina have been living together for two years and now John wants to ask her to be his bride, but is worried that he won't be able to put together a classically romantic proposal. When the Fab 5 enter his life, they realize that with his Southern charm and classic tall, dark and handsome looks, John will need very little work to make him better. Nevertheless, the transformation that ensues is based around specific interventions that are designed to maximize the excessive romance of the special event. When Carson takes John to Ralph Lauren, Cary Grant is his couture inspiration. John's appeal to both heterosexual female *and* homosexual male audiences is secured not only in his appropriation of the classic Hollywood glamour of the bisexual Grant, but in Carson's comment that it 'just makes us wish *we* were Tina some more.' Kyan's motivation behind John's manicure is also designed for optimum romantic effect: because he is offering his hand in marriage he should present the best hand possible.

But it is Ted, Thom, and Jai, who arm John with the lessons for getting a 'guaranteed yes'. Ted takes John shopping to feed Tina's love of bittersweet dark chocolate and points out its aphrodisiac qualities. He also suggests when John should propose and how: during dessert, by placing the engagement ring in one of the chocolate dessert boxes. In addition, Jai teaches John how to say 'I love you' in Armenian in honour of Tina's heritage: *yes keh si'rem kezi*. But the centrepiece of the Fab 5's lessons in love here is the spectacular Moroccan-themed tent enclosure that Thom constructs in John's backyard, complete with draping red fabric, candles, cushions, and flower petals. It is an exotic space designed for maximum romantic effect, and which, because of its outdoor location, offers the possibility of even further romance. As Kyan notes: 'If it's a little chilly out, you can take the jacket and put it over her shoulders. That's a guaranteed yes.'

When Tina arrives to see not only her new home but her new boyfriend, Ted notes that John is a true gentleman and 'very chivalrous'. The extent to which the Fab 5 have personally invested in the success of

John's makeover and proposal, is evident in their nervousness back at the loft. They sit together, arms clasped, at the edge of their seats, and when Tina says yes, like the self-anointed 'fairy godmothers' that they are, Carson declares yet 'another happy ending' and 'our first *Queer Eye* wedding'. Carson concludes proceedings with a toast, and declares, 'A night of classic romance... our best work yet!' It may be the show's first wedding, but it isn't the last. These lessons have not only been for John's use in wooing and winning the love of Tina, but are explicitly positioned as lessons for all straight guys watching: do these things and you too will be a successful man.

Success is the name of the game for Kevin (episode 18) who also wants to ask long-time love, Matilda, to be his bride. Interestingly, Kevin's girlfriend has refused to set foot in his apartment for the past five months because of the state of disarray it is in. But after some coaching from the Fab 5, and the enacting of classic heterosexual conventions including champagne and caviar as the quintessentially romantic meal, and calling Matilda's parents to ask for their permission and blessing, Kevin's proposal is accepted with open arms. As the website says, 'we're thrilled to report that *Queer Eye*'s record for marriage proposals accepted remains a perfect two-for-two.'

Cheers, Queers!

Sasha Torres argues that *Queer Eye for the Straight Guy* tells a more complex story than simply placing gay men in the service of heterosexual coupling. What these interventions, and particularly those focused on the marriage proposal, suggest is 'a crisis in the reproduction of heterosexuality so enormous that the Fab Five's interventions constitute at best a drop in the bucket' (2005: 96). As Torres argues, and as I have illustrated here, heteronormativity, as it is currently conceptualized by mainstream society, produces flawed men and models of masculinity. *Queer Eye for the Straight Guy* offers a subversive strategy for reconfiguring these flaws, and for illuminating the complexities and anxieties associated with hegemonic models of masculinity in the post-9/11 era. As Torres writes, 'even as the show positions the queers as just the thing to ease the straight guys' transition from unkempt bachelorhood to happy coupledom, it suggests, sotto voce, the inadequacy of such coupling, and of the heterosexual families such coupling initiates, to teach heterosexual men how to live' (96). In this context, I agree with Kyra Pearson and Nina Reich, who posit that the Fab 5 in fact 'dismantle the system within which they work'

(2004: 230). If the show can be said to reinforce a gay/straight binary by highlighting gay difference via its superiority in this space, it collapses the binary to enable a more fluid interaction between both sides of the sexual divide.

But maybe the point is, as Bech suggests, that there has always been something a little 'queer' about the way men have learned about masculinity from each other. In conventional understandings of homosociality, this 'queerness' is submerged under the regressive veil of macho practices such as sport, sexual bravado, and violence. But here the true nature of the 'sameness' at the core of male bonding practices is more anxiously reproduced. *Queer Eye for the Straight Guy* ultimately sabotages the homosocial order. Here, it is five gay men who define and affirm the appropriateness of each straight guy's masculinity; here the *looking*, *comparison*, and *desires* are distinctly an interest in what heterosexuality is learning from homosexuality about masculinity. In doing this, a representative space is opened that actively challenges the supremacy and security of heteronormativity and, in Bush's America, this is a bold undertaking. As Bruce C. Steele writes: 'As fundamentalist preachers and right-wing politicians demonize and divide, the Fab 5 are doing the Lord's own work with rubber gloves, natural fabrics, and pre-shave oils: Strengthening the family. Abolishing chaos. Fostering fellowship. Cleaning house' (2003: 42–3). For a nation mired in a divisive public battle over who is a citizen and who isn't, the anxiety produced by *Queer Eye for the Straight Guy*'s gay/straight interaction lies here: in this dependent configuration of identification and the hollowness of a hetero-masculinity that must now look outside its fragile parameters for social and cultural validation. Despite current attempts to push gay men back into the closet, it is gay men who are reinvigorating both tired haircuts and national mythologies, gay men who have the power to rewrite and widen our understanding of what is 'normal', what is 'masculine', and what it means to be an American.

Chapter Eleven

MAKEOVER MORALITY

and
Consumer Culture

Guy Redden

This chapter is an attempt to think through the relationships between makeover television and consumer culture, with a view to highlighting historically specific cultural rationalities that mediate forms of economic activity. Makeover shows are about (quite literally at the levels of narrative, character and theme) the modification of attitudes, behaviour and lifestyle so as to enhance personal wellbeing to a putatively life-changing extent. This is effected largely via participants learning how to select and consume goods and services appropriately. The shows project mentalities, ethics and activities associated with consumption, depicting its value in terms of the lived experiences, and social interests, of ordinary contemporary persons. As such, they are a recent addition to the category of lifestyle television that McQuail sees as showcasing the patterns of life associated with consuming under conditions of abundant leisure and income (2002: 428).

In broadcasting contexts that permit product placement in television programming, the shows themselves can function as marketing vehicles. For instance, the US version of *Queer Eye For the Straight Guy* (Scout Productions, 2003–2006) has led to phenomenal sales increases for placed products that are featured as gay guys show straight ones how to live well (Lowrey et al. forthcoming). Yet the link between the media form and consumption is not confined to below-the-line promotion. *Queer*

Eye For the Straight Guy, an international hit, is something more than a sub-genre of marketing communications. Like all makeovers, it focuses ultimately upon transforming the literacies and competencies of people, and channelling them towards certain culturally valued ends. Such consumer transformations are inseparable from processes of identity formation and how they bear upon cultural change or continuity. For example, Jay Clarkson (2005) has shown how the forms of self-care and self-presentation featured in *Queer Eye For the Straight Guy* embed particular notions of gay maleness while recasting heterosexual masculinity in terms of consumption rather than production.

In so reconstructing identities, makeovers simultaneously act as forms of moral guidance, presenting consumption as a generalized late-modern *modus vivendi*. The remainder of this chapter questions how we might understand such 'makeover morality' in light of theories of consumer society. With reference to British makeovers, I argue that the shows articulate a particular cultural logic associated with exigencies of liberal consumer capitalism, which above all enjoins people to find in the marketplace consumer options that satisfy differentiated and personalized notions of value. The piece concludes by questioning both simplistic notions of the self-determining freedom of the 'sovereign consumer' and the extent to which the individualized forms of cultural consumption advocated in makeovers can be seen as indexical of corporate social identity, in particular, class.

Makeover Morality

The makeover genre is constantly proliferating. At the time of writing, the UK appears to have a penchant for pet transformation shows, and the animal industries are no doubt grateful that the ever-spreading makeover theme has jumped the species barrier. Health and personal grooming shows (especially ones involving cosmetic surgery) are also prominent in current schedules, perhaps inevitably taking the vanguard away from the home makeover in the light of a slowing national housing market. However, across variants, basic qualities can be readily defined. The prime ingredient is always ordinary persons, people ostensibly plucked from the population and held up as exemplars of the ordinary and embodiments of an issue (Bonner 2003: 86–9). This does not mean that they belong to a particular cohort that has been reified for its ordinariness. As Brunsdon notes, in the British context, even as makeovers may be accused of contributing to a dumbing down in programming, they seem to effect a kind of 'pluralling up' of the constituencies that can pass for ordinary Britons (2003: 17). Gay, straight, divorced, single, black, white, urban, rural, rich and not yet rich: the characters we meet come complete with their own life worlds, which, as viewers, we are allowed to witness vicariously. While the exigencies of a given show may privilege certain groups of ordinary folk, the diversity of life situations presented in the makeover galaxy is notable.

The other category of persons involved is that of experts (see Powell and Prasad in this volume). They are, of course, the polar opposites of technocrats. They are members of the class of new cultural intermediaries, experts in matters of style whose work is to facilitate broader processes of taste discrimination that are crucial to contemporary markets (Philips 2005: 214). As specialists in aspects of everyday life (personal grooming, fashion, cooking, gardening, home decoration, etc.), their principal role is to guide the ordinary persons through a series of consumer choices in order to achieve a particular goal, typically some kind of breakthrough in personal appearance or appearance of domestic space. The one certain element is that the result is a transformed state of being that contrasts with the original state and becomes a focus for emotional response on final revelation. All of the choices made and activities undertaken combine to create an overall effect: a woman who looks ten years younger, a property now saleable or worthy of the name home, a man who exudes what women really want.

In this, the makeover reproduces a central tenet of commercialism, namely that consumption leads to improved life-experience (Deery 2004: 212). The textuality of consumer culture is elsewhere shot through with optimistic vignettes about lives getting better. This is not simply a narrative tendency, but constitutes a moral vision of consumption as a right action leading to improvement. As Lears (1983) notes, modern advertising is essentially therapeutic. Transcending appeals to immediate use-value, it links products with imaginary states of wellbeing, projected as implicitly achievable by the consumer. The promise is of self-realization, even a secular form of salvation. Ian Woodward's study of attitudes towards home decoration among the Australian middle classes reveals how hopes of self-realization through consumption are lived. According to Woodward, consumption functions 'as a cultural operation that allows people to use the material world as a resource for exercising moral judgements.' Decoration involves value discriminations that meld the aesthetic and the moral – notions of beautiful and ugly, and good and bad – in line with qualities that are seen to define who a person is and their approach to life (2003: 401).

An example from a typical opening of the fashion makeover show *What Not to Wear* ('Lisa', 4.7) reveals a certain moral tone. A hapless woman, a soldier, obviously more than a size 8, is scrutinized by the zero-tolerance fashion gurus, Trinny and Susannah. She is having problems dating. After deliberations that include asking their sartorially challenged charge when she last looked into a full-length mirror and the acute observation 'You're just not happy are you?', the pair conclude their diagnosis with the judgement 'You look what can only be described as an embarrassment.' Luckily, the team is on hand to right all this by demonstrating better choices. At the end, rehabilitated, the woman feels the obligatory 'great' for knowing what kinds of clothes, cosmetics and accessories are suitable for her. The whole thing is a kind of instructional fable in which her guardians exhort change towards a better state, in line with arguments about right and wrong, good and bad.

A themed episode about young women starting out in their careers ('Starting Out', 5.2) illustrates how the experts moralize not about what is right per se, but what is right for the person. Their skill is more sophisticated than subjecting all participants to the same makeover formula. Rather, it lies in interpreting the life situation of the given person, who may represent a certain social category of ordinary people (female soldiers, young professional women, etc.), but is simultaneously represented as a unique individual in body and inclination. Each of the five workers vying for a makeover reveals the peculiarities of their situation. One, who is admonished for showing her belly ('Who's going to give you a job looking like that honey?') has to find a way of dressing that both expresses responsibility and allows her to feel good about herself. Another wants to be taken seriously, in particular by other women. Unlike her over-expressive counterpart, she is a 'geek', who needs to learn how to be comfortable among peers, and above all wants to be able to wear short skirts. One is a young doctor who must achieve a professionalism in apparel that invites trust, while another has to reconcile the mixed messages sent out by her conflicting aesthetic codes of 'tart' and 'student', before she can make her mark in the world of work.

Symbolic violence

The framework of Bourdieu's sociology of consumption is particularly apposite in accounting for the ways that makeover shows present deliberations over matters of taste. In a close reading of an episode of the lifestyle show *Hot Property*, David Giles (2002) describes how the residents of flats that are being featured are presented in their everyday 'naturalistic' settings of home. The expert host reads the domestic spaces critically, seizing upon inappropriate furnishing choices, which indicate that the flat owners have poor levels of taste literacy, and the inhabitants are called upon to explain and justify. Such evaluation is typical of the 'before' stage of the makeover narrative that precedes the rebirth. It sets up the problem to be solved and, according to Philips, always amounts to a discrediting of the person by an expert, who is subsequently vindicated (2005: 223–4). Angela McRobbie (2004: 103) has described this structure as the evaluation of the person's habitus. The 'victim' (McRobbie's term) is enjoined to present the signs of what kind of person they are, for subsequent critique. In so doing their personal details (not only attitudes, but concrete signs of habitual dispositions, including home, family friends and neighbours, and social milieu) come to stand for social categories. It is the performance of class, gender and potentially other forms of identity that come under scrutiny through the individual. McRobbie argues that makeovers such as *What Not to Wear* generate forms of class antagonism between women. The new cultural intermediaries (the experts and hosts) admonish those members of the working class and lower-middle class who lack the taste competencies of the elite, spurring them to change themselves. Hence the makeover can be seen to revolve around the 'expectation of improvement of status and life chances through the acquisition of forms of cultural and social capital' (99).

In this reading, the moralizing tone of the makeover derives from the operation of symbolic violence: the legitimating of the symbolic power of the elite group. In being directly concerned with the operation of taste discrimination, the makeover certainly lends itself to this analysis. The 'Starting Out' episode of *What Not to Wear* highlights how learning to adopt the right signs of identity is depicted as an investment that will yield social power in the workplace. A formula for converting cultural into social and ultimately economic capital is outlined. However, as a genre that exhorts people to transform themselves in matters of attitude, taste and behaviour, the makeover cannot be explained solely in terms of social reproduction. Despite its usefulness as a tool to show how the acquired dispositions and competencies of actors correlate with their social positioning, the concept of 'habitus' itself is of no use in identifying the origins of changes in its own form. Hence, for McRobbie, the habitus modification of the makeover is linked to broader social processes that take a shape in media and popular culture, in particular 'individualization', the requirement that people, including women, bear the responsibility for reinventing themselves in order to adapt to new social demands, and above all those deriving from a changing labour market, gender relations, and consumer culture (2004: 100–1, 108).

Individualization

Makeovers do not amount to a straightforward advocacy of new social hierarchies. They construct themselves as déclassé, and they can also be seen as vehicles of cultural democratization. This is the view of the flamboyant host of one of Britain's most famous home makeover shows, Changing Rooms (BBC, 1997–2004). Lawrence Llewellyn Bowen refers to makeovers as a strand in a movement towards 'design democracy'. He argues that we have passed from the era of elite prescription of tastes and into one where everyone is permitted to have an opinion. With a media (significantly TV and magazines) responsive to this, 'Taste is no longer prescribed by the few for the majority' (cited in Philips 2005: 26). Although she views it as inseparable from the transcription of class and gender, McRobbie also recognizes that redistribution of elite cultural capital takes place and is constructed as culturally democratizing in the televisual text (2004: 106).

Lines of social identity are not drawn uniformly in all shows. The allure of the makeover cuts across classes, ages and genders, and includes ethnic and sexual minorities, resulting in a 'something for everyone' ethos. In the realm of popular British home transformations we find shows featuring successful professionals and upper-middle-class participants in their pursuit of cutting-edge luxury (e.g. *Grand Designs*, Talkback, 2000–2006), shows largely about the lower-middle-class families next door (e.g. *House Doctor*, Talkback, 1999–2006), and shows that mainly involve working-class experts and participants (e.g. *DIY SOS*, BBC, 1999–2006). Other programmes alternate between differently situated 'ordinary persons' week-by-week. It is true that the makeover is a generally middle-class world, in which generally middle-class tastes are purveyed. But the phenomenon does not reduce to a particular class dynamic, except to say that as improvement-via-consumption is showcased in all life contexts, upward class mobility or being a better consumer within one's existing milieu are standard implications. At least in British television, the inclusiveness extends to sexuality and race. Despite the inevitable prevalence of white heterosexuals, such possibilities as young gay hosts advising middle-aged heterosexual couples (*How Not to Decorate*, Ricochet, 2003–6), and regular inclusion of people of non-white British racial and ethnic identity, make the makeover a decidedly liberal seam of programming. This inclusiveness is illustrated by a random sample of makeovers that were broadcast simultaneously at 8pm on three of the five British free-to-air television channels (12 January 2006). In the personal finance show *Pay Off Your Mortgage in Two Years* (BBC, 2006), a black entrepreneur guides a white middle-class family (other weeks he helps both richer and poorer people) through disciplines that could lead to an anticipated 'freed-from-the-mortgage-to-spend-on-lifestyle' consumer nirvana ('Macvean Family', 1.2). Meanwhile, over on Five in *Diet Doctors Inside and Out* (Tiger Aspect, 2006), two white health professionals help a larger black woman to become a better version of herself ('Georgina Hawes', 1.2). And in *10 Years Younger* (Maverick Television Productions, 2004–2006) on Channel 4, a white African presenter heads up a team of three professional experts, another white African and two British Asians, who are responsible for the complete body modification of a white working-class, middle-aged woman, as her black husband and mixed-race children lend moral support ('Winter Sun Bikini Special', 3.1).

How do we account for this inclusiveness? In the televisual discourse (as opposed to critical discourse about it) the subjects of makeovers are not made to stand for categories that are isolated and subject to analysis in social terms. Rather, through intense biographical focus, they are made to stand for individuals. They function as *typifications of individuality* whatever their apparent social category. The contingencies of people's situations come to define their personal uniqueness. Consequently, the diversity presented serves to generalize aspirational individuality across the social field by showing all possible configurations of identity as amenable to transformation. Each episode is an exercise in case management, where enhanced wellbeing is seen to lie in a better combination of elements in the given life. The main personal problem illustrated is that of reflexivity. Consumption is depicted as an heuristic art in which the interpretation of the value of the commodity is intimately linked with a capacity to evaluate one's own needs, construed as one's best interests in a particularized, heavily narrated, life context. The aggregate effect of all the makeovers in the world is a normalization of this kind of reflexive action. An ethic of consumerism is projected onto all, incorporating diverse identities into the larger category of individuals concerned with improving themselves and their possessions via consumption.

A form of media addressing the desires of contemporary persons, in general, to fashion themselves, is consistent with one of the main themes of contemporary social theory: that of the individualization brought about by the fragmentation of institutions and the pluralization of knowledges. In Ulrich Beck's analysis, amid multiple knowledges and options for action, people increasingly enjoy 'precarious freedoms'. They have to plan, calculate and adjust their lives in rapidly changing environments, in which a person's life course is less predetermined (2002: 6). Yet greater freedom to choose is itself no guarantee of wellbeing, which has to be actively and strategically pursued at the same time as forms of social support and predictability lose their force. That is to say that perceived wellbeing increasingly depends upon individuals' reflexive competencies in diverse fields of action. Bauman has argued that the pluralization of knowledge changes the social form of morality. Being right no longer equates with following custom. Increasingly, people have to choose what is right in belief and action, while the grounds of right choice are not socially enforced, but drawn from competing interpretations and traditions (1993: 4). The responsibility for making all kinds of decisions results in the challenge of how one is to fashion personal narratives of purposefulness. One can but deploy resources at hand to construct and reconstruct one's biography reflexively, transforming the tasks of living into projects for the self (Bauman 2001: 21; Giddens 1991: 70–83).

The solutions that makeovers present are not confined to isolated moments of consumption that fulfil logically separable needs. Instead, by examining the logic of the whole life, they bring alignment between both means and ends so as to fulfil larger goals. For instance, the aspirations of the subject of the 'Winter Sun Bikini Special' episode of 10 Years Younger are not confined to the level of functional utility. Heather is not simply a person who has identified her own needs for rhinoplasty, breast enlargement, and better clothes, and then sought expert input regarding her best options. Instead, the team start with a vague set of ideas and preferences that point towards the kind of life desired. In this case, the main goal is to reclaim years lost (implicitly to the exigencies of child-rearing and nest-building) by recovering aspects of Heather's previous self, that is a person who loved beach life and all that it represents (and who had a beach wedding with a beach body to match). The experts contribute to a project already in hand. She has completed an astounding diet (taking her from size 20 to size 8). The expert's intervention is her reward for being such a morally deserving subject and, with their intimate knowledge of such recalcitrant phenomena as dieters' skin flaps and smokers' 'yellowed tombstone teeth', they help her across the line. She becomes the subject of a narrative resolution in which disparate elements are synthesized to create a final congruence. It is precisely holistic in the sense that the parts, when combined correctly, create a whole that does not reduce to an aggregation of separate items. There is a unifying shift to a qualitatively new level of personal order, a breakthrough amounting to a realization of a personal version of the good life.

In this context, the makeover can be viewed as a media projection of activities of reflexive construction of the life course, acting to show how knowledge of a given practical sphere of action (design/consumption) can become part of a life narrative when applied with apparent success. Individualization theory helps to account for the pedagogic dimension of the makeover. The genre addresses the quintessential high modern problem faced by individuals – that of establishing value amid a plurality of options, and of having no choice but to choose in these matters. Yet, despite their 'middle-classness', makeover narratives do not promote clear universal standards of taste. The genre does *not* serve to demonstrate that this or that commodity is right for all, or even that a given way of living is right or wrong. It takes the given life context and shows how a certain collocation of consumption choices provides a unique and contingent fit with it. The reflexive heuristics sets it apart from prescriptive discourses advocating simple emulation of standards or icons. As Taylor argues, drawing upon Bauman, the expert host is a 'personality interpreter' whose role is not that of the authoritative intellectual, but is confined to assessing the needs of the client in a market setting (2002: 487–8). This denotes a kind of relativist rightness-to-self and the possibility of a radically individual conception of the good embedded within the orderly whole of the individual lifestyle.

Lifestyling

So far I have argued that Bourdieu's sociology of taste and individualization theory both shed some light on how the makeover mediates contemporary social dynamics. Indeed, they address truly distinctive elements of the genre. In a fundamental sense, the entire focus of the programmes is a moral evaluation of tastes. Makeover candidates are analysed in the fullness of their habitus. They are counselled to improve their taste literacies and depicted as acquiring superior cultural capital as a result (Philips 2005: 226–7). This capital is routinely shown being transformed into social power in the ways that it apparently impresses others. But these same processes can also be viewed through the prism of individualization. Makeover morality is one of rightness-as-appropriateness to the life world, rather than straightforward emulation of predefined, universally valid tastes. Amid the generalized legitimating of mainstream symbolic repertoires, there is a marked focus on constructing final value as consisting of what is 'right for the person'.

The two approaches are, of course, ways of conceptualizing the same mediated processes of evaluation of the life world and its improvement via consumption. However, they may appear incompatible. Various writers have criticized the implication that the reflexivity of persons under individualized conditions amounts to apparent freedom of action, and thus reproduces the liberal myth of the self-determining individual. This is equated with the replacing of traditional sources of social authority and structures of belonging with 'the biographical project of the reflexive self' (Wood and Skeggs 2004: 205). For these reasons, Wood and Skeggs are wary of reading the apparently déclassé freedom of choice depicted in the 'new ethical selves' of lifestyle television as a sign of individualization. For them, 'self-making in televised scenarios re-routes class and gender categories, rather than freeing up traditional structures as suggested by the individualization thesis' (207).

However, I would like to argue that the reconstructions of identity (including class identity), that are presented in makeovers are indissoluble from individualization. Yet in order to avoid the charge that reflexive lifestyle construction constitutes freedom from determination, it is vital to emphasize that individualization is socially shaped. Governmentality theory is useful here, as it stresses that the ability to choose is not an autonomous property of the subject. It is the result of institutional techniques that encourage actors to channel their agency in ways compatible with the rationalities of advanced liberal capitalism (Andrejevic 2005: 485). The dominant neo-liberal discourses in a range of social fields, including work, politics and consumption, guide citizens to pursue the forms of private self-interest consonant with marketization of social provision. Choice is an ideal not only championed in politics and business, but also operationalized. The behaviour of the putatively 'free subject' in the school, home or shopping mall is highly monitored so that its performances can be made calculable by institutions that administer the resources made available

(Dean 1999: 205–6). Techniques of expertise are, in turn, applied to such information to create persuasive discourses designed to enrol people into activities that suit the interests of state and business.

Of course, one of the key fields in which this takes place is that of marketing, with all of its psychological and communications techniques for 'forming connections between human passions, hopes, and anxieties, and very specific features of goods enmeshed in particular consumption practices' (Miller and Rose 1997: 2). The expansion of consumer markets is effected by cultural processes in which commodities are invested with meanings by those who sponsor them. As Andersen points out, it is a fundamental condition of commodity fetishism that 'a vast array of arbitrary meanings can be assigned to products at the convenience of marketers' (1995: 88). By definition, all consumption derived from commodity exchange with others is mediated by communications surrounding and facilitating exchange. However, beyond direct commodity promotion, the media of a society in which personal activity and, in particular, leisure, are increasingly imbricated with commodity consumption are also bound to carry broader messages about ordinary life which revolve around enculturated patterns of consumption itself. According to Hartley, the popular media and, in particular, TV – as that medium which most palpably provides images of how people behave – is an important source from which people draw notions of conduct for comparison and possible emulation (1999: 154). However, mixed in with the public affairs that address the audience member as citizen are the lifestyle choices that construct them as a knowledgeable consumer. Hence, 'the generalised addressee of TV is now a mixture of consumer and student' (156). Knowing about consumption is inseparable from knowing how to live. TV itself is a major resource of information about possible ways of living reflexively. John Ellis argues that the main feature of contemporary programming is that it captures and 'works through' the mass of available information about life. It takes the raw material of what happens in the world and processes it. 'Television attempts to define, tries out explanations, creates narratives, talks over, makes intelligible, tries to marginalise, harnesses speculation, tries to make fit and, very occasionally, anathematizes' (1999: 55). These dynamics, however, ensure a lack of overall closure, generating more and more information and interpretation (55–8).

I would now like to propose that the makeover is one channel of 'working though' that seizes upon how consumption apparently happens in the everyday, narrativizes it and theorizes its hows and whys. However, the key to understanding the peculiarities of the genre lie in the ways that the constructions of ordinary life it purveys incorporate the broader discourses of consumer culture at a particular stage in the development of capitalism.

Lifestyle has become something to be produced and constantly reproduced through resources supplied by the media, culture and leisure industries (Taylor 2002: 479–82). The move into so-called consumer society denotes a historical trend born of the problem of how to grow consumer markets in proportion with radically enhanced productive capacity. In short, a continual-growth economy cannot be sustained by simply producing, marketing and consuming more of the same, in the same old way. It relies on qualitative social and cultural shifts, especially with regard to the systemic 'production of consumption desires' (Woodward 2003: 410). With the diversification of products and media channels for promotion, marketing has grown in sophistication in order to find ways to differentiate goods symbolically through appeals to culture and lifestyle (Featherstone 1991: 86). The resulting socio-economic environment is one of niche markets in which the strategic problem of business is not only creating a greater range of products, but also communicating differentiated options to the right potential consumers, ones for whom a given product can be deemed suitable. This is the flipside of the problem for consumers, which is that of how to find the goods and services that are right for oneself from the massive array on offer.

The operationalization of lifestyle in marketing has become an important functional requirement in the niche market economy. In the words of Andrejevic, 'In an era of mass customization, niche marketing and agile, mobile markets, enterprise culture entails proliferation of information gathering strategies and increasingly fine-grained forms of monitoring and individualization' (2005: 485). Lifestyle modelling is superseding demographics and psychographics as the vanguard of consumer research (Vyncke 2002: 447). Advances in information processing now make it possible to profile consumer behaviour through multiple variables, resulting in lifestyle composites. These correlate data about people's attitudes, values, behaviours, social status, identity, provenance, credit history, consumer and media choices, etc., so as to generate powerful predictive models about goods and services that may be compatible with particular, and ever more particularized, kinds of people and lifestyle segments.

If the makeover is not itself a form of marketing communications, it partakes of the individualizing logic of niche markets. However, it does so from the consumer point-of-view, working out from the attitudes, behaviours, and values of the person and the demands of their situation, to calculate the most appropriate collocation of purchase decisions. The life styling processes depicted represent the subject 'doing the work' of the niche market society by taking on the role of an active consumer, someone who is intent on developing their literacies to the levels of sophistication required so as to make personal order from a multitude of options. In this regard, the makeover itself can be viewed as a technique of individualization – one that works through the problems of choice attendant upon reflexive life, and claims to solve, even transform, them by radical demonstration of ever-more individuated skills of fitting commodities into one's lifestyle successfully. This is in no way a matter of reflexivity constituting self-determination. Rather, the reflexivity portrayed and advocated is that of the person learning to apply the discourses of industry experts. It takes the form of monitoring oneself and changing oneself to economically productive ends. The makeover depends upon a perfectly ideological conceit. Individual satisfaction is celebrated but is never completely freed from context-defined calculative social interests. Transformations of appearance in the body, person or home are investments that rely upon being exchanged for the recognition of others in broader, collective, if unstable, economies of value (a more saleable house, a more attractive body...). Consumption is rendered not only economically, but also socially productive.

Conclusions

The new ethical selves of makeovers are not people freed from social structures in their apparent self-realization. However, theorizing individualization as a freeing up from traditional structures into an implied self-determination misses the possibility that the techniques through which it is effected perform a function of loosening ties to extant structures in order to bind people into ones representing current and changing systemic requirements of capitalism.

British cultural studies has a genetic concern with class-based culture. The culturalism of Hoggart and Williams was animated by a desire to legitimate working-class ways of life, conceived as sets of distinctive, shared and communally experienced elements. In Thompson's words: 'class happens when some men (sic), as a result of common experiences (inherited or shared), feel and articulate the identity of their interests as between themselves, and as against other men whose interests are different from (and usually opposed to) theirs' (1980: 8–9). However, such formulations have always been haunted by the possibility that other, 'industrial' forces that administer culture have the power to mediate and undo such solidarities. The lifespan of the discipline has seen radical economic reconstruction. The signal development has been the increased importance of working-class consumers to capitalism, alongside the continued development of consumer markets through product innovation. Consumerism itself revolves around the continual symbolic reconstruction of taste. The received habits that makeover morality enjoins us to transcend are the marks of a non-productive clinging to the old ways. There is no cultural imperative greater for contemporary capitalism than getting people to refashion their lives, whatever their social identities.

As long as uneven distribution of resources creates economic classes, differences in the ways classes appropriate goods and services, and are seen to do so by others, are inevitable. According to John Frow, 'The primary business of culture is distinction, the stratification of tastes in such a way as to construct and reinforce differentiations of social status which correspond, *in historically variable and often highly mediated ways,* to achieved or aspired-to class position' (1995: 85, his italics). However, the historical variability and mediation of taste cultures that Frow emphasizes is key. He goes on to argue that in advanced capitalist societies the cultural system is no longer organized in strict hierarchies, in the same way as in highly stratified societies, where culture is closely tied to class structure (85). This is not to deny material inequality or the existence of class as an economic category. However, the simple quantity of options forces people to live reflexively (Chaney 1996: 52). The fact that they are increasingly free to elect how they live within the constraints of available resources is precisely what leads to reconstructions of class and other social identities traditionally associated with particular ways of life. So it is that received ways of life become interwoven with and fragmented by lifestyle choice (Chaney 1996: 93).

It is possible to concur with McRobbie, Wood and Skeggs that makeovers reconstruct or re-route class and gender. However, in so doing they do not articulate anything like the traditional forms of class-consciousness derived from stable vocation and attendant patterns of cultural consumption. Rather, they serve to undo it by teaching that, whatever one's social identity may be, one can remake oneself in the sphere of consumption. Makeovers enjoin people to use their capacity to choose to become individuals whose route to the good life is to be found in ever-more individuated consumption in the all-inclusive, culturally democratic sphere of consumer markets. The normative expectation – purveyed by consumer culture media in general – is that by aligning consumption with characteristics of the self you can find those things that are right for you. While there is a long tradition of the guidance of taste, the makeover reifies personal lifestyle to the extent that it becomes the moral framework for an individualised vision of wellbeing. The aspirational agent is putatively capable of such a level of self-transformation that they can determine and realise any value that can be shown to be germane to their specific life. Such value is revealed to be a context-defined state of rightness-to-self, more than compliance with transcendent standards. Of course, this rightness involves channelling one's agency towards consumption consistent with what is deemed socially acceptable and productive in one's situation. That is how self-realization is constituted by makeover experts, and such shaping of reflexivity is the sleight of hand of any discourse of individualization. However, the particular ideological force of personal transformation in the makeover is precisely one in which consumer choice becomes equated with self-realization, not the realization or pursuit of corporate identity, collective interests or action towards them. With such ample sources of guidance at hand these days, it appears so much easier to make over oneself, than to make over society.

Chapter Twelve

EXTREME MAKEOVER: HOME EDITION

An American
Fairy Tale

Gareth Palmer

It's a fairy tale. It's a guaranteed happy ending (Forman 2005).

ABC's *Extreme Makeover: Home Edition* (hereafter *EMHE*) was one of the top ten programmes of the 2004/05 season in America and winner of the 2005 EMMY for Outstanding Reality TV Programme. *EMHE* tells a fascinating story about modern-day America where the return of a strong right-wing ideology privileges the traditional family and the interests of business, yet also affords a glimpse of the crises affecting ordinary Americans. In the model of community proposed by the programme, the state has no role to play: in its place are people coming together out of fellow-feeling for their neighbours. But the repair work is so extreme it throws into relief the mundane quality of most American homes. In promoting such a perspective both in the programme and through its various affiliated enterprises with Sears etc., ABC are championing an America which resonates with its mythical past but which is utterly un-representative of family life for most Americans. The programme is, in short, a fairy tale where magic is represented by selfless communities, free goods, labour, and dreams coming true.

I will proceed by considering how the following elements knit together to produce this modern portrait of American life. The centrality of the *family* is the first and primary theme in what follows. Which families have been chosen and why? What do they represent? I then consider the ways in which the programme helps construct the *community* as a natural mechanism founded not on self-interest but on the simple concept of neighbourliness. I then look at how the state has almost completely retreated, and how its work has been replaced by a *magical market* where items such as labour have no price. In the final section I consider the ways in which the programme represents another dimension in the changing role and function of *television*. Rather than being an apparatus that records a world external to it, television is now an increasingly active agent in changing it. The very fact that well over 50,000 people per series have written in to be on the programme is testimony to the fact that, as far as many people are concerned, television can and perhaps even should change their lives. I conclude by considering the programme in the context of the American economy.

The Family

> Representations have become a critical battleground in the conflicts
> over family and family values leading to the spectacularization of the
> family as the platform on which society's profound debates about
> sexual and personal morality are performed (Chambers 2001: 176).

EMHE starts every week with a sequence in which the assorted designers who will lead the re-design of the house are situated in a van watching the targeted family's videotape. Team Leader Ty Pennington gives the background to this family and the rest of this sequence involves reaction shots of all involved. What is remarkable about this sequence, at least for this British viewer, is that these video-diary sequences sent in by the family are all extraordinarily revealing about the state of America.

In many cases the desperation of families is a direct result of the fact that agencies of the state have abandoned them. For example, in one case a family had to watch their son die because ambulances and police refused to go into their neighbourhood for fear of their lives. In another video we see a family whose son is dying because he is ineligible for medical aid. In yet another typical episode, an Iraq War veteran has materials provided for him, as the state does not support veterans very generously. Week after week we see first hand video testimony that the state is in retreat and only those lucky enough to have many friends, family and neighbours are able to survive. But it is those who have slipped below ordinary levels of subsistence that form the centrepieces of *EMHE*. As Frances Bonner writes when describing 'ordinary' television: 'When... it has to deal with death... and given its fascination with medical matters and with hard luck stories (tragedies) it must do this with some regularity – placing it within a 'plucky' family is the principal way to do things' (Bonner 2003: 111).

After watching their tape for a few moments the crew arrive, and the family to be chosen is woken very early in the morning, on the doorstep of their home. This magical moment is only the first of many such other-worldly touches in the narrative. After meeting the team and crying tears of gratitude, the family is then whisked away for a week-long holiday while crew, enlisted community, and contractors go about the business of changing their home.

What follows is a monumental effort to effect the transformation. But why has all this energy been devoted to making the home so central? In the last ten years, makeover shows have become a mainspring of TV schedules in Britain and America. In each case a person with limited resources is assisted into a new look and given the confidence he or she needs to progress. However, at the centre of these 'reveals' is the family. In examples ranging from *This Old House* to *The Swan* it is the family that has inspired the change and the family who are focused on in their reaction to it. In this way the home is remade as a machine for keeping families together, the place to retreat to. It need hardly be said that such an approach brings to mind long and powerful myths about the centrality of the family. Anthony Giddens describes the family as, 'The site for the democratisation of intimate relationships, the family becomes a major platform on which debates about moralities and ethics gets staged' (Giddens 1999: 165).

The makeover show turns individuals into family members, foregrounds the family and makes it a part of the wider community. It is hard to imagine a clearer message about the centrality of the home and the importance of keeping the family together come what may. But, as Young has pointed out, 'The family can of course teach adherence to the values of the community but the presence of a strong family does not magically entail community' (Young 1999: 155).

It might be argued that there are two families at work in *EMHE* – the subject of the makeover and the extended family of the design team. It is after all this family that we get to know every week through their work and their relationships with one another. It is they who represent a modern family with no fixed relationships and no permanent 'home' they can call their own. We might also note that the five men exhibit some of the camp characteristics that are now a trademark of the genre: only in this sense can the hint of homosexuality be tolerated, in a space marked-off from ordinary life. In a sense, the *EMHE* team represent the fluid upwardly mobile petit bourgeoisie against the time-worn virtues of the proletariat. This divide between the classes ensures that the working class are always receptive and thankful for the 'good taste' bestowed upon them by the middle class. But while it is the role of the working class to be properly grateful, the designers are all seen to be humbled by their experience, which extends beyond the show and is maintained through letters and notes pinned to a message board. The coming together of these two family groupings is about 'learning' – a theme that dominates so much American television. While the working class learn taste, the petit bourgeoisie learn about 'real people' (i.e. the sort of people they would not normally ever encounter in their lives as designers for the rich and famous). This learning is a means of bringing groups together, the wider theme that animates the series and which keys it into the classic picture of an America constituted of families connected to communities making one nation (Morley and Robins 1995: 109).

At the end of the show the ramshackle house, held together by the depth of the bonds between the family members, is replaced by a magnificent home. Crucial here is the show's reveal which takes place after a bus is moved aside to show the transformed home. (It has even inspired the catchphrase 'Bus Driver. Move that Bus!') As Charlotte Brunsden has written, 'It is the reaction, not the action, that matters' (Brunsden 2001: 35).

As we are lead through the magically transformed home at the same time as the family, we too can be awestruck by the changes wrought by the designers and of course the wider community. In one sense, we marvel at the high quality of the work achieved but perhaps more significant is the fact that we are reminded that this transformation is also a reward – it is because people have held the family together in very difficult situations that they deserve this home. In clips and segments that remind us of the past, we are moved to see that these people have got what they deserve. The home is an extension of the love that the family hold for one another. By undergoing this transformation as a reward for their dedication to the family, the individuals go from being objects of our pity to ones of our envy.

It seems almost churlish to mention it in the presence of so much joy, but this portrait of a family transformed is so unrealistic it might even be counter-productive. This is a classic example of what Chambers calls 'the massive discrepancy between complex lived experiences of human relationships and those popular discourses that invent and promote an imaginary nuclear familiarism' (Chambers 2004: 175). But such discrepancies are hidden in the magic of transformation.

Community

'A better community – get involved and help – click here' (ABC website).

Makeover programmes are the most overt sign of the ways television perceives itself to be engaged in a project of advising ordinary viewers about their transformation into happier, more satisfied, up-to-date versions of their selves (Bonner 2002: 136).

The community plays a central role in *EMHE*. It is made clear throughout the programme and in all accompanying materials that it is the community that are responsible for making the whole thing come together. While it may be designers who provide the creative impetus, it is the community that are seen doing all the unglamorous heavy work. Unlike the virtual shadow-communities inspired to 'call the cops' in response to televised police appeals which dissolve once their contribution is made, *EMHE* features real communities showing us all how to work together.

To begin with, the community has often been the sponsor of the families who are featured. As Forman has said: 'Most of the families we end up doing are nominations. The kind of families we're looking for don't say "Gee, I need help". They are quietly trying to solve their problems themselves and it's a neighbour or co-worker who submits an application on their behalf' (Forman 2005).

We see the community, shortly after the programme begins, giving testimony to the deserving family, then later throughout the show at work in various jobs. They play small but significant roles in the drama as the glue in the cracks of the community holding everything together. And yet they are also there in the reveal. They 'star' here because of what they have done to bring about these changes. Whether as contractors, friends, tradesmen or simply labourers, all have a role to play and are defined not so much as individuals but as part of a greater whole. No individual pulls focus: it is always about the larger community. But what actually constitutes this community?

It is important to see the entire series in context as a trigger for activating a wide variety of communities. For example, the local press are often keen to highlight the series if a local family is involved. In Salt Lake City we learn of the '1,500 workers and volunteers working 24 hours a day to build a bigger home for the Johnson family.' In the *Boston Globe* we read about how residents had 'been routing for more than a year for a family to be picked up by the show.' Once they had been selected, the community were all too keen to get involved.

Two allied supporters of this community effort are local businesses and the Church. John McMurria has pointed out how Sears has benefited from the programme (McMurria 2005). But plenty of other local services are represented in *EMHE*, not as profit-led businesses but as benevolent organizations. The value of PR here can be enormous as big cardboard cheques are presented to tearful local residents. As one business said of a veteran – 'He has such a sweet and humble spirit and we wanted to thank him for the way he loves for his country and his family.'

It is important also to note that American Christian groups have been generous in praising the show. As Evangelical journalist Holly Vincente Robaina wrote, 'It's a rare phenomenon. Believers of every age, ethnicity and denomination are embracing the primetime television show ABC's *Extreme Makeover: Home Edition*' (Robaina 2005).

Executive producer Tom Forman was specifically asked whether any plan was made to 'include elements that would connect specifically with Christian values.' Forman responded that the show appealed because 'good things happen to good people. That's possibly why it resonates with the Christian community and all of our viewers' (Forman, ABC interview).

Church leaders are quoted by the local press, such as Mr A. Wigston in the *Cass County Democrat of Missouri*. 'It was really neat to see God working through the hearts of the designers for people with disabilities.' Some other churches have set out on 'copy-cat' schemes in which members decorate or attempt mini-makeovers of their own in just the way that producer Forman had hoped they would. Not only does this imitative practice privilege the role of the Church in the community, but the reporting and celebration of this role presents a clear ideological message on the centrality of helping heterosexual families. But is this at the expense of other communities?

These timeless myths of the American 'heartland', featuring the happy smiling community working for nothing but love, bring to mind classic American TV fictions such as *Little House on the Prairie* and *The Waltons*.

These idealized versions of perfect family life may be instructive about nostalgia in the 1970s and 1980s, and for settled family life in a time of great upheaval. But of course these fictions were located in the past when such a myth may have been feasible. But what are we to make of *EMHE*'s portrait of American life, which suggests such ideals are here with us now?

It is of course possible to take a different view of the community. A few questions might be worth asking here: what other possible communities may be excluded here? To what extent are alternative family groupings given time and attention? Or perhaps a more useful question might concern the location of this community. In almost every edition of the show, the house to be modified is placed centre screen without any sort of context. What are the neighbour's houses like? What else is on the street? The framing of the house in this way also helps us to consider the home as somehow separate from others, but it excludes any arguments we might make concerning the collapse of American communities. What if we were to see other broken-down homes? The danger here might be that we could make wider arguments about poverty and the role played by corporate America as it seeks to maximize profit without any thought for communities. I think here of Flint, Michigan in Michael Moore's *Roger and Me* where the collapse of the community after the departure of Chrysler is denoted in showing hundreds of boarded-up homes. But there are no shortage of communities who have borne the brunt of America's economic boom and bust. For example, on Public Housing, the Bush administration has twice proposed the elimination of the HOPE VI programme, which provided for the revitalization of more than 20,000 severely distressed public units as well as the demolition of another 63,000 severely distressed units (Alliance for Healthy Homes).

To try and deal with change on this scale would perhaps be a makeover too far. Furthermore, according to the embedded logic of the industry, such a programme would not be 'good television'. As the old maxim goes 'The death of millions is just a statistic: the death of one is a tragedy.'

But to return to the programme as it currently stands: is it small-minded to think of the after-show effect? Is it just possible that, after the cameras have gone, the community become jealous of the fact that their neighbour's house now towers above them all? Will the idealized family always be so well thought of by other members of the community? One wonders how the community will fare after one of its members has been both symbolically and financially elevated.

The Magical Market

What I want to do in this section is analyse how the market is disguised as part of the magical narrative of *EMHE*. One of the most unusual factors about the programme for British viewers is the complete absence of cost. In contrast to many UK makeover shows, costs are never mentioned in *EMHE*. Why is this? The instinctual answer has to be that costs have no place in a fairy tale. Do we know where the Prince bought the glass slippers? Of course not – these are crass questions. It is our role simply to be enchanted by the transformations wrought. But, at the risk of breaking the spell, there are various economic elements that I think merit discussion, for they speak to the real and entirely non-magical base of the programme.

In the first place, we might consider the costs of labour. What would it cost to hire such designers or to employ upwards of 150 people for 24 hours a day, seven days a week? Secondly, we might look at the cost of the furnishings, the materials and the many other artful purchases that go into the ideal home. It is only at the end of the show that we have any sort of opportunity to calculate the cost of this transformation, but by then we are too emotionally involved to make such calculations. The point is that all of these costs are hidden in the service of repairing families. But not mentioning costs makes these repairs appear free or even magical. As most communities know, the economic is determining and not at all magical. The fact is that there are many who profit enormously from the show.

While it is clearly the case that one family will benefit from the makeover, the Public Relations benefits to others involved are extraordinary. The most obvious recipient of good PR is the Sears corporation. The programme's website makes it clear that the company is a major partner in the production of the show. It is worth noting that Sears also sponsor *EMHE* host Ty Pennington. Pennington's 'can-do' attitude represents something that Sears wants – as long as the 'can-do' he recommends is connected to Sears products. As PR, Pennington legitimates Sears as a caring company through his leadership of such obvious good works.

But Sears is only the most high profile of sponsors. Every week we hear of many other local organizations that have devoted their goods and services to the families in need. At this point we are encouraged to think of local businesses not as profit driven but as charitable organizations. The PR benefit of this publicity is enhanced when favourable coverage appears in the local papers about the *EMHE* projects in their town. This would be a good time for local businesses to place adverts reminding consumers of their modest role in the transformation.

Thirdly, and perhaps most obviously, the benefits to ABC will be very considerable. Firstly, there are the benefits in revenue that accrue to shows that are doing well. This factor is particularly important when competition from other stations and other media is more intensive than ever before. During the show the families often thank ABC while the presenters and others also make subtle mention of how the programme has only been possible through the good offices of the station. Again, this will represent an invaluable opportunity for the station to define itself as family-driven in contrast to its more ruthless rivals CBS, Fox and NBC. This benefit sometimes informs the company's well-advertised outreach programmes and also helps to inspire other shows. The praise heaped on the programme by churches and other religious groups helps ABC reposition itself in the family market. The Disney channel owns the station, whose sponsorship of gay-friendly corporate policies and broadcast of gay-themed sitcoms such as *Ellen* has resulted in criticism from Christian groups. *EMHE* redefines ABC as a wholesome family station.

Finally, is it not also the case that the programme is of enormous benefit to the eight designers who appear on the show? The 'good works' they do here will drive business to their companies as well as raise their price in the celebrity market as guest speakers, seminar leaders etc.

But what is crucial to all of this is that the market appears to be driven not by the hunt for profit but by the simple desire to do 'good works'. In this way, capitalism is sold to audiences as a warm and responsive mechanism reacting to community needs rather than a system for maximizing profits. It is not money that pulls people together, but a sort of magic.

But might it be possible to read the lavish life styling of these homes in another way? Might we also look at this extravagance as masking a sort of crisis? Barthes would describe such lavish furnishings as a 'spectacle of excess', behind the exuberance of which we can detect some deeper crisis (Barthes 1988). Can we read the excesses of *EMHE* as a frantic attempt to disguise the actual breakdown of families (caused in no small part by the logic of capitalism) with an over-abundance of consumer goods?

One useful historical antecedent to *EMHE* is the 'Ideal Home Exhibition'. These perfect platforms for family styling first arrived in the 1950s. Such extravaganzas were – and still are – hosted in giant pavilions offering families the chance to see how they ought to be living (according to absent remote designers). It is interesting to note that for 45 years the event has been sponsored by *The Daily Mail* – the most right wing of all UK newspapers and one that makes the most powerful declarations in the name of the traditional family. My point is simply that the ideological work of keeping families and communities together takes place in a number of spheres and national contexts and that consumption is perhaps more to the fore than ever before. It is only the excesses of *EMHE* that make it exceptional – desperate, even.

Television That Works

'An ethics of care as presented in lifestyle programmes is primarily about care and responsibility... good and bad ways to live their lives' (Hill 2005: 184).

EMHE is part of a growing number of television programmes that are not simply recording or reflecting on society but becoming active elements, working practically and ideologically to change the world. As Jack Bratich points out in this volume, 'Reality TV may be less about representing reality than intervening in it, less mediating and more involving.'

In one sense, television has always done this. Magical solutions to practical problems for everyday people have been the staple of quiz and games shows for decades. But the past twenty years have seen a distinct rise in the number of programmes that focus on intervening in the lives of the public. In a curious historical quirk, commercial television is engaging with the public in a way that PBS can no longer afford to do. But commercial interests inspire all these interventions. *Wife Swap*, *Big Brother* and *Temptation Island* are not there to help the public (despite the rhetoric) but to offer mutual exploitation opportunities. They work, however, and this fact is proved night after night in reality TV shows, makeover shows, talk shows, cosmetic surgery shows, and many other programmes made at the behest of commercial institutions. Like any other product maker, the apparatus of ABC has a vested interest in producing 'good' (i.e. repeatable) results. Furthermore, if it does this in a way which makes it look socially responsible, then it gets a double-whammy. Not only does this help to keep the profile of the medium high but it also foregrounds television as a site for the validation of the person. To be on television is now one of the highest honours that can be accorded someone.

There is another significant point underscoring and helping to guarantee the effects of *EMHE* and others in the lifestyle genre: and it is in the craft of performance. *EMHE* is a very polished production that pulls together emotionally moving performances with the use of music, lighting and photography. Not only does the styling of the show borrow creatively from drama, it also emphasizes a theatrical transformation that will impress children – the next generation whose devotion to the medium all stations need to cherish. It is also interesting to note that many of the designers have experience in drama. Of the eight designers in the 2004/5 season, four have stage or screen credits in theatre or television – i.e. they know how to emote on screen. The rest all have experience on makeover shows of one kind or another that make them perfectly primed for *EMHE*'s excesses. This is not suggesting anything as crude as engineering but, given their histories, it is certainly significant. Those on screen know how to enhance their performances of concern. Television works here because the effects on all the participants are plain to see – crying, hugging, laughing, etc.

It would be comforting to think that our own responses to the transformations, led by the families and designers, heralded some sort of emotional literacy, but even if we try to gain comfort from this we cannot escape the fact that this is all wrought for commercial profit (Littler 2002: 20). It is sad to reflect upon, but the radical changes to one family's life that we see in *EMHE* would simply not happen if it were not for television. Despite the powerful and manipulative devices that bring forth our involvement, at base the programme is a device for selling audiences to advertisers. It is not an engine for social change.

Television works here in four ways – as a mechanism for information and entertainment, as a space for validation and legitimating, as an apparatus that can effect transformations and, last but by no means least, as a way of embedding consumer goods in our lives. More than ever – symbolically, economically and commercially – 'television works.'

Conclusion

Commercial culture does not manufacture ideology, it relays and reproduces and processes and packages and focuses ideology that is constantly arising set forth both from social elites and from active social groups and movements throughout the society (Gitlin 1994: 518).

We have seen that *EMHE* produces a vision of America that has powerful emotional resonances. Its view of the world articulates connections with families, the Christian right and the neo-conservative policies of the Bush era. Yet the programme also provides gaps and fissures through which we can see massive cracks appearing in the American Dream. Although *EMHE* might seem like an unadulterated paean of praise to Capitalism, it fails to completely convince because of what it reveals as the inspirations to the makeover: things have got to be so bad because of the retreat of the state, that radical, even magical, consumer surgery is necessary.

Any acquaintance with government sources, such as the Census Bureau, provides plentiful evidence that America is a rich country that is systematically neglecting its poor. For the past five years all indexes indicate that poverty is rising year-on-year. According to the 2004 Census, 35.9 million people live below the poverty line in America. Furthermore, programmes to assist the poor such as 'America's Second Harvest' record that, since 1997, 2 million more people have turned to them, making a total of 23.3 million people requesting emergency food. We might, for example, compare the *EMHE* children whose tear-soaked faces of joy at the makeover contrast with the 33 per cent of children whose parents cannot secure full-time year-round employment (Toppo 2005). It is against these harsh economic facts that we ought to understand the work that ABC does to promote the family.

The fact is that in modern-day America many families and communities have been wrecked by policies that force them to uproot and look for work elsewhere. While the statistics attest to the breakdown of the family unit, ABC is doing the massive ideological labour of shoring it up. In the face of this breakdown *EMHE* deploys its excesses. The revamped houses look like sets because they are there to provide ideal templates for the performance of family roles.

As capitalism continues to deepen divisions between rich and poor, ABC offers the cold comfort of the *EMHE* fairy tale, the belief that if the family holds together despite everything that can be thrown against it, then the reward will eventually come.

Hope may be all they have.

Chapter Thirteen

'NOW I AM READY TO TELL HOW BODIES ARE CHANGED INTO DIFFERENT BODIES...'

Ovid, The Metamorphoses

Kathryn Fraser

In February 1936, *Mademoiselle* magazine featured an article (not insignificantly, titled 'Cinderella') detailing the first makeover as we now know it of an 'average' reader – Barbara Phillips – who had written in for advice as to how to 'make the most of herself'. Ms Phillips entreated the editors with a letter describing herself as 'homely as a hedgehog', asking '[Do you] know someone who could tell me how to do my hair, powder my nose, cultivate sex appeal...?' (1936: 56). Still later, 'I am homely, too skinny and know none of the feminine wiles that my more attractive sisters seem to have been endowed by nature with [sic]... I don't want to become a frigid old maid... I want to be good-looking, well dressed and have at least a chance of giving Kit Cornell [a popular stage actress of the time] a run for her money' (ibid.). An 'inventory' is then taken, reducing Ms Phillips to a series of 'parts' to be overhauled: 'And now the several sections of Barbara Phillips were ready for the assembly line' (60). Through a series of cosmetic and sartorial interventions, Ms Phillips is thus instructed in the proper use of make-up and clothing in order to make the most of her 'good' features and 'minimize' those deemed 'bad'. The end result is a glamorous photo spread and an editorial by the stylist describing each of the techniques used in the transformation of his subject. In this we can see the establishment of the main themes informing the Cinderella-cum-makeover narrative in all of its incarnations: 1) the presentation of the self as a 'problem' in need of external expertise ('Do you know someone...?'); 2) the idea that transformation will improve a person's life and life chances ('I wanted to be an actress'); 3) the democratization of beauty: everyone has the ability to transcend their appearance ('It followed naturally that if Barbara Phillips could be transformed, so could anyone' [56]); 4) the aim being to become more attractive to the opposite sex – heteronormativity – (she doesn't want to become a 'frigid old maid'); 5) consumption/self-commodification (she learns how to dress and make herself up); 6) passing/class-transcendence and celebrity emulation or identification (she wants to 'give Kit Cornell a run for her money'); 7) that the self is malleable, plastic.

All of these themes signify each other and speak to the emergence of a particular brand of femininity – one forged through consumerism. In fact, the 'tremendous response' to *Mademoiselle*'s 'first Cinderella feature' was such that it became a regular series in the magazine, soon copied by other women's magazines, and now exploding into every arena of modern life. Turn on the television and you will undoubtedly come across a makeover of some sort. On various talk shows, women are regularly paraded in front of approving audiences after having been transmogrified by a team of 'specialists' and instructed in techniques of femininity and taste. The Learning Channel even has an entire series devoted to cosmetic and sartorial transformations called *A Makeover Story*. Magazines no longer simply take readers from a dull 'before' to a glamorized 'after'; now the makeover is applied to everything from recipes ('Comfort Food Makeovers', *Eating Light*, winter 2001) and financial planning ('Do you Need a Money Makeover?', *O: The Oprah Magazine*, February 2001) to home decor (*Before and After*, *Trading Spaces* and, of course, *Extreme Makeover: Home Edition*). Evidently, the makeover is great entertainment. In fact, the makeover has become so ubiquitous that it has been incorporated into our everyday lexicon, so much so that (as opposed to when I first started writing about the topic 12 years ago) my computer's spellchecker doesn't even identify it as an unknown word!

However, perhaps the most significant development in the makeover-as-entertainment has been the introduction of plastic surgery – a branch of medicine originally intended to treat pathology, but which, in this instance, produces it. This paradox underscores the already manifest contradictions of the makeover's aforementioned themes: self-love and/or acceptance can only be achieved at the expense of self-loathing, where the feminine self is always deficient and in need of intervention. Consequently, in order to make sense of television programmes devoted to surgical transformations like *Extreme Makeover*, I believe it is useful to first delineate the taxonomy of its modern antecedents. In this chapter, then, I will trace the consumerist origins of the cosmetic makeover and its relationship to identity in order to point up its thematic paradoxes and the way in which it informs identities (particularly 'feminine' ones) in a culture increasingly negotiated through the possibilities of transformation. I will conclude by asking 'what happens *after* the "after"?' This is the prohibited question of all makeover narratives and particularly *Extreme Makeover*'s really only penultimate conclusion of 'Happily Ever After'.

Consumerism and Self-Commodification

Prior to the makeover's familiar appearance, it was at least already implicit in the new era of advertising in the 1920s made possible by the proliferation of cosmetics in the marketplace and a growing emphasis on personal appearance. In western culture, which is increasingly inclined toward spectatorship and display, cosmetics made possible the assertion of new selves and identities for women now solidly engaged in public activities. Earlier fears about the hazards of cosmetics (legitimated by the centuries-old practice of using arsenic, white lead and other toxic 'beautifying' enamels), and anxieties about the 'painted woman' were assuaged by the regulation of the cosmetics industry and cosmetics' new-found respectability among middle-class women flocking to New York and Paris-based beauty salons. Up until this point, cosmetics had been limited to ointments and salves, medicinal creams and soaps purchased with health and hygiene in mind, not the adornment of the physical self. At this stage, however, as Kathy Peiss (1998: 142) points out, 'cosmetic ads endlessly reminded women that they were on display, especially conspicuous in a world peopled by spectators and voyeurs.' Advertisements thus played upon women's new-found self-consciousness (or social selves) by appealing to 'negative feelings such as shame, envy, and fears about social acceptability' (Zuckerman 1998: 173). Earlier views of cosmetics as vanity or artifice thus gave way to cosmetics as a route to self-confidence and control.

As the industry segmented into diverse product lines, and a multitude of beauty aids such as rouge, mascara, eyeliner and lipstick appeared, advertising presented cosmetics as a means not only to a confident public self, but as a way for a woman to 'remake herself and her life chances' (Peiss 1998: 144). The equation of cosmetics use and personal transformation with improved social mobility is apparent in an ad for Hagan's Magnolia Balm – a skin bleach marketed to white women since the late nineteenth century. In one (albeit insidious) ad employing the 'before and after' trajectory, not only has the woman using the balm undergone a transformation of appearance, but seemingly of racial identity as well. Her previous, stereotypical 'black' features and wiry hair are all seemingly 'reversed' by the product, and the abjured image of otherness remade into that of a conventional white 'lady'.

The trend of appealing to the possibility of changing identities gained momentum throughout the Depression and into the 1940s and 1950s even while critics 'stressed the unrealistic hopes the ads created, promising women physical transformations' that were obviously quite impossible in reality. Meanwhile, as advertisers set out to change the way women viewed their external appearance, 'they drew on new perceptions of the inner self beholden to psychology and psychiatry' (Peiss 1998: 155) not to mention the notion that male desire was the key to female subjectivity. Thus, in the 1920s, sex became a marketing tool – the 'sexual sell' – with cosmetics positioned as a means by which to attract and then keep a man. Earlier anxieties about perceived female defects – vanity, deceit and desire – thus soon came to be seen as normal constituents in the delineation of the average female mind and women's presumed singular goal of becoming attractive to men. Though male desire would remain a constant driving force behind women's magazines and advertisements from the 1920s onwards, things would change somewhat in the 1960s when women's magazines themselves underwent a transformation of significant proportions. More and more beholden to the advertising dollar, and taking into consideration the growing popularity of what was often pejoratively termed 'Women's Lib', magazines had to reposition themselves to reflect changes in women's realities. Increasingly identified with activities outside the home, women were also interacting more with other women. So while advertising promoted cosmetics as a means to winning and keeping a man, as a cultural practice, however, using make-up, or making oneself over, was often more indicative of women's relationships to each other as opposed to their relationships with men. Demographic studies further revealed that many readers were single and in pursuit of a career (Craik 1994; Zuckerman 1998; Ballaster et al. 1991), and magazines raced to acknowledge this change. In light of any anxieties that might have been created as a consequence of women gaining more power in the social realm and thereby becoming more 'masculine', cosmetics use would come to serve as the ultimate signifiers of women's still-strong ties to femininity, not to mention the capacity of all women to achieve beauty.

This apparent democratization of beauty, then, obviously has much to do with the increasing role played by cosmetics. Cosmetics advertising had been a staple of women's magazines since the 1920s, but might be seen to have reached its zenith today, if only due to the substantially greater number of products and lines on the market. From the 1920s to the 1950s the most frequent cosmetics advertised were face powder and 'beauty bars' often endorsed by emerging young movie stars, and heralded as rendering beauty achievable by all. Indeed, the transformative abilities of cosmetics would seem to speak to all women, regardless of size, class or even race. As Kathy Peiss (1990: 148), puts it:

> By making the complexion, rather than the bone structure or physical
> features, more central to popular definitions of beauty, [the cosmetics
> industry] popularised the democratic idea that beauty could be
> achieved by all women if they used the correct products and treatment.

An ad for Max Factor 'Pan-Cake Make-Up' taken from *Cosmopolitan*, April 1943, reads 'Create flattering new Beauty... in a few seconds. What a thrill the first time you try Pan-Cake Make-Up and find that you can actually create a new complexion, lovely in colour, smooth and flawless... in just a few seconds.' The direct address to 'you', which has proven so effective that it has become a magazine and advertising mainstay, is a further illustration of the democratization process, and may be seen to serve as a subjectivizing *and* an objectifying function where consumer and commodity seem to collapse into one. What takes place is a sort of inversion between subject and object, where the object or commodity becomes linked with the potential consumer or subject almost to the point of inextricability. Robert Goldman (1992: 121) argues that such a process means that women are encouraged 'not merely to adorn themselves with commodities, but also to perceive themselves as objectified surfaces.' In other words, magazines position the reader as a sort of 'tabula rasa' to be determined and defined by the products they display, and even by the magazines themselves, as commodities.

In the heady new era that legitimated cosmetic use, the makeover was as much an instruction in making up as it was a device to sell products and, in turn, the magazine. In virtually every makeover in the years to follow, we are presented with a photograph of the person to be transformed. Each is barefaced, and sports what can be construed as a natural look. We are then taken through the various stages which culminate in a presumably improved new look – a look which reflects the fashion, coiffures and make-up techniques of the time. Before her makeover, one *Mademoiselle* candidate is quoted as saying: 'I want <u>my</u> hair back' (August 1980), the assumption being that its transformation will return to her an *authentic* aspect of herself. After her makeover, and somewhat contradictorily, she goes on to announce that not only has her 'look' been changed, but that her very self has been transformed: 'I'm a new person.' The newness of self and the expression of delight in having discovered it is a declaration that would become the hallmark of the makeover's claim to fame. As much about promoting the products (which figure prominently in the accompanying copy), makeovers promised new identities, new configurations of self and, in them, the promise of a better future: as one made-over woman happily declares, 'I'm not holding on to a fantasy anymore!' Now she has presumably become it. In this way, the makeover paradoxically suggests that not only can you discover your 'true' or authentic self, but a whole new one entirely, illustrated also by the frequent proclamation, 'I feel like a movie star' (a point I will return to later).

What becomes immediately apparent in these narratives is the problematic nature or instability (not to mention reflexivity) of (unmediated) feminine identity. The makeover ethos promises to turn woman into a subject of consumerism, a position that ironically requires she first become an object for consumption. Female spectators are thus lured to images of other women in the throes of transformation (whether it be the ads on the pages of magazines, films like *Pretty Woman*, or television programmes like *Extreme Makeover* or *What Not to Wear*), on the one hand, by the possibilities of identification or sameness and, on the other, by occupying the position of what John Berger famously describes as 'the surveyor'. A circuit of desire is therefore posited in response to the problem of feminine identity or selfhood. By becoming objects of desire, women can be the paradoxical subjects of desire – *if* they desire to be desired. Women's subjective experience as objects of exchange informs their identity as realized (and realizable) through men and has in part created what we might call the 'problem of female subjectivity'. This is not simply a discursive formulation, but a very real, historical phenomenon. Women have rarely been addressed or considered outside of their so-called contingent identities. Their existence has been relegated to the margins of society, with their subjectivity positioned as a negation (as 'not men', though they are forged and constituted by the same structures that allow men to come into social existence). The problem of female subjectivity, of women's identity, has been addressed by psychoanalysis with Freud's possibly apocryphal articulation, 'What does woman want?' The coterminous emergence of consumerism has proffered an answer: to consume, and so be consumed, endlessly. In this formulation, desiring to be desired emerges in response to an array of commodities, which – in both Freudian and Marxist terms – promise to fetishistically complete the woman.

The relationship between feminine subjectivity and commodity consumption has been theorized seemingly endlessly, but Mary Ann Doane (1989: 31) has perhaps summarized this relationship most succinctly:

> Commodification presupposes that acutely self-conscious relation to
> the body, which is attributed to femininity. The effective operation
> of the commodity system requires the breakdown of the body into
> parts – nails, hair, skin, breath – each one of which can constantly be
> improved through the purchase of a commodity.

Though of course all identities are subject to commodification in the late twentieth and twenty-first centuries, for women the relationship is more intimate. For instance, feminine identity or subjectivity can be likened to the commodity, not only in structural terms, but also in terms of appearance. Indeed, it is the commodity's appearance on display amidst other commodities that endows it with value, or desirability, just as it is women's appearance and competition amongst other women that determines their currency. If we take up this argument that defines woman as a commodity under patriarchal capitalism, and if we consider this in relation to the solicitation of woman as a consumer, then it is easy to see how the makeover is also and equally an invitation to self-commodification. In this way, the makeover promises to invest woman with the authority or identity of the consumer at the same time as it reinscribes her status as the consumed.

Identification: How the Makeover Works

The success of the makeover's encouragement of self-commodification relies on the viewer/reader's investment in the fantasy of the 'after' prefigured by identification with the unsatisfactory image – we might say 'sameness' – of the 'before'. That is, the woman must be able to interject the image of the woman on the page (or on the screen) and then reconfigure that same image substituting herself as the object of transformation. This is to say that the woman must be able to imagine herself in both images, as simultaneously the subject *and* the object of transformation. Such dialectic can be understood as determining women's narcissistic relation to consumerism: commodity acquisition, which usually distances subject from object, is here conflated. The woman, it seems, is incapable of separating herself from the commodity she buys. As Mary Ann Doane (1987: 32) has determined, consumerism depends upon the woman's relationship to her own body – that is, upon her considering it in much the same way as she would an object:

> The body becomes *the* stake in late capitalism. *Having* the
> commodified object – and the initial distance and distinction
> it presupposes – is displaced by *appearing*, producing a strange
> constriction of the gap between consumer and commodity.

In this, we might note, the image of the 'after' does not always inspire feelings of pleasure. Rather, the perfected image can succeed only insofar as it is able to convince the would-be consumer that her non-commodified appearance is somehow incomplete. John Berger (1972: 134) explains:

> The spectator-buyer is meant to envy herself, as she will become if
> she buys the product. She is meant to imagine herself transformed
> by the product into an object of envy for others, an envy which will
> then justify her loving herself. One could put this another way: the
> publicity image steals her love of herself as she is, and offers it back to
> her for the price of the product.

Class Transformation: Pygmalion

I have tried to show how the makeover is addressed first and foremost to women as relational and consuming subjects: all makeovers present the idea of the unmediated self as a problem, if not *the* problem, to be remedied by self-commodification. Self-transformation is always promised as a means of self-empowerment on the surface, but the ideology of the makeover is a fiction which narrates self-empowerment as self-commodification, and as giving oneself over to, and actively pursuing, what in the end amounts to conjugal, or what we might call 'relational', status. Transformations thus represent empowerment as desirability where, as Robert Goldman (1992: 113) puts it, 'women enhanc[e] their social and economic power *vis-à-vis* men by presenting themselves as objects of desire.' For now, what is important is the idea that woman on her own (either independent or undefined by male desire) is *the* problem – a problem which finds its first critical articulation in what might be considered the structural blueprint for what we have come to call the makeover, and to which Barbara Phillips makes reference in her letter to the editors of *Mademoiselle*: George Bernard Shaw's *Pygmalion* ('If you have any Pygmalion in you, please be a sport and help me out' [56]).

Shaw's play takes its name from a tale in Ovid's *Metamorphoses*. The fifteen tales Ovid relates comprise a mythical history of transformations, which are seen to provide the very foundation of human (and divine) existence. The title of the tales itself indicates, of course, that transformations are universal – perhaps even integral – subjective processes. Pygmalion's particular situation is one that deals explicitly with the necessity of transformation in the construction of an ideal femininity. Pygmalion was something of a misogynist who, 'revolted by the many faults which nature ha[d] implanted in the female sex... long lived a bachelor existence,' and carved himself the 'perfect woman' out of ivory. What is important in this myth is the idea that the perfect woman for a man is a woman conceived *by* him, and that when left to define herself, woman is corrupt, immoral and, therefore, undesirable. We can see here the foundation for the contemporary makeover: the construction of female subjectivity as something akin to a disorder, and the presentation of male desire and/or male intervention as its remedy. Pygmalion, however, 'starts from scratch', improving not on an existing subject, but creating one entirely anew. In this, the makeover is equally about the construction of a model femininity. The woman Pygmalion conceives – Galatea – conforms to classical ideals of what a woman should be. She is, above all else, passive. She is immobile and essentially decorative. During a time when Aristotelian notions of femininity constructed woman as little more than companion to man and repository for his reproductive seed, the conclusion to the myth, which might be seen as the 'ur' conclusion to the makeover in general, is decidedly ominous: Galatea, brought to life by Venus who has heard Pygmalion's pleas to '[give] as my wife... one like the ivory maid' (Garland edition, 232), turns immediately to Pygmalion as his wife and, shortly thereafter, gives him a son. She has no thoughts of her own, no ambitions nor desires. She exists for male desire and for reproduction, not as an autonomous, desiring subject in her own right.

Set in early twentieth-century London, George Bernard Shaw's critical rewriting of the myth represents Galatea not as an object for male desire and pleasure, but as a subject who ultimately becomes aware of the object-like status that has been thrust upon her. Prior to Eliza Doolittle's metamorphosis under the tutelage of Henry Higgins, her appearance as a woman alone on the streets indicates, first, that she is outside of male control and influence and, second, that this is what her makeover should, and will, attempt to alter. In a time that was struggling to reconcile the notion of separate spheres with the emergence of greater mobility for women, Eliza's presence on the streets is highly suspicious. Previously, if a woman was alone on the streets it could only mean that she was a prostitute; 'ladies', on the other hand, stayed at home. Eliza is highly sensitive to the possible interpretation that she is, simply because she is not a lady, a prostitute, and is anxious to defend herself against the implication ('My character is the same to me as any lady's' [Longman edition, 226]). She is aware of her precarious situation as a woman alone in public, but is equally aware of the lack of alternatives available to her.

For Shaw, this 'crisis in femininity' was primarily a crisis of class. A socialist, Shaw was a key member of the Fabian Society, a group comprised, interestingly enough, of middle-class critics of capitalism. The Fabians held that the gradual reform of institutions, and not revolution, would bring about the desired egalitarian state, and that that state would not be proletarian but, rather, middle-class. On the one hand, this was seen as a matter of pure practicality, for surely everyone would desire to be educated and privileged. On the other hand, there were also the Fabians' decidedly middle-class tastes and the presumption of their natural superiority. To this end, they disdained the working classes even as they sympathized with their collective plight. Shaw's disinclination to romanticize the working classes is represented in *Pygmalion* by Henry Higgins's purely aesthetic approach to Eliza. He treats her, he claims, as he treats everyone – the same ('I treat a duchess as if she were a flower girl'), but his approach with her is patriarchal – even colonial – as if she were a 'savage' being taught the proper way to behave and speak. For Eliza the change to come must enable her to 'pass' as a duchess

– in effect, to attain the appearance and other European trappings of femininity. Indeed, the unmediated Eliza – that is, the 'unmade-over' Eliza – hardly conforms to the ideals of 'correct' femininity particular to the surrounding culture, if only because of her class. Eliza is a common flower vendor who, the stage directions tell us, 'is not at all an attractive person' (219). She is not attractive, we are made to understand, because her clothes are soiled and mismatched and she needs a bath. The play on class and gender is thus established as Shaw notes, '[s]he is no doubt as clean as she can afford to be; but *compared to the ladies* she is very dirty' (220, my emphasis).

The instability of class identities, and the era's greater anxieties about the erosion of class boundaries, is played upon throughout *Pygmalion*. This is first hinted at in the opening scene where, on a busy London street, characters from all walks of life seek refuge from a downpour (significant because water promises to wash away all visual markers of class difference and make everyone appear the same). The disparateness of the classes assembled on stage is signified by the various dialects of English represented, yet none of the accents we are to hear is so 'horrible' as Eliza's. After identifying the exact street from which she comes based on her diction, Higgins describes Eliza's speech as consisting of 'depressing and disgusting sounds' (227). What is so apparently horrible about Eliza's accent is that it is a marker of her low class, and the transformation to come must endeavour to elevate her from it.

Of course, what will rescue her from the misfortune (and indignity) of her class are both a makeover and a marriage, since, as we have seen, Eliza's problem is twofold. Firstly, her low class – indicated primarily by her accent but also by the clothes she wears – makes her presence in the street highly dubious. She works the same streets as the prostitutes, albeit from the margins ('off the kerb'), and is seemingly outside of the control of masculine authority. Like the prostitutes with whom she shares geography, and the shop girls with whom she shares the legitimate job of vending, Eliza is quite autonomous. Secondly, in order for her to attain the mark of respectability, she must be able to engage in the activities which define femininity (defined, in turn – and paradoxically considering the allure of department stores to the new and feminine bourgeoisie – by its containment within the domestic realm). Eliza, according to the dictates of femininity and middle-class morality, must be made over for either a marginally respectable job as a shop girl, or as a potential candidate for a middle-class – ergo respectable – marriage. The important thing (the thing which the play laments) is that she must be transformed and then transported into a controlled space, a space under the dominion of male authority. In relation to the structure of the makeover, what is most important is that Eliza becomes domesticated, and feminized, signified in part by her acquired genteel speech and clothes, but also by the fact that she has been left fit for little but marriage. 'What am I fit for? What have you left me fit for?' (280), she asks, knowing full well that the alternatives open to her now are really no better (if not worse) than before her metamorphosis. To Higgins, the problem of Eliza's future has, for the most part, been resolved by the transformation of her appearance: 'you're what I should call attractive... You go to bed and have a good nice rest; and then get up and look at yourself in the glass; and you won't feel so cheap' (ibid.). Higgins reiterates here the ideology of the makeover, which promises to remedy all dissatisfaction through the commodification of the subject's appearance, the ultimate reward being a flattering self-image and the added 'bonus' of marriage.

Yet, although the makeover comes at Eliza's request, it is not because she wishes to become eligible for marriage. Rather, she wants to remain independent, and to find work in a respectable flower shop. Here is the framework for the contemporary makeover, which attempts to pass itself off as a means of self-improvement and empowerment: Eliza initially believes in the makeover's promise to improve her economic status and, therefore, her social power. But, of course, in keeping with this same structure, it is assumed from the outset that the problem of Eliza's low class, as well as her lack of power, is to be solved by the solicitation of heterosexual (though, also middle-class) male desire ('By George, Eliza, the streets will be strewn with the bodies of men shooting themselves for your sake before I've done with you' [238]). Therefore, if we consider the parallel between class and gender arranged at the beginning, it is easy to see how Eliza is only superficially transformed into the feminine by being only superficially transformed into a member of the class definable by its ability to consume. What thus becomes increasingly obvious in all manifestations of the makeover is an implied romantic ('happily ever after') conclusion in the form of male recognition and/or desire as a remedy to the problem of the feminine self. It is perhaps not surprising that the makeover takes on the form of a romantic narrative considering, as Anthony Giddens (1992: 40) points out, '[t]he rise of romantic love more or less coincided with the emergence of the novel: the connection was one of newly discovered narrative form.' Hence we are interpellated by the 'transformative powers of love', and the idea that 'love reinvents us'. But, in the makeover, the situation is reversed: the makeover is seen to render romantic love/attention possible, rather than the reverse.

Extreme Makeover

As discussed thus far, consumption and, by implication, transformation, is offered as a means of self-(re)creation. It promises at least the appearance of autonomy over one's bodily representation. Indeed, as Anne Friedberg (1993: 118) notes in *Window Shopping*, 'the historical relation between feminism and consumerism… (made emphatic in Stanton's rallying cry: "GO OUT AND BUY")' might be seen to offer feminist theory an alternate way of viewing consumption. Instead of theorizing female consumerism in terms of ideological coercion and condemning its pleasures as guilty ones, the impermanence of cosmetic transformation might alternatively be seen to offer women access to the construction of a multiplicity of selves. As a consequence, the makeover might provide a form of critique: women can pick and choose from a variety of identities, which can be worn as easily as cosmetics.

With the proliferation of cosmetic surgery, however, the makeover has moved beyond the simpler questions of identity vis-à-vis consumption. No longer is it enough to *have* the items *to be like* the ideal, now the aim appears to *become* it. Like its magazine counterpart, *Extreme Makeover* encourages 'readers' (viewers) to take stock of themselves and consider what might be (and surely is) lacking. Unlike the magazine makeover, however, here transformation is considered to be not only permanent, but a means by which the psychological reality, or authenticity, of the subject can be externalized.

The programme plays upon all of the themes discussed so far: candidates write in hoping to improve their social and/or romantic status through a transformation of their appearance. They identify their 'deficiencies' as being outside of their own capacity to change, and look to the Pygmalion-surgeons to mould ('carve') their flesh and create them anew in the paradoxical aim of revealing their 'true selves'. Further, they often cite the individual parts of celebrities (Angelina Jolie's lips, Michelle Pfeiffer's cheekbones, etc.) that they would like to 'have' themselves. Without exception, all of the subjects to be made over are working or lower-middle class hoping to 'pass', or transcend, what Pierre Bourdieu calls their 'habitus' – the set of social and cultural circumstances into which a person is born which then inform her/his tastes, values, etc.

Therefore, not only are surgeons required, but taste-makers as well: stylists, shoppers, make-up artists and so on.

Each show is structured in the same way: we are introduced to the subject to be made over and then her 'problem areas' are identified by the surgeons who recommend a series of surgical procedures to 'correct them'. Invariably, cosmetic dentistry, rhinoplasty, breast augmentation and liposuction are suggested (as well as dermabrasion, Lasik – refractive laser surgery to correct visual acuity in order to eliminate the need for glasses or contact lenses – and other less invasive 'corrective' procedures). We are shown the candidates as they go through each process, while frequently being reminded of what they looked like before through flashbacks to their 'before' selves. Whilst recovering from their various operations, and signalling the impending conclusion to the hour-long broadcast, candidates are taken on a shopping spree with stylist Sam Saboura, who shows them how to make the most of their figures. In one episode, Saboura explains, '*everyone* has the potential to look fantastic: you just have to understand what clothes to wear, what to buy, and where to shop,' oblivious to the fact that not everyone – certainly not the candidates appearing on the programme – has the capital (financial and/or cultural) to possess the items he endorses (otherwise, why would they need him?). In this, there is the assumption that good taste or distinction is both natural and unnatural: it can be *learned* by anyone because, paradoxically, despite surfaces, we 'are all the same', and it is this promise of sameness that makes the makeover so appealing.

Indeed, sameness – or the quest for it – is closely aligned with identification. In the cosmetic variety of makeover, sameness with an ideal is an illusion, something ephemeral, changeable. With surgical transformations, however, the promise of sameness is forever: in fact, the aesthetic indelibly inscribed on each candidate's body is the same in every instance resulting in a very homogenized look. As mentioned previously, this look can be related back to various celebrities, themselves the products of myriad makeovers of one sort or another. They are what Jean Baudrillard has called 'copies without originals', ideals that never existed in the first place but which, through the apparatus of the screen and the apparent superiority of celebrities' taste, are made to seem 'natural'. In the end, the newly transformed women are revealed not only to loved ones and the audience, but also to themselves. Appraising themselves from a position of difference, frequently candidates exclaim 'I look like a movie star', 'I'm beautiful' or, 'Oh my God! It doesn't look like me: I love it!'

The conflicting notions of achieving sameness, on the one hand, and of creating an entirely new person, on the other, are never explored by the show or its participants. Further, the self-love returned to them is expected to translate into the romantic field as well: in one episode where the self-proclaimed 'Gobbler Girls' (triplets) are transformed, their reward for their 'hard work' is a vacation on a singles' cruise where it is assumed their improved self-images will translate into currency on the marriage market. Of course, this is the 'happily ever after' ending assumed from the start, and integral to every makeover narrative. But what happens *after* the 'after'? What happens when the stylists, nutrition consultants, personal trainers and personal shoppers are no longer available to impart their expertise and the cameras are turned off? Apart from the permanent changes in bone structure and breast size, are the lives of these women also transformed forever?

Bourdieu would answer 'no'. Like Cinderella's midnight deadline lest she be caught out, the contemporary made-over subject's 'original' identity might similarly be in jeopardy of discovery, for the 'after of the after' can only be, if Bourdieu is correct, an ultimate return to the before. One need only watch as the Fab 5 of *Queer Eye For the Straight Guy* survey the made-over subject on CCTV at the end of each episode worrying/hoping he might regress to his former tastes and/or behaviours (which, in most cases, he does, to lesser and greater degrees). This is because the habitus, which makes up so much of our identity, can never be fully left behind. Caught up in a regime of self-class loathing (or what Bourdieu calls 'class racism'), transformation is articulated in ideological terms where the makeover is represented as levelizing, democratizing. The accoutrements of wealth (or of middle-classness) become enchanted – fetishized – endowed with almost magical powers of transformation. *Extreme Makeover*, however, would have us forget that one needs capital to acquire the items and undergo the procedures defining the *lifestyle* to which the participants aspire, just as much as the makeover in general glosses over the fact that the distribution of aesthetic knowledge is uneven between classes.

Central to this idea of taste is the presupposition of 'absolute freedom of choice', a freedom that is decidedly bourgeois because it is born not out of necessity but financial capacity. Much like the consumption-based makeover that preceded it, the surgical transformation as exemplified by *Extreme Makeover* is equally an illusion, though the stakes are that much higher. And while the metamorphosis of a person's appearance may allow her to superficially pass or transcend her class, it can really only ever be temporary as eventually she must return to her former life and the various exigencies that prompted her search for help in the first place.

Conclusion

We are thus faced with a set of related contradictions. First, as I have argued throughout, the pleasures of consumption/self-transformation for women are available only at the cost of their self-abnegation, of accepting the presumption of their 'deficiency'. In other words, the pleasures of consumption, of self-appreciation, hinge on the precondition of personal displeasure. The made-over woman, therefore, may obtain some desired goals (such as social/visual approbation and an attendant improved self-image), but it is not the liberating process it is made out to seem. Instead, self-transformation provides only a tenuous sense of recognition misdirecting feminist and political activity in the direction of heterosexual desirability. The second dilemma is one long familiar to cultural/feminist studies: how do we reconcile acknowledging the pleasures of self-re-creation with our critical analysis of the makeover's ideological participation in sustaining a world of middle-class, not to mention masculine, privilege? While it is a desire for recognition that may drive the makeover, such a desire is ultimately tragic for it insists on feelings of incompleteness and a falsely assumed sense of female power and agency. While as yet there has been very little academic work on lifestyle television – and even less on the currency of the makeover as part of its structuring mythos – I hope that these questions will begin to find their answers in this new and increasingly prescient area of critical inquiry.

Chapter Fourteen

'MAKEOVER MADNESS'

The Designable Body and Cosmetic Surgery
in Steven Meisel's Fashion Photography

Anne Jerslev

Even though it seems like a contradiction in terms, *Italian Vogue*, in July 2005, inscribed cosmetic surgery into fashion photography by way of a 70-page, glamorously extravagant fashion editorial titled 'Makeover Madness'. The many spreads form a narrative of cosmetic surgery and the models' fashioned bodies are arranged spectacularly in highly stylized backstage scenarios from various operating rooms and the luxurious hotel suites where the post-operational healing and caring takes place.

The power of contemporary fashion photography has been linked to its ability to 'define what the here and now means' (Poschardt 2002: 13) and 'to capture the spirit of an era' (Craik 1994: 92). Obviously inspired by the proliferation of cosmetic surgery in general but also by television makeover programmes and drama series, distinguished American fashion photographer Steven Meisel who, himself, understands his work as 'a reflection of my times' (*The Fashion Book* 1998: 316) directed the feature, which opened with the statement: 'There is much too little discussion – for or against – cosmetic surgery: aesthetics, "obsession" or a tendency between art, realism, and irony?'. Obviously, the aim of the editorial is to enter into dialogue with a 'hot issue' and, in doing so, it constructs itself as more than just a fashion fantasy. Even though 'Makeover Madness' seems to criticize a decadent and narcissistic bourgeois culture through irony and satire, and despite the fact that it obviously comments on fashion itself, the series is primarily interesting because it so strikingly pinpoints, albeit in an ironic and highly ambivalent way, a contemporary 'culture of quick-change' (Sobchack 2000).

The 'Makeover Madness' editorial includes typical 'before' (mostly b/w) and 'after' (colour) pictures and scenarios from operating rooms, where the models/women pose in designer clothes on the operating table, lying, slouching or seemingly being operated on, surrounded by surgeons and nurses, operating tools, syringes and bloodstained cloth, and with surgical crayon marks or bloody stitches on their bodies. Likewise, there are close-ups of faces in pain or models self-absorbedly looking at themselves in hand mirrors. And, finally, there are photographs taken in corridors and suites in an extremely luxurious hotel where the women are supposedly staying during recovery. In the tableaux from the suites the models/women are again surrounded by doctors, nurses and piles of medical supplies. They are bandaged, suffering and wrapped in blankets, fur or thick hotel dressing gowns, lazily loafing in their beds watching television, having their afternoon tea or eating breakfast from exquisite silver trays, talking or, more likely, negotiating on their mobile phones, contemplating piles of shoes that might have been brought to them by personal shoppers or giving business instructions to fashionably dressed male assistants who seem to endlessly and obediently wait in the background for their next instructions.

Even though 'Makeover Madness' is very extensive compared to most other Meisel series, it is not remarkable for its length, as Steven Meisel has directed many lengthy fashion series for *Italian Vogue* during the past years. Nor is 'Makeover Madness' particularly remarkable for its narrative form. Narrative sequences has been an aesthetic drive in fashion photography at least since the beginning of the 1960s when Richard Avedon, in the September 1962 issue of *Harper's Bazaar* (at the same time that Andy Warhol created his newspaper paintings with gossip headlines) published his famous ten-page fashion spread performing a mock newspaper-gossip article with paparazzi-style, grainy and slightly out-of-focus photographs of a couple of unhappy celebrities on the run from paparazzi. Irony has also been used in fashion photography before, for example by Meisel himself in his extended October 1997 editorial for *Italian Vogue* titled *The Good Life*, where he imitated a 1950s advertising style and constructed brightly coloured and campily exaggerated, slightly uncanny 'front stage' images of the optimistic all-American healthy and happy normal family (some of the images were featured at the *Fashioning Fiction in Photography*

Since 1990 exhibition at MOMA, New York, 2004).

However, 'Makeover Madness' *is* remarkable, in the sense that it actually situates the model body where it has never been seen before in fashion photography – that is, on the operating table – and further stigmatizes it with blue lines and circles from crayons or a liposuction cannula. The series seems to turn upside down that which has generally – except for the interest taken in the realist, non-glamorous *Imperfect Beauty* (Cotton 2000) by a range of young photographers and stylists in the 1990s – been a defining element in fashion photography: the model's body as finished and timeless. But in Meisel's makeover photographs, the body is quite literally constructed as unfinished, in the act of being (re)designed into something else. The question is, nevertheless, whether the series actually challenges the notion of the body in fashion photography and offers an alternative to the abstract, perfectly impenetrable body so often performed in Meisel's pictures as well as in fashion photography as a whole.

I shall start addressing this question by, first, discussing the notion of *the morph* and, then, framing Steven Meisel's 2005 series within two central tendencies in fashion photography from the 1990s onward: a *realist* tendency in the 1990s, which borrows its style from snapshot and documentary photographs; and a *post-realist* tendency to which Meisel's works belongs and which includes a range of different styles united by their filmic look, a glamour 'that tolerates the impure' (Poschardt 2000: 29) and a polished body where 'the corporeal is avoided in a particular tasteful manner. All that remains of the pores of the skin, the muscles and sinews, of pubic hair, is some polished, made up and retouched shadows' (33). I will argue that in the case of Meisel's work, as is also the case in a series of other post-realist photographs, the body is constructed as a *designable* body, designed and always ready to be redesigned. This flawless polished body bears some similarities to the statuesque body in fashion photography and star publicity stills from the 1930s and 1940s, but there is no metaphysical meaning attached to it and it is inscribed in time in a much more ambivalent way, without the melancholic traces of the irreversibility of time that we find in the earlier fashion photographs and publicity stills. Correspondingly, it differs in crucial ways from the construction of the realist body in the influential *realist* trend in fashion photography in the 1990s. In the last part of the article, I'll discuss in more detail the 'Makeover Madness' series. My argument here is that even though the series inscribes the models in the narrative as both women and models and even though it self-reflexively comments upon the world of fashion, it manages to maintain the designable body on the operating table as a *mediated* construction of the body and thus in a sense excludes from the realm of cosmetic surgery the *real* model's *real* body.

'Makeover Madness' and the Cosmetic Morph

In Vivian Sobchack's characterization of contemporary visual culture in *Meta-Morphing* (Sobchack 2000), *morphing* stands as both a digital practice and 'a *cultural* imaginary that links a present digital practice to a much broader history and tropology of metamorphosis and its meanings' (Sobchack 2000: xiv). In contemporary culture, boundaries are fluid and anything can be transformed into something more suitable and desirable; consequently, *morphing* may be understood metaphorically as 'a marker of our time, a time in which morph like activities and events are overwhelming our sense of boundaries, space, direction, identity, and time' (Krasniewicz 2000: 54). The body is the privileged utopian site of transformation in today's visual culture, in art, ads, music videos, and television programmes, documentary as well as fiction. Thus, the morph and morphing stand as metaphors for a historically specific understanding of the body, which, in Sobchack's words, covers 'the "artifice" of a body that can be transformed not only through digitization but also through "naturalized" cosmetic surgery' (xv). As such, morphing is 'both an inscription and transformation of bodies' (Duckett 2000: 209). The metaphor inscribes the body in the logic of design and places it most identical to itself on the operating table as *cosmetic morph* (ibid.) or when it takes the stage in makeover programmes where anyone can be designed as a beauty.

The cosmetic morph is both a real and a mediated body which harbours the capacity for what Vivian Sobchack calls 'marvellous transformation' (Sobchack 2000: xv) and embodies both the reversibility of time and the simultaneous existence of past, present and future. Technically speaking, morphing is a reversible and on-going process of transformation of one visual object into another by means of computer technology. Printed fashion photographs in magazines are, of course, fixed tableaux. They have most likely used image manipulation techniques to produce the actual bodily appearances, but photographs cannot, like film or television, use morphing as an *effect* to procure the time-bound procedure of metamorphosis in front of our eyes. Likewise, television makeover shows like *The Swan* and *Extreme Makeover* and a drama series like *Nip/Tuck* only use digital morphing on rare occasions (for example, in order to illustrate the ritualized metamorphosis from a hideous 'before' to a marvellous and beautiful 'after' – or vice versa), just like the 'retouching' of girls' bodies is mentioned as a necessary procedure, but is never actually *revealed* in *America's Next Next Top Model*. The point is, however, that no matter how much actual digital image manipulation is done, *morphing metaphorizes a specific cultural inscription of the body in a digital era*. Meisel's fashion photographs stage this notion of the body as a site of 'quick-changes' very literally and ironically in the form of cosmetic morph; they are not only captured in the act of (re)designing but also act as if this is the most natural thing in the world. The 'Makeover Madness' series may well be regarded as an ironic commentary on female executives' busy lives in the fast lane of big business, where appearance is an indisputable part of the game and cosmetic surgery a common part of their self-centred way of life, not an exception to it. Cosmetic surgery is constructed as an expensive but absolutely affordable commodity in line with the glamorous accessories and expensive clothes. The body itself is commodified and performed as an aestheticized cosmetic morph, a transmutable object in the course of being subjected to cosmetic quick-changes with as little loss of valuable work-time as possible. The photographs comment self-consciously on the ongoing discussion about cosmetic surgery as an intervention into an otherwise 'natural' body: we see in one of the photographs an open magazine with pictures of Tom Cruise and Katie Holmes under the caption 'Are They Faking It?' The celebrity couple may fake their romance, but the series seems to argue that not only is the made-over body not fake, but a natural part of contemporary life.

Steven Meisel's Designed Bodies

Meisel's editorial features for *Italian Vogue* from the new millennium have typically been inspired by films and he has borrowed his aesthetics from many different film genres and scenarios, for example, film noir in 'Killer Vogue' (September 2005), science-fiction retro ('Trendspotting', July 2004), a trashy trailer park in a hot and dusty desert surrounding ('Couture', September 2004), gangster decadence ('Pulp – His Kind of Woman', July 2004), and noirish escape scenarios in 'Underworld' (October 2005). But he is also inspired by other photographers, most notably Cindy Sherman, whose *Untitled Film Stills* from the second part of the 1970s has been a recurrent point of reference in his works for more than a decade, for example, in some of his non-pornographic photographs in Madonna's audacious *Sex* (1992), an *Italian Vogue* feature in July 1995 (cf. Miller 1997), and – although somewhat more loosely interpreted – in his famous 2001 campaign for Versace, *Four Days in L.A.* (also exhibited in White Cube 2 in London).

But whereas the rather wealthy woman in the 1960s-style furnished living room in Sherman's *Untitled Film Still no. 50* seems to occupy her home without inhabiting it, the glamorous and monumental women in Meisel's Versace photographs who gaze directly at the viewer are completely at home in their luxurious Los Angeles mansions. The interiors function as set pieces for their self-presentation and at the same time their posing bodies are, just like the furniture, details in the photographs' overall construction of a specific Versace style. The women seem to be forever frozen in an oddly eighteenth-century bourgeois representative pose, as if they were subjected to an old-fashioned camera with a slow exposure time; a gesture of immobilization that renders the models' perfect bodies as statuesque and inhuman mannequins. Bodies are hard and impenetrable in these Meisel photographs after the year 2000. The models are constructed as impressive, polished and cool femme fatales or they are immobilized into more fragile-looking inorganic dolls.

Jennifer Craik argues that modelling constructs 'the ideal technical body' (1993: 91), a body that can perform any attitude according to prevalent ideals of beauty and gender. But when it comes to the mediatized fashioned body, or, in other words, the posing body in fashion photography, it seems rather to harbour the ideal *plastic* body; the body as a perfectly mouldable material in the hands and in front of the lens of the fashion photographer. Contrary to the staging of a 'natural' body in fashion photography in the 1960s and 1970s, the working body situated in everyday surroundings in the 1980s, and the realist vulnerable body in the 1990s, fashion photography's body has in recent years to a large extent returned to its earlier idea of abstraction and the sculptural. The crucial difference is that it is deprived of relations to the metaphysical. Rebecca Arnold claims that the fashioned body in recent fashion history 'is drawn ever further from the organic' with 'clothing, make-up and accessories as artificial elements used to disguise the living flesh' (2001: 85); however, it seems that the body itself has, today, been transported into the realm of *design* and transformed into a material morph (Duckett 2000).

Steven Meisel's body is a designed body which, digitally manipulated, retouched or just striking a pose, may be given any shape, beautiful or not, life-like or not, meaningful or without any meaning at all. The body in much contemporary fashion photography is neither well-proportioned nor trained; by means of digital image manipulation and the ideas and taste of the individual fashion photographer, it is often made into a 'genetically modified' (or 'mutant' (Calefato 2004)) body with, for example, extremely long legs, an extremely slender waist or completely flawless, polished and hard-looking skin that seem to contain no pores or 'natural' marks at all. The body is, in this kind of post-realist photograph, often situated in an uncanny field between living and dead, between animate and inanimate, between model and mannequin, the body turned into a material morph that bears only a vague resemblance to its owner or may be doubled into an uncanny likeness to its same.

The construction of the generalized, flawless, designed body may be seen as a reaction to the much discussed so-called 'heroin chic' aesthetics (cf. Arnold 1999; Kismaric & Respini 2004) which started in the wake of grunge culture in the mid 1990s. Inspired by snapshot and documentary aesthetics (cf. Hartley & Rennie 2004), this aesthetic constructed what Caroline Evans, with a more precise term than 'heroin chic', calls 'a wasted look' (2003: 100) and an individualized, realist, vulnerable and intimate body. Meisel's photographs are consistent with the shabby realism, but his are the result of an effort to create artificial worlds or image worlds. His long snapshot-paparazzi editorial from January 2005 is specifically *not* an authentic representation of reality but a post-realist merging of media and reality, a citational gesture which points to a world of images, at the same time as he confers upon his filmic scenarios a sense of realism. Paul Jobling (2002) sees the difference between the realist and the artificial photographs as a difference between 'Romantic Realists', who primarily work with analogue equipment and in realist environments, and 'Master Manipulators', who work digitally and create simulated environments. However, stylist Anna Cockburn's (Cotton 2000: 65) idea that 'there has to be an element of something mildly uncomfortable in fashion images' does not apply to the realist photograph alone; even though interpreted in a much different manner, Steven Meisel's images are often made to convey the same feeling.

The realist fashion photographers who worked for sophisticated magazines like *The Face, Dazed & Confused* and *i-D Magazine* in the 1990s were not interested in the beautiful body. But neither is Meisel and other non-realist or post-realist photographers. Their aim is to create conspicuous and glamorous image-narratives, and digital techniques can provide the model's body with proportions, capacities and a surface that fulfils the photographer's vision. The paradoxical thing is that at the same time as fashion models have become more individualized – many of them are celebrities we know by name – their appearance becomes more dehumanized and their bodies unreal, reduced – or retouched – to workable material, frozen in significant but non-signifying poses and inserted on the image surface to form part of a conspicuous composition. The visual style in Meisel's 'Killer Vogue' series, for example, points self-consciously to the digitized image-production process and it constructs the fashionable designer items – the clothes and the model's body – as identical digitized wonders; as such, the bodies are no more human than their virtual surroundings.

In Meisel's stylized series, the designed body is not the result but the *embodiment* of the digital process; hence the body has, in a sense, already inscribed post-productional procedures in its moment of posing for the photographer. In her interesting discussion of the pose, Kaja Silverman argues that the pose 'needs to be more generally understood as the photographic imprinting of the body' (1996: 205) and she refers to Craig Owens who claims that to pose is to 'freeze, as if anticipating the still I am about to become… inscribing across the surface of my body, photography's "mortification" of the flesh' (Owens 1992: 210). Posing is essential in understanding the mediatized body in fashion photography; the term may help us bear in mind that the body is *always* posing no matter how realist and authentic it may seem. The "wasted look" of the 1990s is exactly a look, which *stages* 'the authentic as posed' (Poschardt 2002: 11). However, it seems that the metaphors of death attached to the concept of posing and further underlined with the reference to Roland Barthes' seminal work *Camera Lucida* (Barthes 1981) are especially eloquently embodied in many of Meisel's series through his performance of the model as mannequin or doll.

With its even and polished surface, the transformable body in contemporary fashion photography often appears sculptured and statuesque and it brings to mind the glamorously posing film stars and models in the production stills and fashion photography of the 1930s. However, always without the antique statuesque harmony, the ideal of classical beauty, and the idealized and unattainable vertical monumentality of the 1930s female body (see, for example, Ducros 1998; Kobal 1976). This is also true for one of the most sculptural bodies in recent years, namely model Sophie Dahl posing in the nude for Yves Saint Laurent's perfume, Opium. Her voluptuous marble body reclining on a velvety podium is transformed into the very flacon that is absent from the ad and as a consequence it is absolutely profane.

Even though today's model often poses as if she had fallen from her pedestal or is captured reclining, the body is still even and sculptural and glamorous, even though glamour in the contemporary photograph does not come from a staged inner radiance, a metaphysical body, or a distanciating pathos. Meisel's picture of Madonna posing as a fallen sculpture from Versace's spring 1995 campaign (featuring Madonna) is interesting in this respect. In the photograph we see Madonna lying with her head down on a stone staircase, as if she had stumbled and fallen. She is 'armoured through glamour' (Evans 2003: 237), wrapped in a shiny and tight lilac gown. Her eyes are open and staring and in her right hand she has a half-eaten red apple. It is hard to say whether the model is alive or dead, and thus whether only the glittering garment is alive. Like so many other models in Meisel's photographs, she is captured in an in-between state. The brownish flesh of the apple suggests that she has been lying there for a while, and it confers upon the image a notion of *nature morte*. She may be still alive but she is also a *still life*, and the passing of time which is suggested by the apple may point to the mortification of the body. But the brown trace of time may also just prosaically point to the time-consuming staging of fashion photography. *Still life* is thus how close Meisel gets to the motif of death and disaster which has otherwise been a recurrent theme in fashion photography in the past decade (Arnold 2001; Evans 2003); it is also how close he gets to a melancholic notion of the body.

Fashion Surgery and Natural Beauty

In the extravagantly luxurious and ambivalent scenarios of 'Makeover Madness', the models are staged with a twinkle as glamorous versions of the kind of 'assembly-line beauty' (Balsamo 1997: 58) that we find in *The Swan*. Only here the final result is not yet disclosed; except for a few images, they are bandaged on their heads in exactly the same way. In one black and white photograph we see two models sitting in wheel chairs in the same bent-over way, wearing their bandaged heads with the same mixture of suffering and indolence, cosmetically embellished but also made into the same.

Other spreads stage surgical procedures as well. In one, the model lies as a beautifully dressed corpse, her face covered with a cloth and her breasts bared and marked with a crayon. Only the open mobile phone in her left hand reveals that she is still alive. In another photograph, the model lies with her eyes wide open on the operating table, clad in a yellow and green flowered chiffon dress. Her head is bandaged, seemingly from a former procedure. Her left arm with its wide pleated sleeve hangs relaxed from the table and the right hand grasps one of the surgeons by his arm. Like the Madonna figure, she is constructed as a still life, but without the sign of passed time that is inscribed on the Versace photograph. She is seemingly unaware of the procedures being performed on her body, the traces of which are visible in the foreground of the image in the many bloody cloths and the two transparent jars filled with fat and blood.

Even though there is an abundance of traces of the material morph in the two photographs, the body posing as cosmetic morph is as abstract as ever in fashion photography, an image accessory in a staging of a contemporary fashionable operating theatre. The body is in the course of being redesigned, and thus the photograph might be regarded as a striking illustration of Anne Balsamo's notion of 'fashion surgery' (Balsamo 1997: 62), surgery performed for no functional reason but to transform the body into a fashionable appearance. It is not an old body being fixed but an old-fashioned body being replaced by an updated one.

This 'statement' is at once underlined and contested by Meisel's use of Linda Evangelista as one of the recurrent models. She is one of the 1990s supermodels and was around the age of forty when 'Makeover Madness' was shot; thus, she indisputably belongs to the target group for cosmetic surgery. In one of the Evangelista spreads we see her sitting relaxed and self-absorbed on the operating table looking at her face in a hand mirror. Her pose is insignificant and she seems to have been captured by a passing camera. In another remarkable, soft and authentic-looking close-up, which differs from most of the other photographs, she is seemingly captured without make-up and also absorbed in the intimate activity of watching herself in a hand mirror. There are remnants of blood on her eyelids and forehead, and the light from a window falls sharply, revealing the left side of her face where we can see every little pore and pit in the skin, every freckle and every change of colour in her complexion. Except for the gorgeous, glittering evening dress in the first of these images, she seems in the two photographs to project realism and the 'natural' – as if she is posing as herself in the pictures and has actually undergone the procedures, the traces of which are so obvious in her face. But the pictures, and especially the close-up, might just as well tell the exact opposite story. We are allowed to get close to the model and see for ourselves that the only fakery is the blood and the other traces of surgery. Her careful effort to loosen a piece of bandage from her nose seems to anchor the authenticity of the picture; the face is not made-up, her complexion is varied and her skin soft. In contrast to the smooth and polished retouched surfaces of the model in the other Meisel examples, Evangelista's face seems here to be delicately unretouched and real. By means of this picture, the series seems to deny that Linda Evangelista, herself, needs cosmetic surgery.

Digital image manipulation makes the creation of artificial bodies possible. However, these designed photographic bodies do not deny the existence of a unique and 'natural' beautiful model behind the frozen pose or sculptured and designed body. The digital morph makes the body's 'marvellous transformation' possible in fashion photography, whereas both the cosmetic morph and the body as a material morph, according to 'Makeover Madness', are absent from the world of fashion – except as a pose.

'Makeover Madness' does not question the 'natural' uniqueness of the body of the models whose names are included in the credit information. The printed information on the many before and after spreads, where the model's seemingly ordinary 'before' face is placed side by side with a glamorous 'after' photograph in colour, refers equally to the barely visible clothes and to make-up brands; thus the brief commodity information anchors, not least, fashion photography as a field of (digital) image manipulation. In 'Makeover Madness' the cosmetic morph is therefore constructed solely as a *mediated* idea of the body. Meisel's photographs of cosmetic surgery confirm rather than deny that the model remains exceptional and the fashion world remains filled with exceptionally beautiful women.

The series refers to the world of fashion in another way, too. It might be regarded as a statement about the realist, snap-shot photography and the wasted look, claiming this style to be absolutely over. It thus functions as a tribute to Meisel's own post-realism. By using 1990s icon Linda Evangelista, the series seems almost demonstratively to posit the use of ordinary people in fashion photography as unfashionable at the same time as it points out that Linda Evangelista's natural beauty is real.

The cover of the July issue of *Italian Vogue* and the closing photograph in the 'Makeover Madness' series seem to be connected narratively. On the cover, a woman (Linda Evangelista) is walking down a hotel corridor and in the final image we see the same woman after she has left the

hotel and is captured by the photographer in the street between two rows
of shiny black cars. She is escorted by a nurse in a white uniform in
both pictures. In the corridor, the nurse holds the woman's arm and
supports her. In the street the nurse is almost hidden behind the woman
who still has her head bandaged but conveys an air of indisputable self-
confidence from under her black man's hat and behind her large dark
sunglasses. Like the typical 1980s fashion photography, she is seemingly
caught in motion in a recognizable metropolitan reality; the photograph
is glamorous, dispersing glamour to all areas of the picture while
maintaining an impression of immediacy.

Like many other Meisel photographs, this one refers to other
photographs, not in art history but in the history of fashion photography.
In this case it refers to Richard Avedon's controversial fake gossip-
magazine article called "Mick Nichols Suzy Parker Rock Europe" with
its staged paparazzi photos from the September 1962 issue of *Harper's
Bazaar* mentioned above. In one of the unfocused paparazzi images we
see the model Suzy Parker seemingly leaving a hospital. She hides her eyes
behind dark glasses and wears a large black hat. She is also, as in Meisel's
images, supported by a nurse in a white dress who holds her arm and on
her left is director Mike Nichols with a cigarette in his mouth. Her head
is not bandaged, but her wrists are; the short sleeves on the coat reveal
that she has tried to kill herself. Avedon's gossip narrative is 'a fiction of
a failed suicide attempt' and 'a comment on the implications of what he
was photographing' (Harrison 1991: 132). In 'Makeover Madness', on the
other hand, Steven Meisel has the woman leave triumphantly, seemingly
without scars on her perfect body and self-confidently transforming the
bandage around her head into one more fashionable accessory. Contrary
to Avedon's narrative, with the fragile pose and the construction of an
imperfect and penetrable body with the marks of death written on it, the
'Makeover Madness' narrative triumphantly seems to confirm fashion
photography's impenetrable and abstract body which has left blood and
other traces of specificity behind in the operating room. Staging a cosmetic
surgery narrative is a new idea in fashion photography and it touches
upon both hot and delicate issues. However, the body constructed in the
many spreads is a recognizable Meisel body, which corresponds well with
the optimistic notion of the designable body elsewhere in contemporary
visual culture.

BIBLIOGRAPHY

Abt, V and M Seesholtz. 'The Shameless World of Phil, Sally and Oprah: Television talkshows and the deconstruction of society'. *The Journal of Popular Culture*. 28:1 (1994): 171–91.

Agamben, Giorgio. State of Exception. Chicago: University of Chicago Press. 2005.

Allen, Ted, et al. *Queer Eye for the Straight Guy: The Fab 5's Guide to Looking Better, Cooking Better, Dressing Better, Behaving Better and Living Better*. Sydney: Bantam, 2004.

Alliance for Healthy Homes. (June 2005) www.afhh.org.res/res-alert.

Altman, Rick. *Film/Genre*. London: British Film Institute, 1999.

Andersen, Robin. *Consumer Culture and TV Programming*. Boulder, Colorado: Westview Press, 1995.

Andrejevic, Mark. 'The Kinder, Gentler Gaze of Big Brother: Reality TV in the era of digital capitalism'. *New Media & Society*. 4:2 (2002): 251–70.

——. *Reality TV: The Work of Being Watched*. Lanham, Maryland: Rowman & Littlefield, 2003.

——. 'The Work of Watching One Another: Lateral Surveillance, Risk and Governance'. *Surveillance and Society*. 2:2 (2003): 479–97.

Arnold, Rebecca. 'Heroin Chic'. *Fashion Theory*. 3:3 (1999): 279–96.

——. *Fashion, Desire and Anxiety*. London and New York: I.B.Tauris, 2001.

Austin, D. *The Complete Workout*. United States: Parade, 1988.

——. *Shrink Your Female Fat Zones*. United States: Lionsgate, 2003.

Ballaster, Ros and Margaret Beetham, Elizabeth Frazer and Sandra Hebron. *Women's Worlds: Ideology, Femininity and the Woman's Magazine*. London: Macmillan, 1991.

Balsamo, Anne. *Technologies of the Gendered Body. Reading Cyborg Women*. Durham and London: Duke University Press, 1996.

Banks, Andrew. 'Review: *Chaotic*'. *The Sunday Mail*. 28 December 2005. www.thesundaymail.news.com.

Banner, Lois W. *American Beauty: A Social History Through Two Centuries of the American Idea, Ideal, and Image of the Beautiful Woman*. New York: Knopf, 1983.

Barbie. *Dance! Workout with Barbie*. United States: Gee Whiz Kids Video, 1991.

Barker-Benfield, GJ. *The Horrors of the Half-Known Life: Male Attitudes Toward Women and Sexuality in Nineteenth-Century America*. London: Routledge, 2000.

Barlow, David M et al. *The Media in Wales: Voices of a Small Nation*. Cardiff: University of Wales Press, 2005.

Barthes, Roland. *Camera Lucida*. London: Jonathan Cape, 1981.

——. *Mythologies*. London: Paladin, 1988.

Baudrillard, Jean. *Selected Writings*. (ed. Mark Poster) Cambridge: Polity Press, 1988.

Bauman, Zygmunt. 'Consuming Life'. *Journal of Consumer Culture*. 1:1 (2001): 9–29.

——. *Freedom*. Minneapolis: University of Minnesota Press, 1988.

——. *Intimations of Postmodernity*. London: Routledge, 1992.

——. *Postmodern Ethics*. Oxford and Cambridge, Massachusetts: Blackwell, 1993.

Bech, Henning. *When Men Meet: Homosexuality and Modernity*. [1987] (trans. Teresa Mesquit and Tim Davies) Cambridge: Polity Press, 1997.

Beck, Ulrich. *Risk Society: Towards a New Modernity*. London: Sage, 1992.

Beck, Ulrich and Beck-Gernsheim, Elisabeth. *Individualization: Institutionalized Individualism and its Social and Political Consequences*. London and Thousand Oaks, California: Sage, 2002.

Berger, John. *Ways of Seeing*. London: Penguin, 1972.

Bird, Sharon R. 'Welcome to the Men's Club: Homosociality and the Maintenance of Hegemonic Masculinity'. *Gender and Society*. (April 1996): 120–32.

Biressi, Anita and Heather Nunn. *Reality TV: Realism and Revelation*. London and New York: Wallflower Press, 2005.

Black.White. Producers RJ Cutler, Mat Alvarez and Ice Cube. FX Network. www.myspace.com/blackwhite.

Blackman, Lisa. 'Self-help, Media Cultures and the Production of Female Psychopathology'. *European Journal of Cultural Studies*. 7:2 (2004): 219–56.

Blanks, B. *Tae-Bo: Advanced*. United States: Ventura, 1998.

Bonner, Frances. *Ordinary Television: Analyzing Popular TV*. London: Sage, 2003.

Bordo, Susan. *Unbearable Weight: Feminism, Western Culture, and the Body*. Berkeley: University of California Press, 1995.

Boston Globe, The. (2005) www.boston.com.

Bourdieu, Pierre. *Distinction: A Social Critique of the Judgment of Taste*. (trans. Richard Nice) Cambridge, Massachusetts: Harvard University Press, 1984.

——. *On Television and Journalism*. (trans. Priscilla Parkhurst Ferguson) London: Pluto, 1998.

Brabazon, T. 'Time for a Change or More of the Same? Les Mills and the Masculinization of Aerobics'. *Sporting Traditions*. 17 (2000): 97–112.

Branston, Gill and Roy Stafford. *The Media Student's Book*. London and New York: Routledge, 1999.

Britney & Kevin: Chaotic Reviews. Internet Movie Database. (September–December 2005) www.imdb.com.

Brunsdon Charlotte. 'Lifestyling Britain: The 8-9 Slot on British Television'. *International Journal of Cultural Studies*. 6:1 (2003): 5–23.

Brunsdon, C, C Johnson, R Moseley and H Wheatley. 'Factual Entertainment on British Television: The Midlands TV Research Group's "8-9 Project"'. *European Journal of Cultural Studies*. 4:1 (2001): 29–62.

Busk, Malene. 'Micropolitics: A Political Philosophy from Marx and Beyond'. In P Pisters and M Lord, eds. *Micropolitics of Media Culture*. Amsterdam: Amsterdam University Press, 2002: 103–23.

Butler, Judith. *Gender Trouble: Feminism and the Subversion of Identity*. New York: Routledge, 1990.

Calefato, Patrizia. *The Clothed Body*. Oxford and New York: Berg Publishers, 2004.

Calhoun C, ed. *Habermas and the Public Sphere*. Cambridge, Massachusetts: MIT Press, 1992.

Campbell, C. *The Romantic Ethic and the Spirit of Modern Consumerism*. Oxford: Blackwell, 1989.

Carpignano, P, R Anderson, S Aronowitz and W Difazio. 'Chatter in the Age of Electronic Reproduction: Talk television and the "public mind"'. *Social Text*. 25:6 (1990): 35–55.

Carr, David. 'I'm in Love. Why Shouldn't I Be Paid?' *The New York Times*. 20 June 2005. www.lexis-nexis.com.ezp.bentley.edu.

Cashmore, Ellis. *... and there was television*. London: Routledge, 1994.

Cass County Democrat Missourian. 7 October 2005. US Census Bureau (2004).

Cavender, Gray. 'Community in *America's Most Wanted* and *Survivor*'. In Su Holmes and Deborah Jermyn, eds. *Understanding Reality Television*. London and New York: Routledge, 2004: 154–72.

Chambers, D. *Representing the Family*. London: Sage, 2001.

Chaney, David C. 'From Ways of Life to Lifestyle: Rethinking Culture as Ideology and Sensibility'. In J Lull, ed. *Culture in the Communication Age*. London: Routledge, 2001.

Chaney, David C. *Lifestyles*. London: Routledge, 1996.

Cher. *CherFitness: A New Attitude*. United States: Isis Productions, 1991.

——. *CherFitness: Body Confidence*. United States: Isis Productions, 1992.

Clarkson, Jay. 'Contesting Masculinities Makeover: *Queer Eye*, Consumer Masculinity and 'Straight-Acting' Gays'. *Journal of Communications Inquiry*. 29:3 (2005): 235–55.

Clissold, Bradley D. '*Candid Camera* and the Origins of Reality TV'. In Su Holmes and Deborah Jermyn, eds. *Understanding Reality Television*. London and

New York: Routledge, 2004: 33–53.

Connell, RW. *Masculinities*. London: Polity Press, 1985.

Constantine, Susannah and Trinny Woodall. *What Your Clothes Say About You: How to Look Different, Act Different and Feel Different*. London: Weidenfeld and Nicolson, 2005a.

——. *What You Wear Can Change Your Life*. London: Weidenfeld and Nicolson, 2005b.

Corner, John. 'Afterword: Framing the New'. In Su Holmes and Deborah Jermyn, eds. *Understanding Reality Television*. London and New York: Routledge, 2004: 290–9.

——. 'Performing the Real: Documentary Diversions'. *Television & New Media*. 3:3 (2002): 255–69.

Cotton, Charlotte. *Imperfect Beauty. The Making of Contemporary Fashion Photographs*. London: V&A Publications, 2000.

Couldry, Nick. 'Teaching Us to Fake It: The Ritualized Norms of Reality Television'. In Susan Murray and Laurie Ouellette, eds. *Reality Television: Remaking Television Culture*. New York: New York University Press, 2004: 57–74.

Craik, Jennifer. *The Face of Fashion: Cultural Studies in Fashion*. London and New York: Routledge, 1994.

Crawford, Cindy. *Shape Your Body Workout*. GoodTimes Home Video, United States, 1992.

Davis, Kathy. *Reshaping the Female Body: The Dilemma of Cosmetic Surgery*. New York: Routledge, 1995.

Dean, Mitchel. *Governmentality: Power and Rule in Modern Society*. London and Thousand Oaks, California: Sage, 1999.

Deery, June. 'Trading Faces: The Makeover Show as Prime-Time "Informercial"'. *Feminist Media Studies*. 4:2 (2004): 211–14.

——. 'Spare Change: Reality TV and the Female Object'. Paper presented at *Console-Ing Passions: The International Conference of Feminism and Television, Video, New Media, and Audio*. (30 May – 2 June 2004) New Orleans, Louisiana.

Deleuze, Gilles. 'Control and Becoming'. In *Negotiations*. (trans. M Joughin) New York: Columbia University Press, 1990a: 169–176.

——. 'Postscript on Control Societies'. In *Negotiations*. (trans. M Joughin) New York: Columbia University Press, 1990b: 177–82.

DeLuna, Amy. '"Chaotic" Stinker'. *New York Daily News*. 18 May 2005. www.nydailynews.com.

Dinnerstein, M and R Weitz. 'Jane Fonda, Barbara Bush, and Other Ageing Bodies: Femininity and the Limits of Resistance'. In *Sex, Self, and Society: The Social Context of Sexuality*. (ed. TL Steele) Belmont, California: Thomas Wadsworth, 2005: 322–31.

'DivorceKevin.com'. *The Jason Cage Radio Show*. 21 November 2005. www. divorcekevin.com.

Doane, Mary Ann. *The Desire to Desire: The Women's Film of the 1940s*. Bloomington: Indiana University Press, 1987.

——. 'The Economy of Desire: The Commodity Form in/of the Cinema'. *Quarterly Review of Film and Video*. 11:1 (1989): 22–33.

Dorfman, R. 'The Future of Reality... Television'. *Exquisite Corpse*. Cyber Issue 11 (Spring/Summer 2002) www.corpse.org.

Dover, C. '"Crisis" in British Documentary Television: The End of a Genre?' *Journal of British Cinema and Television*. 1:2 (2004): 242–59.

Dovey, Jon. *Freakshow: First Person Media and Factual Television*. London: Pluto Press, 2000.

——. 'Reality TV'. In Glen Creeber, ed. *The Television Genre Book*. London: British Film Institute, 2001: 137–8.

Duckett, Victoria. 'Beyond the Body. Orlan and the Material Morph'. In Vivian Sobchack, ed. *Meta-Morphing. Visual Transformation and the Culture of Quick-Change*. London and Minneapolis: University of Minnesota Press, 2000.

Ducros, Francoise. 'The Dream of Beauty. Fashion and Fantasy'. In Michel Frizot, ed. *A New History of Photography*. Köln: Könemann, 1998.

Dworkin, Andrea. *Pornography: Men Possessing Women*. London: The Women's Press, 1981.

Dyer, Richard. 'Entertainment and Utopia'. *Movie*. 24 [1977]. Reprinted in Simon During, ed. *The Cultural Studies Reader*. London and New York: Routledge, 1999: 371–81.

——. *Stars*. (new edition) London: British Film Institute, 1988.

——. *Heavenly Bodies: Film Stars and Society*. London: British Film Institute, 1986.

——. *Light Entertainment*. London: British Film Institute and TV Monograph, 1973.

——. *White*. London and New York: Routledge, 1997.

Dyer-Witheford, Nicholas. *Cyber-Marx: Cycles and Struggles in High Technology Capitalism*. Urbana: University of Illinois Press, 1999.

Ellis, John. 'Mirror, Mirror'. *Sight and Sound*. 11:7 (2001): 12.

——. *Seeing Things: Television in the Age of Uncertainty*. London and New York: I.B.Tauris, 2002.

——. 'Television as Working Through'. In Jostein Gripsrud, ed. *Television and Common Knowledge*. London: Routledge, 1999: 55–70.

——. *Visible Fictions: Cinema, Television, Video*. (second edition) London: Routledge, 1992.

Evans, Caroline. *Fashion at the Edge. Spectacle, Modernity and Deathliness*. New Haven and London: Yale University Press, 2003.

Everett, Anna. 'Trading Private and Public Spaces @ HGTV and TLC: On New Genre Formation in Transformation TV'. *Journal of Visual Culture*. 3:2

(2004): 157–81.

Faking It. 'Alex the Animal'. (18 September 2000, BBC).

Faking It. 'Faking It... as a Stuntman'. (30 October 2002, BBC).

Faking It. 'Faking It... as a Yachtswoman'. (11 December 2002, BBC).

Faking It. 'Cellist Turns DJ'. (17 April 2001, BBC).

Faking It. 'Drag Racer to Drag Queen'. (29 March 2003, The Learning Channel).

Faking It. 'Ivy League to Big League'. (1 March 2003, The Learning Channel).

Faking It. 'Lady Lisa'. (25 September 2000, BBC).

Faking It. 'Painter to Artist'. (1 May 2001, BBC).

Faking It. 'Simple Life to Social Life'. (20 October 2004, BBC).

Faking Changed My Life. (27 September 2002, BBC).

Faking Changed My Life (II). (3 February 2004, BBC).

Fashion Book, The. London: Phaidon Press, 1998.

Featherstone, Mike. *Consumer Culture and Postmodernism*. London: Sage, 1991.

Felski, Rita. *The Gender of Modernity*. Cambridge, Mass: Harvard University Press, 1995.

Fetveit, Arild. 'Reality TV in the Digital Era: A paradox in visual culture?' *Media, Culture & Society*. 21:6 (1999): 787–804.

Fleming, JC and KA Martin Ginis. 'The Effects of Commercial Exercise Video Models on Women's Self-Presentational Efficacy and Exercise Task Self-Efficacy'. *Journal of Applied Sport Psychology*. 16 (2004): 92–102.

Fonda, Jane. *My Life So Far*. New York: Random House, 2005.

Fonda, Jane. *Workout*. United States: Karl Video, 1982.

Forman, T. Interview at official ABC website. (2005) www.abc.go.com/primetime/xtremehome/index.html.

Foucault, Michel. *Discipline and Punish: The Birth of the Prison*. (trans. Alan Sheridan) London: Penguin, 1991.

——. *Power: The Essential Words of Michel Foucault: 1954–1984, Volume 3*. (ed. James D. Faubion) London: Penguin, 2002.

——. *The History of Sexuality, Volume 1: An Introduction*. (trans. Robert Hurley) New York: Vintage, 1990.

——. *The History of Sexuality: The Will to Knowledge, Volume 1*. (trans. Robert Hurley) London: Penguin Books, 1998.

Franks, BD, ET Howley and Y Iyriboz, eds. *The Health Fitness Handbook*. Illinois: Human Kinetics, 1999.

Fraser, Suzanne. 'Woman-Made Women: Mobilisation of Nature in Feminist Accounts of Cosmetic Surgery'. *Hecate*. 27:2 (2001): 115–33.

Freud, Sigmund. *Art and Literature*. London: Penguin, 1987: 335–76.

Friedberg, Anne. 'A Denial of Difference: Theories of Cinematic Identification'. *Psychoanalysis and Cinema*. (ed. E Ann Kaplan) New York: Routledge, 1990.

——. *Window Shopping: Cinema and the Postmodern*. Berkeley and Los Angeles:

University of California Press, 1983.

Friedman, James, ed. *Reality Squared: Televisual Discourse on the Real*. New Brunswick, New Jersey: Rutgers University Press, 2002.

Fries, Laura. 'Britney & Kevin: Chaotic'. *Variety*. 19 May 2005. www.lexis-nexis.com.ezp.bentley.edu.

Frow, John. *Cultural Studies and Cultural Value*. Oxford: Oxford University Press, 1995.

Gallagher, Mark. '*Queer Eye* for the Heterosexual Couple'. *Feminist Media Studies*. 4:2 (2004): 223-6.

Gammage, KL, KA Martin Ginis and CR Hall. *Journal of Sport and Exercise Psychology*. 26 (2004):179-90.

Gamson, Joshua. *Claims to Fame: Celebrity in Contemporary America*. Berkeley: University of California Press, 1994.

Garay, Ruben. *World of Britney* [WoB] fansite. October 2002. www.worldofbritney.com.

Gates, Anita. 'These Old Houses: A TV Genre is Built'. *The New York Times On the Web*. 11 February 2005. www.nytimes.com/.

Gauntlett, D. *Media, Gender and Identity: An Introduction*. London: Routledge, 2002.

Gergen, Kenneth. 'The Decline and Fall of Personality'. *Psychology Today Online*. November 1992. http://health.yahoo.com/centers.

Giddens, Anthony. *Modernity and Self-identity: Self and Society in the Late Modern Age*. Stanford, California: Stanford University Press, 1991.

——. *Runaway World: How Globalisation is Reshaping our Lives*. London: Profile Books, 1999.

Gilbert, Matthew. '"Chaotic" shows desperate Spears using stale script'. *The Boston Globe*. 18 May 2005. www.lexis-nexis.com.ezp.bentley.edu.

Giles, David C. 'Keeping the Public in their Place: Audience Participation in Lifestyle Television Programming'. *Discourse and Society*. 13:5 (2002): 603-28.

Gillan, Jennifer. 'From Ozzie Nelson to Ozzy Osbourne: The Genesis and Development of the Reality Star Sitcom'. In Su Holmes and Deborah Jermyn, eds. *Understanding Reality Television*. London and New York: Routledge, 2004: 54-70.

Gitllin, T. 'Prime Time Ideology: The Hegemonic Process in Television Entertainment'. In Horace Newcomb, ed. *Television: The Critical View*. Oxford: Oxford University Press, 1994.

Goffman, Erving. *Gender Advertisements*. New York: Harper and Row, 1979.

Goldman, Robert. *Reading Ads Socially*. New York: Routledge, 1992.

Goodwin, Andrew. *Media Studies for Adults*. London: British Film Institute Education, 1988.

Griffen-Foley, B. 'From Tit-Bits to Big Brother: A century of audience participation in the media'. *Media, Culture and Society*. 26:4 (2004): 533-48.

Grimshaw, J. 'Working out with Merleau-Ponty'. In J Arthurs and J Grimshaw, eds. *Women's Bodies: Discipline and Transgression*. London: Cassell, 1999: 91–116.

Grindstaff, Laura. *The Money Shot: Trash, Class, and the Making of TV Talk Shows*. Chicago: University of Chicago Press, 2002.

Gudrun, P. *Aerobic Training*. Oxford: Meyer and Meyer Sport, 2002.

Haiken, Elizabeth. 'The Making of the Modern Face: Cosmetic Surgery'. *Social Research*. 67:1 (2000): 81–97.

Hain, A. *Total Rewind: The Virtual Museum of Vintage VCRs*. (2005) www. totalrewind.org/vhs.htm.

Halliwell, G. *Geri Yoga With Katy Appleton*. United Kingdom: Video Collection International, 2001.

Haralovich, Mary Beth and Michael W Trosset. 'Expect the Unexpected': Narrative pleasure and uncertainty due to chance in *Survivor*'. In Susan Murray and Laurie Ouellette, eds. *Reality Television: Remaking Television Culture*. New York: New York University Press, 2004: 75–96.

Harbour, Maggie, Jeff Samuels and Jennifer Pearson. 'Britney – Divorce Kevin Now!' *The Star*. 28 November 2005: 44–47.

Hardt, Michael. 'The Withering of Civil Society'. In Elizabeth Kaufman and Kevin J Heller, eds. *Deleuze & Guattari: New Mappings in Politics, Philosophy, and Culture*. Minneapolis, Minnesota: University of Minnesota Press, 1998.

Hardt, Michael and Antonio Negri. *Empire*. Cambridge, Massachusetts: Harvard University Press, 2000.

——. *Multitude*. Cambridge, Massachusetts: Harvard University Press, 2004.

Harrison, Martin. *Appearances. Fashion Photography since 1945*. London: Jonathan Cape, 1991.

Hart, Kylo-Patrick R. 'We're Here, We're Queer – and We're Better Than You: The Representational Superiority of Gay Men to Heterosexuals on *Queer Eye for the Straight Guy*'. *The Journal of Men's Studies*. 12:3 (2004): 241–53.

Hartley, John. *Uses of Television*. London: Routledge, 1999.

——. 'Daytime TV'. In Glen Creeber, ed. *The Television Genre Book*. London: British Film Institute, 2001: 92–3.

—— and Ellie Rennie. 'About a Girl. Fashion Photography as Photojournalism'. *Journalism*. 5:4 (2004): 458–79.

Hatch, Kristen. 'Daytime Politics: Kefauver, McCarthy, and the American Housewife'. In James Friedman, ed. *Reality Squared: Televisual Discourse on the Real*. London and New Brunswick, New Jersey: Rutgers University Press, 2002: 75–91.

Hay, James. 'Helping Ourselves: Men in the Kitchen'. Paper presented at *Console-Ing Passions: The International Conference of Feminism and Television, Video, New Media, and Audio*. (30 May – 2 June 2004) New Orleans, Louisiana.

Hearn, Alison. '"Tom, a 22 year-old firefighter from Kansas": On the incorporation
          of identity and the spectacularization of the "self" in the age of reality
          television'. Paper presented at the *Fifth Annual International Crossroads in
          Cultural Studies Conference*. (June 2004) Urbana, Illinois.

Heller, Dana, ed. *The Selling of 9/11: How a National Tragedy Became a Commodity*.
          New York: Palgrave Macmillan, 2005.

Hermes, J. *Reading Women's Magazines: An Analysis of Everyday Media Use*.
          Cambridge: Polity, 1995.

High-Tech Productions. *The History of Television*. (2005) www.high-techproductions.
          com/historyoftelevision.htm.

Hill, Annette. '*Big Brother*: The Real Audience'. *Television & New Media*. 3:3 (2002):
          323–40.

——. *Factual TV: The Reception of News, Documentary and Reality TV*. London:
          Routledge, forthcoming.

——. *Reality TV: Audiences and Popular Factual Television*. London: Routledge, 2005.

—— and Gareth Palmer. 'Editorial: Big Brother'. *Television and New Media*. 3:3
          (2002): 251–4.

Hilmes, Michele. *Radio Voices: American Broadcasting, 1922–1952*. Minneapolis:
          University of Minnesota Press, 1997.

Hochschild, Arlie. 'The Commercial Spirit of Intimate Life and the Abduction
          of Feminism: Signs from Women's Advice Books'. *Theory, Culture and
          Society*. 11:2 (1994): 1–24.

Hollows, J. 'Oliver's Twist: Leisure, labour and domestic masculinity in *The Naked
          Chef*. *International Journal of Cultural Studies*. 6:2 (2003): 229–48.

Holmes, Sue. '"But this Time You Choose!": Approaching the "Interactive" Audience
          in Reality TV'. *International Journal of Cultural Studies*. 7:2 (2004): 213–31.

——. '"All You've Got to Worry About is the Task, Having a Cup of Tea, and
          Doing a Bit of Sunbathing": Approaching Celebrity in *Big Brother*.' In
          Su Holmes and Deborah Jermyn, eds. *Understanding Reality Television*.
          London and New York: Routledge, 2004: 111–135.

—— and Deborah Jermyn. 'Introduction: Understanding Reality TV'. In Su
          Holmes and Deborah Jermyn, eds. *Understanding Reality Television*.
          London and New York: Routledge, 2004: 1–32.

Instone, A. *Phat Moves*. United States: Firefly Entertainment, 2004.

Irigaray, Luce. 'Women on the Market'. In *This Sex Which is Not One*. (trans.
          Catherine Porter) Ithaca: Cornell University Press, 1985: 170–91.

Jobling, Paul. 'On the Turn – Millennial Bodies and the Meaning of Time in Andrea
          Giacobbe's Fashion Photography'. *Fashion Theory*. 6:1 (2002): 3–25.

Kagan, E and M Morse. 'Women's Search for Empowerment and Self-
          Transformation'. *TDR*. 32 (1988): 164–180.

Kellner, Douglas. 'Popular Culture and the Construction of Postmodern Identities'.

In Scott Lash and Jonathan Friedman, eds. *Modernity and Identity*. Oxford: Blackwell, 1992.

Kilborn, R. 'The Docu-soap: A critical assessment'. In J Izod and R Kilborn with M Hibberd, eds. *From Grierson to Docu-Soap: Breaking the Boundaries*. Luton: University of Luton Press, 2000.

Kismaric, Susan and Eva Respini. *Fashioning Fiction in Photography since 1990*. New York: The Museum of Modern Art, 1994.

Kocieniewski, David. 'After $12,000 There's Even Room to Park the Car'. 20 February 2006. *The New York Times On the Web*. www.nytimes.com/.

Kooijman, Jaap. 'They're Here, They're Queer, and Straight America Loves It'. *GLQ: A Journal of Lesbian and Gay Studies*. 11:1 (2005): 106–9.

Krasniewicz, Louise. 'Magical Transformations. Morphing and Metamorphosis in Two Cultures'. In Vivian Sobchack, ed. *Meta-Morphing. Visual Transformation and the Culture of Quick-Change*. London and Minneapolis: University of Minnesota Press, 2000.

Kraszewski, Jon. 'Country Hicks and Urban Cliques: Mediating race, reality, and liberalism on MTV's *The Real World*'. In Susan Murray and Laurie Ouellette, eds. *Reality Television: Remaking Television Culture*. New York: New York University Press, 2004: 179–96.

Kristof, Nicholas D. 'Time for an Extreme Makeover at the White House'. 21 February 2006. *The New York Times On the Web*. www.nytimes.com/.

Langer, J. *Tabloid Television*. London: Routledge, 1998.

Lawrence, M and J Germov. 'Future Food: The Politics of Functional Foods and Health Claims'. In J Germov and L Williams, eds. *A Sociology of Food and Nutrition: The Social Appetite*. Victoria: Oxford University Press, 1999.

Learning Channel website. (28 September 2004) tlc.discovery.com.

Lears, TJ Jackson. 'From Salvation to Self-Realization: Advertising and the Therapeutic Roots of the Consumer Culture, 1880–1930'. In Richard Wightman and TJ Jackson Lears, eds. *The Culture of Consumption: Critical Essays in American History 1880–1980*. New York: Pantheon, 1983: 1–38.

——. 'The Resurrection of the Body: Medicine and the Pursuit of Happiness'. *The New Republic*. (26 April 2004): 25–34.

Levy, Ariel. *Female Chauvinist Pigs: Women and the Rise of Raunch Culture*. New York: Simon & Schuster, 2005.

Lewis, Justin. 'The Meaning of Real Life'. In Susan Murray and Laurie Ouellette, eds. *Reality Television: Remaking Television Culture*. New York: New York University Press, 2004: 288–302.

Littler, J. 'Making Fame Ordinary: Intimacy, Reflexivity, Keeping it Real'. *Mediactive*. 2 (2004): 8–25.

——. Editorial. *Mediactive: Celebrity* 2. London: Barefoot Publications, 2003

Live With Regis and Kelly. Hosts Regis Philbin and Kelly Ripa. 28 October 2004.

Buena Vista Television. ABC. WVEC Norfolk, Virginia.

Lobstein, T, N Rigby and R Leach. *EU Platform on Diet, Physical Activity and Health: International Obesity Task Force EU Platform Briefing Paper*. International Association for the Study of Obesity, 2005. www.iotf.org/media/euobesity3.pdf.

Losano, A and BA Risch. 'Resisting Venus: Negotiating Corpulence in Exercise Videos'. JE Braziel and K LeBesco, eds. *Bodies Out of Bounds: Fatness and Transgression*. Berkeley, California: University of California Press, 2001: 111-25.

Lowney, Kathleen S. *Baring Our Souls: TV Talk Shows and the Religion of Recovery*. New York: Aldine De Gruyter, 1999.

Lowrey, Tina M, LJ Shrum and John A McCarty. 'The Future of Television Advertising'. http://faculty.business.utsa.edu/ljshrum/KimmelChapter.%20Final.pdf: 1-32. Forthcoming.

Lury, C. *Consumer Culture*. Cambridge: Polity, 1996.

MacPherson, E. *Sports Illustrated Super Shape-up Program: Stretch and Strengthen with Elle MacPherson*. United States: The Time Inc. Magazine Company, 1989.

Magder, Ted. 'The End of TV 101: Reality Programs, Formats, and the New Business of Television'. In Susan Murray and Laurie Ouellette, eds. *Reality Television: Remaking Television Culture*. London and New York: New York University Press, 2004: 137-56.

'Makeover Madness', *Italian Vogue* (July 2005), 270-340.

Marina Plastic Surgery Associates. www.marinaplasticsurgery.com/video.cfm.

Markula, P. 'Firm but Shapely, Fit but Sexy, Strong but Thin: The Postmodern Aerobicizing Female Bodies'. *Sociology of Sport Journal*. 12 (1995): 424-53.

Marshall, PD. *Celebrity and Power: Fame in Contemporary Culture*. Minneapolis: University of Minnesota Press, 1997.

Massumi, Brian. 'Realer than Real: The Simulacrum According to Deleuze and Guattari'. 1987. www.Anu.edu/HRC/first_and_last works/ realer.htm.

McCarthy, Anna. '"Stanley Milgram, Allen Funt, and Me": Postwar social science and the first wave of Reality TV'. In Susan Murray and Laurie Ouellette, eds. *Reality Television: Remaking Television Culture*. London and New York: New York University Press, 2004: 19-39.

McCarthy, William. *Hacking Matter: Levitating chairs, quantum mirages, and the infinite weirdness of programmable atoms*. New York: Basic Books, 2003.

McChesney, Robert W. 'Corporate Media, Global Capitalism'. In Simon Cottle, ed. *Media Organization and Production*. London: Sage, 2003: 27-39.

McDonald, DG and JA Hodgdon. *The Psychological Effects of Aerobic Fitness Training: Research and Theory*. New York: Springer-Verlag, 1991.

McGuigan, J. *Culture and the Public Sphere*. London: Routledge, 1996.

McKee, Robert. *Story: Substance, Structure, Style, and the Principles of Screenwriting*.

London: Methuen, 1998.

McMurria, John. 'Desperate Citizens'. *Flow*. 3:3 (2005). http://jot.communication.
utexas.edu/flow/?jot=view&id=1047.

McQuail, Denis. 'The Media and Lifestyle: Editor's Introduction'. *European Journal
of Communication*. 17:4 (2002): 427–8.

McRobbie, Angela. 'Notes on *What Not to Wear* and Post-Feminist Symbolic
Violence'. *Sociological Review*. 52:2 (2004): 99–104.

Meyrowitz, J. *No Sense of Place: the Impact of Electronic Media on Social Behaviour*.
Oxford: Oxford University Press, 1985.

Millea, Holly. 'Britney's Big Adventure'. *Elle*. October (2005): 388–94, 434.

Miller, Barbara L. 'Sherman's Mass Appeal'. *Afterimage*. November/December
(1997): 5.

Miller, Peter and Nikolas Rose. 'Mobilizing the Consumer: Assembling the Subject
of Consumption'. *Theory, Culture and Society*. 14:1 (1997): 1–36.

Mittel, J. 'A Cultural Approach to Television Genre Theory'. *Cinema Journal*. 40:3
(2001): 3–24.

Moran, Caitlin and Pete Paphides. 'Sometimes Love is Best Kept Hidden'. *The
Times*. 14 September 2005. www.lexis-nexis.com.ezp.bentley.edu.

Morley, D and K Robins. *Spaces of Identity: Global Media, Electronic Landscapes and
Cultural Boundaries*. London: Routledge, 1995.

Morse, Margaret. *Virtualities: Television, Media Art, and Cyberculture*. Bloomington:
Indiana University Press, 1998.

Moseley, Rachel. 'Makeover Takeover on British Television'. *Screen*. 41:3 (2000):
299–314.

Mulvey, Laura. 'Visual Pleasure and Narrative Cinema (1973)'. *Visual and Other
Pleasures*. London: Macmillan, 1989: 14–26.

Murray, Samantha. 'Locating Aesthetics: Sexing the Fat Woman'. *Social Semiotics*.
14:3 (2004): 237–48.

Murray, Susan and Laurie Ouellette, eds. *Reality Television: Remaking Television
Culture*. London and New York: New York University Press, 2004.

Neale, Steve. 'Questions of Genre'. *Screen*. 31:1 (1990): 45–66.

Negri, Antonio. *Negri on Negri*. London: Routledge, 2003.

Nichols, Bill. *Representing Reality*. Bloomington: Indiana University Press, 1991.

Northwest Medical Laser. 'Cosmetic Surgery Jumps to an $8.7 Billion Industry'.
27 September 2005. www.nwmedicallaser.com/Other%20stuff/
Press%20Release%2009_27_05.pdf.

Ouellette, Laurie. '"Take Responsibility for Yourself": *Judge Judy* and the neoliberal
citizen'. In Susan Murray and Laurie Ouellette, eds. *Reality Television:
Remaking Television Culture*. London and New York: New York University
Press, 2004: 231–50.

Ovid. *Metamorphosis*. (trans. Mary M Innes) London: Penguin, 1955.

——. *Metamorphosis*. (trans. George Sandy) New York: Garland Publishing, 1976.

Owens, Craig. 'Posing'. In Craig Owens. *Beyond Recognition. Representation, Power, and Culture*. Berkeley, Los Angeles, London: University of California Press, 1992.

Poschardt, Ulf. *Fashion Statements. Archaeology of Elegance 1980–2000*. London: Thames & Hudson, 2002.

Palmer, Gareth. '*Big Brother*: An Experiment in Governance'. *Television and New Media*. 3:3 (2002): 295–310.

——. '"The New You": Class and Transformation in Lifestyle Television'. In Su Holmes and Deborah Jermyn, eds. *Understanding Reality Television*. London and New York: Routledge, 2004: 173–90.

Pearson, Kyra and Nina M Reich. '*Queer Eye* Fairy Tale: Changing the World One Manicure at aTime'. *Feminist Media Studies*. 4:2 (2004): 229–31.

Peiss, Kathy. *Hope in a Jar: The Making of America's Beauty Culture*. New York: Metropolitan Books, 1998.

——. 'Making Faces: The Cosmetics Industry and the Cultural Construction of Gender 1890-1930'. *Genders*. 7 (Spring 1990): 143–69.

Philips, Deborah. 'Transformation Scenes: The Television Interior Makeover'. *International Journal of Cultural Studies*. 8:2 (2005): 213–29.

Pilates for Beginners. Australia: Pilates Institute of Australasia, 1999.

Postman, Neil. *Amusing Ourselves to Death: Public Discourse in the Age of Show Business*. London and New York: Penguin Books, 1986.

Powter, S. *Burn Fat and Get Fit*. United States: The Susan Powter Corporation, 1994.

Press, Joy. 'My Brilliant Career'. *Village Voice*. 18 November 2003: 48.

PR Newswire. 5 February 2004. Los Angeles. www.prnewswire.com.

Raphael, Chad. 'The Political Economic Origins of Reali-TV'. In Susan Murray and Laurie Ouellette, eds. *Reality Television: Remaking Television Culture*. London and New York: New York University Press, 2004: 119–36.

Ritchie, Jean. *Big Brother: The Official Unseen Story*. London: Channel 4 Books, 2000.

Robaina, Holly Vincente. 'A Foundation of Faith'. *Christianity Today*. www. chritianitytoday.com. *Salt Lake City Tribune*. (2006) www.sltrib.com.

Rogers, Shirley. 'Fox retitles *Family Time* to *Renovate My Family*'. 31 August 2004. www.Reality TVWorld.com.

Rojek, C. *Celebrity*. London: Reaktion, 2001.

Roscoe, Jane. 'Big Brother Australia: Performing the "Real" Twenty-four-seven'. *International Journal of Cultural Studies*. 4:4 (2001): 473–88.

Rose, Nikolas. *Powers of Freedom: Reframing political thought*. Cambridge: Cambridge University Press, 1999.

Scannell, Paddy. '*Big Brother* as a Television Event'. *Television & New Media*. 3:3

(2002): 271–82.

Scholes, Robert. *Structuralism in Literature*. New Haven and London: Yale University
  Press, 1974.

Schreiber, Dominic. 'Formats – Now the Networks Are Taking Notice'. *Format
  News*. (October 2002): 2. *Broadcast* supplement (2 November 2002): 1.

Schulenburg, Caroline. 'Worst TV show of the Week, Britney & Kevin: *Chaotic* on
  UPN'. *Parents Television Council*.18 May 2005. www.parentstv.org.

Seid, RP. *Never Too Thin: Why Women Are at War With Their Bodies*. New York:
  Prentice Hall Press, 1989.

Shales, Tom. 'Britney's Home Video: Plumbing the Depths'. *The Washington Post*. 18
  May 2005. www.washingtonpost.com.

Shattuc, Jane M. *The Talking Cure: TV Talk Shows and Women*. London: Routledge,
  1997.

Shaw, George Bernard. 'The Basis of Socialism: Economic' and 'The Transition to
  Social Democracy'. In G. Bernard Shaw, ed. *Fabian Essays in Socialism*.
  London: Walter Scott Publishing, 1889, reprint 1908.

——. *Pygmalion: A Romance in Five Acts*. Burnt Mill, Essex: Longman Group,
  1985.

——. *Pygmalion: A Romance in Five Acts*. New York: Signet Classic, 1980.

Sherwin, Adam. '*Faking It* puts Britain at top of world's reality TV'. *The Times*. 19
  May 2003: 11.

Silverman, Kaja. *The Threshold of the Visible World*. London and New York:
  Routledge, 1996.

Simmons, R. *Sweatin' to the Oldies*. United States: Warner's Home Video, 1988.

Smith Jr, L. *Bodylicious: The Ultimate Dance Workout*. United States: Universal
  Pictures Video, 2004.

Smith, MW. *Reading Simulacra: Fatal Theories for Postmodernity*. Albany: State
  University of New York Press, 2001.

Sobchack, Vivian. 'Introduction'. In Vivian Sobchack, ed. *Meta-Morphing. Visual
  Transformation and the Culture of Quick-Change*. Minneapolis and London:
  University of Minnesota Press, 2000.

Spears, Britney. 'Letter to Fans'. On *Love B: Stream of Consciousness* link. *The Official
  Britney Spears Website*. 4 October 2005. www.britneyspears.com.

Spittle, Steve. 'Producing TV: Consuming TV'. In S Miles, A Anderson and
  K Meethan, eds. The Changing Consumer: Markets and Meanings.
  London: Routledge, 2002: 56–73.

Spitzack, C. 'The Confession Mirror: Plastic Images for Surgery'. *Social Studies of
  Science*. 21 (1991): 279–319.

Spotlight Reviews of *Britney & Kevin: Chaotic*. amazon.com. August–December 2005.
  www.amazon.com.

Stadler, Gustavus T. 'Queer Eye for the Straight "I"'. *GLQ: A Journal of Lesbian and*

Gay Studies. 11:1 (2005): 109–11.

Stanley, Alessandra. 'Murder, Mogul, Marriage: Three Versions of Reality'. *The New York Times*. 24 May 2005. www.lexis-nexis.com.ezp.bentley.edu.

Stasi, Linda. 'X-Rated Britney Gets Raw on TV'. *The New York Post*. 18 May 2005. www.lexis-nexis.com.ezp.bentley.edu.

Stearns, PN. *Fat History: Bodies and Beauty in the Modern West*. New York: New York University Press, 1997.

Steele, Bruce C. 'The Gay Rights Makeover'. *Advocate*. 2 September 2003: 42–3.

Stewart, RJ. *The Living World of Faery*. Lake Toxaway, North Carolina: Mercury Publishing, 1999.

——. *The Underworld Initiation: A Journey Towards PsychicTransformation*. Lake Toxaway, North Carolina: Mercury Publishing, 1998.

Taylor, Ella. *Prime Time Families: Television Culture in Postwar America*. Berkeley: University of California Press, 1991.

Taylor, Lisa. 'From Ways of Life to Lifestyle: The "Ordinari-ization" of British Gardening Lifestyle Television'. *European Journal of Communication*. 17:4 (2002): 479–93.

Tebbel, C. *The Body Snatchers: How the Media Shapes Women*. Sydney: Finch, 2002.

Tebbel, John and Mary Ellen Zuckermann. *The Magazine in America, 1741–1990*. Oxford and New York: Oxford University Press, 1991.

Thompson, Edward P. *The Making of the English Working Class*. Harmondsworth: Penguin, 1980.

Tincknell, Estella and Parvati Raghuram. '*Big Brother*: Reconfiguring the "active" audience of cultural studies?' *European Journal of Cultural Studies*. 5:2 (2002): 199–215.

Todorov, Tzvetan. *The Poetics of Prose*. Oxford: Blackwell, 1977.

Toppo, G. 'Kids Count'. *USA Today*. 2005.

Torres, Sasha. 'Why Can't Johnny Shave?' *GLQ: A Journal of Lesbian and Gay Studies*. 11:1 (2005): 95–7.

Turberville, K. (2005) managing director of Indigo Television, cited in 'Glued to the TV Awards'. http://uk.news.yahoo.com/hot/n/national-tv-awards/background.html. (Accessed 25/10/2005)

Turner, Mimi. '*Faking It* Tops Montreux Awards'. 20 May 2003. *Hollywood Reporter*. www.hollywoodreporter.com/thr/index.jsp.

Veblen, Thorstein. *Theory of the Leisure Class*. London: The Modern Library, 1918.

Virno, Paolo. *A Grammar of the Multitude*. Los Angeles, California: Semiotext(e), 2004.

Vyncke, Patrick. 'Lifestyle Segmentation: From Attitudes, Interests and Opinions to Values, Aesthetic Styles, Life Visions and Media Preferences'. *European Journal of Communication*. 17:4 (2002): 445–63.

Warner, Marina. *Fantastic Metamorphoses, Other Worlds: Ways of Telling the Self*. Oxford: Oxford University Press, 2002.

Weisser, Susan Ostrov. 'Introduction'. In *Women and Romance: A Reader*. New York: New York University Press, 2001: 1–8.

Welch, R. *A Week with Raquel*. United States: Total Video, 1986.

Who Needs Breast Implants? 007 Breasts. www.007b.com/who_needs_breast_implants.php.

Willis, S. 'Work(ing) Out'. *Cultural Studies*. 4 (1990): 1–18.

WoB Fan Forums. November–December 2005. www.worldofbritney.com.

Wolf, Naomi. *The Beauty Myth*. London: Vintage, 1991.

Wolk, Josh. 'Britney & Kevin: *Chaotic*, Shooting Her Own Foot. *Entertainment Weekly*. 18 May 2005. www.ew.com.

Wood, Helen and Beverley Skeggs. 'Notes on Ethical Scenarios of Self in British Reality TV'. *Feminist Media Studies*. 4:2 (2004): 205–8.

Woodward, Ian. 'Divergent Narratives in the Imagining of Home amongst Middle Class Consumers: Aesthetics, Comfort and the Symbolic Boundaries of Self and Home'. *Journal of Sociology*. 39:4 (2003): 391–412.

Wright, E. *Classes*. London: Verso, 1985.

Young, J. *The Exclusive Society*. London: Sage, 1999.

Zipes, Jack. *Breaking the Magic Spell: Radical Theories of Folk and Fairytales*. Austin: University of Texas Press, 1979.

——. Interview by Kenn Bannerman. (2002) Available at: www.bitingdogpress.com/zipes/zipes.html.

——. *Spells of Enchantment: The Wondrous Fairy Tales of Western Culture*. New York: Viking, 1991.

Zuckermann, Mary Ellen. 'A History of Popular Women's Magazines in the United States, 1792–1995'. *Contributions in Women's Studies*. No. 165. Westport: Greenwood Press, 1998.

INDEX